Pronunciation Celebration

ESL Listening and Speaking
A Complete High-Intermediate Text

Evelyn Uyemura • Nitza Llado • Debra Mochidome

El Camino College

Kendall Hunt
publishing company

Cover image © Shutterstock.Inc.
Interior images © Shutterstock.Inc. Under license from Shutterstock, Inc.

Kendall Hunt
publishing company

www.kendallhunt.com
Send all inquiries to:
4050 Westmark Drive
Dubuque, IA 52004-1840

Copyright © 2011 by Evelyn Uyemura, Nitza Llado, Debra Mochidome

ISBN 978-0-7575-8890-7

Kendall Hunt Publishing Company has the exclusive rights to reproduce this work,
to prepare derivative works from this work, to publicly distribute this work,
to publicly perform this work and to publicly display this work.

All rights reserved. No part of this publication may be reproduced,
stored in a retrieval system, or transmitted, in any form or by any
means, electronic, mechanical, photocopying, recording, or otherwise,
without the prior written permission of the copyright owner.

Printed in the United States of America
10 9 8 7 6 5 4 3 2

Dedication

This book is dedicated to our students, who have taught us the real meaning of the word "dedication." Their dedication to learning, their willingness to leave behind a familiar world and to struggle with a new language in order to fulfill their dreams for themselves and their families, has inspired us each day. So we dedicate this book to our students, who teach us so much.

Contents

Acknowledgments viii
To the Instructor ix

Part 1 The Big Picture 1

Chapter 1 You, Me, and Arnold Schwartzenegger 2
Chapter 2 Spelling Bee: English Spelling and the IPA 9
Chapter 3 Can You Hear Me Now? Voiced and Unvoiced Sounds 13
Chapter 4 I've Got Rhythm: Stressed Syllables and Compound Words 17
Chapter 5 Don't Stress the Small Stuff 23
Chapter 6 Can I Ask You a Question? 28

Part 2 A Mouthful of Vowels 37

Chapter 7 The Real Cheese Deal (/iy/) 38
Chapter 8 The Big Pig Jig (/ɪ/) 45
Chapter 9 The Red Hen's Dead End (/ɛ/) 50
Chapter 10 The Whale's Tail (/ey/) 55
Chapter 11 The Rat Pack Attack (/æ/) 61
Chapter 12 All Together Now *(Review of Chapters 7–11)* 66

Chapter 13 Love a Lucky Duck (/ʌ/) 71
Chapter 14 Banana Extravaganza (/ə/) 78
Chapter 15 Watch that Octopus (/a/) 85
Chapter 16 I Thought I Saw a Hawk (/ɔ/) 89
Chapter 17 Together Again *(Review of Chapters 13–16)* 94

Chapter 18 Go Rope a Goat (/ow/) 100
Chapter 19 Cute Cuckoo's Clues (/uw/ and /yuw/) 105
Chapter 20 Look, a Wolf in the Bush! (/ʊ/) 111
Chapter 21 Tiger, Tiger Smiling Bright (/ay/) 115
Chapter 22 A Noisy Oyster (/ɔy/) 120
Chapter 23 Mouthy Cow Sounds (/aw/) 124
Chapter 24 Come Together *(Review of Chapters 18–23)* 129

Chapter 25   Nerdy Bird's Word Search (/ɝ/ and /ɚ/)   133
Chapter 26   The Boring Boar (/ɔr/)   138
Chapter 27   Park Your Car in the Yard (/ar/)   144
Chapter 28   Weird Deers and Bears There (/ɪr/ and /ɛr/)   149
Chapter 29   Together We Can Make It *(Review of Chapters 25–28)*   154

Part 3   Conquering Consonant Confusion   159

Chapter 30   Lucy Loves Robby Rabbit (/l/ and /r/)   160
Chapter 31   Ed's Endings (/t/, /d/, and -ED endings)   168
Chapter 32   Susan Saves the Zoo (/s/, /z/, and -S endings)   176
Chapter 33   Three Thumbs Up (/θ/ and /ð/)   185
Chapter 34   Shop 'n' Chop (/ʃ/, /tʃ/, and CH)   190
Chapter 35   A Treasured National Vision
             (/ʃ/ and /ʒ/, -TION, -SION, -CIAN, and -SURE)   196
Chapter 36   Together, Baby *(Review of Chapters 30–35)*   202

Chapter 37   You'll Jump for Joy (/ʤ/ and /y/)   212
Chapter 38   Ban the Van and Face the Pace (/b/, /v/, /f/, /p/)   219
Chapter 39   We Will Win the Victory (/w/ and /v/)   226
Chapter 40   Kin to the Golden King (/k/, /g/, /m/, /n/, and /ŋ/)   231
Chapter 41   Silence is Golden   238
Chapter 42   Together at Last *(Review of All Consonants)*   249

Part 4   Projects for Practice and Improvement   259

Chapter 43   Listening Logs   260
Chapter 44   Two Thumbs Up   269
Chapter 45   Getting to Know You   280
Chapter 46   On the Hot Seat   284
Chapter 47   May I Ask You a Few Questions?   299
Chapter 48   Room for Debate   311
Chapter 49   Think on Your Feet   317
Chapter 50   Going Solo   322
Chapter 51   A Panel of Experts   328
Chapter 52   Scenes from American History   332

Appendix   352

Acknowledgments

We would like to thank our dean, Mr. Tom Lew, and our Vice President of Academic Affairs, Dr. Francisco Arce, for their support as we worked on this book. We would also like to thank our family members for their faith in us. Special thanks to Dr. Alicia Class, who contributed to an earlier draft of this book.

To the Instructor

Our intention in this book has been to create a relaxed atmosphere in the classroom, so that students can work on pronunciation and listening comprehension without anxiety or self-consciousness.

In planning your syllabus, you will probably want to include Chapter 1 at the beginning of the course. However, other chapters in that section can be integrated into the course as you see the need. You may want to alternate between vowel and consonant chapters, rather than covering all the vowels first and then moving on to consonants.

The activities in the last section of the book can be implemented throughout the course. You may decide to do either a debate or a panel discussion but not both. The chapter on job interviews will not be suitable for every class. If you are teaching in a non-English-speaking environment, you may not be able to include the interview and survey chapters. However, thanks to the Internet, almost every class will be able to include listening logs and film reviews.

We hope you and your students will celebrate their growth as speakers of English and will enjoy using this textbook.

PART I

The Big Picture

CHAPTER 1
You, Me, and Arnold Schwartzenegger

Do you have an accent when you speak English? Of course you do. So does actor and former governor of California, Arnold Schwartzenegger. So does the queen of England. So do we. Everyone who speaks English speaks it with a particular accent, and your accent can give other people a hint about where you grew up and what other language or languages you speak.

English is spoken as a first language in Great Britain, where there are many different regional accents. It is spoken in Ireland with a distinctive Irish accent. It is spoken with different accents in New Zealand, Australia, and South Africa as well as several other African countries. It is spoken in Canada and the United States with many different accents. It is spoken by millions of second-language users, who all have their own distinct accents as well.

You have probably noticed the differences between British and American English, which includes not only differences in individual sounds, but also intonation patterns, vocabulary, and spelling. In fact, there's an old joke that Great Britain and the United States are two countries separated by the same language. Americans think the British have an accent, and British people think Americans have an accent.

Within the United States, you will notice differences in pronunciation if you visit Boston, New York, Kentucky, Mississippi, Chicago, Los Angeles, or Hawaii. You will notice that African American people and European American people often have differences in their pronunciation. The three authors of this book grew up in Puerto Rico and New York, Boston, and Los Angeles, and they notice some differences in each other's pronunciation. We all have an accent!

So having an accent is not something to be ashamed of. Most researchers believe that it is unusual for anyone who learned a second language after the age of about 12 years old to sound like a native speaker. Eliminating your accent is probably not a realistic goal.

So what goal is realistic? First of all, we hope that this book will help you improve your listening comprehension. Listening and speaking are closely related. If you gain an understanding of the sounds of English, it will help you create new pathways in your brain, which will enable you to pronounce words more accurately. After all, it's not likely that you will be able to pronounce a word correctly if you are not able to "hear" it correctly. So let's talk about that for a moment.

As we learn our first language, we unconsciously categorize the sounds we hear into "boxes." So, for example, babies learning English put the sounds /l/ and /r/ into two separate boxes.

Babies learning Japanese have one "box" for a sound that is somewhat similar to both the English /l/ and /r/ sound. As a result, an English speaker will "hear" the difference between "late" and "rate," while a Japanese speaker will have difficulty noticing the difference. Similarly, Japanese speakers will "hear" the difference between a single vowel and double vowel (/a/ or /aa/), while an English speaker will have a hard time noticing the difference. This is not a matter of physical "hearing," of course, but is something that happens in our brains when we try to understand what we hear.

One of the things this book will do is focus your attention on "hearing" the sounds of English one by one. Research has shown that adults can "retrain" their brains to notice differences that their native language doesn't make. One "box" in our brains can be divided into two boxes through listening practice.

For this reason, most chapters begin by asking you to *listen carefully* as your instructor reads some words. Many students automatically want to *listen and repeat*. We feel that it's important **not** to do that right away. If you do, instead of hearing what your instructor is saying, you will be hearing yourself and your classmates. You might end up reinforcing the "boxes" you already have in your brain—the boxes that match your native language rather than the English language. So listen first. Listen carefully. Practice hearing the differences. Your brain will start to respond to the English sounds. That's a realistic goal.

This book will also explain some of the ways that English spelling can help you with pronunciation, and also the many ways that English spelling can cause confusion. For example, we always spell the regular past ending of verbs –ED. But we actually use three different pronunciations. Understanding the phonetic principles can help you improve not only your listening but also your speaking. If you expect –ED to be pronounced /ɪd/ every time, you might think that Americans just don't bother with past tense endings when they say *walked* /walkt/. Becoming aware of these sounds will help you start to "hear" them, which can help you start to pronounce them as well. Using phonetic rules to improve your pronunciation is another realistic goal.

In addition to structured practice in which you focus on just one or two sounds, each chapter of this book includes discussion topics to help you gain fluency and confidence expressing your ideas in English. Too much focus on sounds alone can make you self-conscious and can actually make your overall pronunciation worse. In most cases, the context of what you are saying will make it clear whether you mean "late" or "rate" or "ban" or "van."

Also, keep in mind that most people who might make you feel bad about your accent probably only speak one language themselves, while you have the ability to use at least two languages. As Eleanor Roosevelt once said, "No one can make you feel inferior without your permission." Keep working on making your English easier for people to understand, but never let anyone make you feel bad about the way you speak. Arnold wouldn't like it if you did!

Ice Breakers

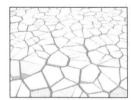

It's the first day of class, and everyone is feeling a little nervous. Even the teacher may be nervous! How are we all going to get to know each other? Will you make friends in this class? Will the teacher and your classmates know your name?

The following are suggestions for activities that will "break the ice." Can you guess what that idiom means? Soon you will feel warmer and more relaxed and comfortable.

Your instructor may choose to use one or more of the following activities. If students are joining the class at different times, the activities might be done on several different days.

A. The Name Game

Work with a partner to ask and answer the following questions. Afterward, your instructor may ask pairs of students to come to the front of the room and explain their names to the class. How many names can you remember at the end of class? Can the instructor remember most or all of the students' names?

1. What is your first name (your given name, the name your family chose for you)? How do you pronounce it? How do you write it in your language?

2. What is your last name (your family name)? How do you pronounce it? How do you write it in your language?

3. Do you have a middle name? A maiden name? A nickname? Any other names? Has your name ever changed?

4. Who chose your name and why? Can you explain the meaning of your name?

5. Have you ever met anyone who has the same name as you?

6. Do you like your name? Why or why not?

7. Can you give us a suggestion for how to remember your name?

© E. Uyemura, N. Llado, D. Mochidome. Permission is granted for instructor to make one copy for each student during the first week of class.

B. Line Up!

This activity will require you to get up and move around and to ask other students some questions.

1. Line up by the month you were born in. People born in January should be on the left, followed by February babies, and so on. If there are several people born in the same month, line up by date—March 1st before March 3rd, for example. (Pay no attention to the year you were born!) Did you find anyone who has the exact same birthday as you?

2. Now line up by how long you have been in this country. The newest newcomer should be on the left, and the person who has lived here the longest on the right. Is there anyone who arrived on the same day as you?

3. This time, line up in alphabetical order by first name. Aaron might be first in line and Zoila would be at the end.

4. Finally, can you organize yourselves into a map of the world? Organize yourselves into continents and countries based on where you come from, and try to make the shape of your country. North and South America should be on the left, with Europe, Africa, the Middle East, and Asia moving to the right.

C. Find Someone Who...

Walk around the classroom asking questions until you find someone who fits the description, and then write that person's name in the blank.

1. Find someone who comes to school by bus _____
   (Ask: Do you come to school by bus?)

2. Find someone who has 3 or more sisters _____
   (Ask: How many sisters do you have?)

3. Find someone who is a parent _____
   (Ask: Do you have any children?)

4. Find someone who plays the piano _____

5. Find someone who is a soccer fan _____

6. Find someone who knows how to swim _____

7. Find someone who has a pet (cat, dog, etc.) _____

8. Find someone who is taking math _____

9. Find someone who likes to dance _____

10. Find someone who speaks more than two languages _____

11. Find someone who is left-handed _____

12. Find someone who drinks tea every day _____

© E. Uyemura, N. Llado, D. Mochidome. Permission is granted for instructor to make one copy for each student during the first week of class.

8 Part 1 The Big Picture

D. Get-Acquainted Sheet

Your instructor may ask you to complete this in class or for homework. The information will be used to help your instructor get to know you better. It will not be shared with other members of the class.

1. Name:
2. Male/Female:
3. Age:
4. Country:
5. Languages(s) you speak:
6. Career or occupation in your country:
7. Career or occupation now:
8. Career goal:

9. How long have you been studying English (in your country and/or in the U.S. or other English-speaking country?)

10. What other classes are you taking?

11. What other responsibilities do you have? (hours of work per week, children, other family responsibilities, etc.)

12. What are your hobbies or interests?

13. How do you hope this class will help you?

14. What worries or concerns do you have about this class?

15. Anything else you want your instructor to know about you?

© E. Uyemura, N. Llado, D. Mochidome. Permission is granted for instructor to make one copy for each student during the first week of class.

CHAPTER 2
Spelling Bee: English Spelling and the IPA

English may be the only language in which children compete in contests to spell words. These contests, known as Spelling Bees, are even broadcast on television. Why is spelling a competitive sport in English? It's because English spelling is so difficult! The alphabet we use to write English was originally created to write Latin. When Latin-speakers first tried to write down the English language, they discovered that English had many more sounds than Latin. Latin only has 5 vowel sounds, but English has 15 or more vowel sounds. It also has some consonant sounds that Latin doesn't have.

The smart solution would have been to invent some new symbols, but perhaps the Latin-speakers didn't think of that. Instead they used the letters they had and combined them in various ways to try to represent this strange language. Since they didn't have the sounds at the beginning of the word *the* or *she*, they used two letters to represent one sound. They didn't have the vowel sound in the word *book*, so again they combined some letters to represent the sound.

That would have been bad enough, but just at the time that the spelling of English was being standardized, English underwent what is known as The Great Vowel Shift. The pronunciation of English changed, but the spelling didn't. In addition, English has borrowed many words from other languages, sometimes keeping the foreign spelling but changing the pronunciation to fit English, and other times keeping the foreign pronunciation as well. So we have words like *ballet* and *champagne*, *yacht* and *sauna*, *chemistry* and *pneumonia*, *coyote* and *karaoke*, in which the spelling and pronunciation don't follow the usual English spelling rules.

English also lost some of its own sounds shortly after it began to be written. The silent E at the end of words, the silent GH in words like *daughter*, *right*, and *night*, and the silent K at the beginning of *knife* and *knuckle* used to be pronounced, as did the H in words beginning with WH, such as *white* and *why* (a few people still pronounce words like *white* and *why* with the sound /hw/).

The result of all these mismatches, borrowings, and changes is that English spelling has many irregularities and exceptions. This causes difficulty for English-speaking children learning to read, and it also causes difficulty for speakers of other languages trying to learn English.

The International Phonetic Alphabet (IPA) is a system of symbols that has been created to attempt to represent every sound used in every language in the world. It uses symbols based on the Latin alphabet as well as other symbols to create a one-to-one correspondence between the symbol and the sound. That is, there should be no exceptions or other confusion if we use the IPA symbols to spell the sounds of English.

Most of the symbols for consonants are the same as the usual spelling of that sound in English. So the symbol for the first sound in *nut* is /n/. (We use slash marks to indicate an IPA symbol.) If we want to show someone how to pronounce the word *knight*, we can write it in IPA: /nayt/.

This book uses a slightly simplified version of IPA, using the symbol /r/ to represent the English R sound, and /d/ to indicate the middle sound in *kettle*. We have also made the choice to represent the first sound in *joy* and *job* with the symbol /j/ and to use the symbol /y/ to represent the first sound in *yellow* as well as the second part of the vowel sounds /ey/, /iy/, /ay/, and /ɔy/ (as in the words *bay, bee, buy,* and *boy*). We don't indicate the difference between the sound of the letter P in *pin* and *spin* (the first is aspirated, with a puff of air added to it while the second one is unaspirated.) As Einstein said, we wanted to make things as simple as possible but no simpler.

Your instructor may ask you to learn how to write words in IPA symbols, or he or she may choose to ask you only to recognize the symbols but not write them yourself. It is important to be able to pronounce words based on their ordinary English spelling, so we will explain the most common spellings for each IPA sound. This is especially important with vowel sounds, which often have several common spelling patterns plus some exceptions.

Many people over the centuries have made suggestions for ways to improve the English spelling system, but so far none of these ideas have been accepted. In fact, sometimes these "improvements" have only made things worse. Noah Webster tried in the early 1800s to improve the spelling of English; his new spelling rules were accepted in the United States, but not in England or Canada. So now we have even more confusion! *Color* or *colour? Theater* or *theatre? Analyze* or *analyse?* In each case, the first spelling is the American spelling while the second is the British.

Be patient with yourself as you learn to make connections between English sounds and spelling, and be patient with English, too! It's not always logical and it's not always consistent, but we have to work with what we've got. In the chapters that follow, we will introduce each of the symbols and explain how to pronounce the sounds and how those sounds are usually spelled.

The charts on the following page give you an overview:

VOWEL SYMBOLS						
	A	**E**	**I**	**O**	**U**	
"short vowels"	/æ/ bat bad	/ɛ/ bet bed	/ɪ/ bit bid	/ɔ/ bought August awesome	/ʌ/ but bud	/ʊ/ book foot should
"long vowels"	/ey/ bait made	/iy/ beet bead	/ay/ bite wide	/ow/ boat rode	/uw/ /yuw/ boot food music	
r-colored vowels	/ar/ bar park	/ɛr/ bear care	/ɪr/ beer fear	/ɔr/ bore war	/ɚ/ /ɜ˞/ burn her bird	
other vowels	/a/ father drama box			/ɔy/ boy voice /aw/ bound now		/ə/ banana away

The letters at the top of the vowel chart give a hint of the possible spelling of words, but as you will see, there are many exceptions. All vowels are voiced.

CONSONANT SYMBOLS	
Unvoiced	**Voiced**
/p/	/b/
/f/	/v/
/t/	/d/
/k/	/g/
/s/	/z/
/θ/ (*th*in)	/ð/ (*th*en)
/ʃ/ (*sh*in)	/ʒ/ (*g*enre)
/tʃ/ (*ch*in)	/dʒ/ (*j*ob)
	/l/
	/r/
	/m/
	/n/
	/ŋ/ (si*ng*)
	/w/
	/y/ (*y*oung)
/h/	

Slash marks are used to indicate sounds. In this book, we will use capital letters to indicate spelling, and italics to indicate words. For example, CH sounds like /ʃ/ in the word *chef*.

Note: To avoid confusion, this book uses the symbol /y/ to represent the initial sound in *year* and *young* (rather than the official IPA symbol /j/.)

CHECK YOURSELF: Answer true or false to each question, based on the information in this chapter:

1. English spelling is very simple and logical.
2. IPA is used in some countries instead of ordinary English spelling.
3. English has always been pronounced the same as it is today.
4. IPA is a system of symbols to indicate the sounds of a word.
5. The words *write* and *right* are written the same in IPA.
6. We can use IPA to show the difference in pronunciation of the present and past tense of the word *read*.
7. English spelling can give us no hint about how to pronounce a word.
8. It is likely that English spelling will soon be changed to make more sense.

Check Yourself Answers
1. False, 2. False, 3. False, 4. True, 5. True, 6. True, 7. False, 8. False, unfortunately

CHAPTER 3

Can You Hear Me Now?
Voiced and Unvoiced Sounds

A. What is Voicing?

Of course we always use our voice when we speak. But in English, as in many other languages, there are pairs of sounds that are made with our lips and tongue in the same position, but which have a different sound because one is "voiced" and one is "unvoiced."

- **Voiced sounds** are sounds in which the vocal cords in our throats vibrate as a sound is being produced. These sounds are a bit louder and deeper sounding.
- **Unvoiced sounds** are sounds in which our vocal cords do not vibrate. They are very quiet sounds, so we often add an extra puff of air as we make the sound.

One way you can learn the difference between voiced and unvoiced sounds is to:

- put your fingers in your ears
- say *sip*
- say *zip*

You should feel your vocal cords vibrating when you say *zip* but not when you say *sip*. This is because the Z in *zip* is voiced and the S in *sip* is unvoiced. Now, try this again:

- put your fingers back into your ears
- say *fan*
- say *van*

Did you feel your vocal cords vibrate when you said *fan* or when you said *van*? If you said, "*van*," you are correct: the V in *van* is voiced. Here is a list of American English sounds:

Unvoiced Sounds	Voiced Sounds	
/h/ **h**at	all vowels and diphthongs	
/p/ **p**at	/b/ **b**at	/m/ **m**eet
/t/ **t**en	/d/ **d**en	/n/ **n**eat
/k/ **c**oat	/g/ **g**oat	/ŋ/ si**ng**
/f/ **f**an	/v/ **v**an	/l/ **l**ead
/θ/ **th**in	/ð/ **th**is	/r/ **r**ead
/s/ **s**ip	/z/ **z**ip	/w/ **w**eed
/ʃ/ **sh**ow	/ʒ/ trea**s**ure	/y/ **y**es
/tʃ/ **ch**oke	/dʒ/ **j**oke	

13

B. Opposites Attract—Sound Sorter

As you can see from the chart above, in English, there are some pairs of voiced and unvoiced sounds.

- Listen to these word pairs. Pay close attention to the sound in the **bold** print. Mark the correct answer in the box.

	Voiced	Unvoiced		Voiced	Unvoiced
1. **b**ull			17. ta**p**		
2. **p**ull			18. ta**b**		
3. **ch**in			19. nea**t**		
4. **g**in			20. nee**d**		
5. **d**ub			21. ra**ck**		
6. **t**ub			22. ra**g**		
7. pre**ss**ure			23. sa**v**e		
8. mea**s**ure			24. sa**f**e		
9. **s**eal			25. brea**the**		
10. **z**eal			26. brea**th**		
11. **th**is			27. M**s**.		
12. **th**in			28. mi**ss**		
13. **g**ood			29. ru**sh**		
14. **c**ould			30. rou**ge**		
15. **v**ine			31. ba**tch**		
16. **f**ine			32. ba**dge**		

Use the Words—Sentence Practice

Practice saying these sentences. For the words in **bold** print, be careful to voice or unvoice the consonant correctly.

1. The **bull** will **pull** a cart.
2. He has **gin** on his **chin**.
3. Let's **dub** it a "**tub**."
4. A **fine vine** is climbing the wall.
5. They **measure** the **pressure** every week.
6. The **seal** eats with a lot of **zeal**.
7. We don't want it to be **this thin**.
8. **Could** it be that **good**?

9. Don't **tap** on the **tab.**

10. We **need** to be **neat.**

11. Put the **rag** on the **rack.**

12. To be **safe, save** some of this.

13. Take a **breath,** so you can **breathe.**

14. Is it **Miss** Wong or **Ms.** Wong?

15. If you **rush,** you'll smudge your **rouge.**

16. One **badge** is not in the **batch.**

C. Voicing and Vowel Length

In English, a vowel before a voiced consonant is longer than a vowel before an unvoiced consonant. Correct voicing and vowel length are very important because if you make a mistake, the sentence you say may have a different meaning than the one you intend it to have.

Compare these sentences:

It's a **wheat** field.

It's a **weed** field.

In this pair of sentences, the /t/ in *wheat* is unvoiced and the /d/ in *weed* is voiced. You may have noticed that the /iy/ sound in *weed* is longer than the /iy/ sound in *wheat*. Also, you can see that these words have very different meanings.

Practice saying the list of words below. Compare the length of the vowels.

Group A: Words that end in an unvoiced consonant	Group B: Words that end in a voiced consonant	Group C: Words that end in a vowel
1. tote	toad	toe
2. seat	seed	see
3. tight	tied	tie
4. ice	eyes	I
5. safe	save	say
6. beet	bead	be
7. life	live	lie
8. wait	wade	way
9. wrote	road	row
10. leaf	leave	Lee

11. Group ____'s vowels are the shortest.

12. Group ____'s vowels are longer.

13. Group ____'s vowels are the longest.

Use the Words—Sentence Practice

Practice saying these sentences.

1. The **toad** in the **tote** bag bit my **toe.**
2. We **see** the **seed** on the **seat.**
3. Who **tied** this **tight tie?**
4. **I** put **ice** on my **eyes.**
5. Did she **say** it was **safe** to **save** it?
6. The **beet** will **be** the size of a **bead.**
7. Don't **lie** about your **life** on **live** TV!
8. **Wait** before you **wade** that **way.**
9. That **row** of students **wrote** on the **road.**
10. **Leave** the **leaf** with **Lee.**

CHAPTER 4
I've Got Rhythm: Stressed Syllables and Compound Words

Stress creates the rhythm of a language, just as a drum creates the rhythm in music. A stressed syllable is pronounced a bit more loudly, with a higher pitch, and with an unreduced vowel, while in unstressed syllables, the vowel is often reduced to schwa /ə/. Unfortunately, there is no simple rule to tell us which syllable to stress. In longer words, there may be two levels of stress: primary stress, which is strongest, and secondary stress, which is weaker, as well as unstressed syllables. For example, in the word *constitutional,* the primary stress is on the third syllable (**con** -sti -**TU**- tion- al), but the first syllable is also lightly stressed.

A. Feel the Stress

Listen as your instructor reads the following words and circle the syllable that has primary stress.

1. volunteer   vo-lun-teer
2. collect   col-lect
3. angry   an-gry
4. embarrassment   em-bar-rass-ment
5. sprinkle   sprin-kle
6. newspaper   news-pa-per
7. tomorrow   to-mor-row
8. cargo   car-go
9. professor   pro-fes-sor
10. elevator   el-e-va-tor
11. forgetful   for-get-ful
12. invitation   in-vi-ta-tion
13. surplus   sur-plus
14. rebuild   re-build
15. distraction   dis-trac-tion
16. opinion   o-pin-ion
17. duration   du-ra-tion

18. pronunciation   pro-nun-ci-a-tion
19. biology   bi-ol-o-gy
20. magnetic   mag-net-ic
21. festival   fes-ti-val
22. problematic   prob-lem-at-ic
23. embassy   em-bas-sy
24. oxygen   ox-y-gen
25. visible   vis-i-ble

B. One Word, Two Ways

In English, some words can be either a noun or a verb. The noun is usually stressed on the first syllable and the verb on the second syllable. Compare these sentences:

> He is a <u>re</u>bel.
> They will re<u>bel</u>.
> I worked on that <u>pro</u>ject.
> We pro<u>ject</u> that it will take a week to complete.
> This wine is an <u>im</u>port.
> They want to im<u>port</u> more products.

Circle the noun or verb your instructor is saying

Nouns	**Verbs**
1. <u>ad</u>dress	ad<u>dress</u>
2. <u>de</u>crease	de<u>crease</u>
3. <u>com</u>bat	com<u>bat</u>
4. <u>con</u>duct	con<u>duct</u>
5. <u>con</u>flict	con<u>flict</u>
6. <u>con</u>test	con<u>test</u>
7. <u>con</u>tract	con<u>tract</u>
8. <u>con</u>vict	con<u>vict</u>
9. <u>ex</u>port	ex<u>port</u>
10. <u>im</u>port	im<u>port</u>
11. <u>in</u>crease	in<u>crease</u>
12. <u>in</u>sult	in<u>sult</u>
13. <u>ob</u>ject	ob<u>ject</u>
14. <u>per</u>mit	per<u>mit</u>

15. pre<u>s</u>ent   pre<u>sent</u>
16. <u>pro</u>duce   pro<u>duce</u>
17. <u>pro</u>gress   pro<u>gress</u>
18. <u>pro</u>ject   pro<u>ject</u>
19. <u>pro</u>test   pro<u>test</u>
20. <u>re</u>cord   re<u>cord</u>

C. Where the Stress Falls

Different forms of the same base word are often stressed on different syllables.

Listen as your instructor reads the words below and underline the primary stress in each word form.

Verbs	**Nouns**	**Adjectives**	**Adverbs**
1. democratize	democracy	democratic	democratically
2. elevate	elevation	elevated	
3. economize	economy	economical	economically
4. evolve	evolution	evolutionary	evolutionarily
5. exaggerate	exaggeration	exaggerated	
6. excel	excellence	excellent	excellently
7. illustrate	illustration	illustrated	
8. memorize	memory	memorable	memorably
9. neglect	negligence	neglectful	neglectfully
10. transport	transportation	transportable	
11. unite	union	united	
12. prepare	preparation	prepared	
13. revolt	revolution	revolutionary	
14. appreciate	appreciation	appreciably	
15. authorize	authority	authoritarian	
16. propose	proposition	proposed	
17. apply	application	applied	
18. substantiate	substance	substantial	substantially
19. testify	testimony	testimonial	
20. repeat	repetition	repeated	repeatedly

D. Same or Different?

Listen to your instructor read each pair of words below. Circle **same** if the primary stress in the word pair is the same. Circle **different** if the primary stress is different.

1. neglect   direct   *same*   *different*
2. dinner   destroy   *same*   *different*
3. daily   prairie   *same*   *different*
4. pineapple   example   *same*   *different*
5. determine   suggestion   *same*   *different*
6. something   comment   *same*   *different*
7. community   celebrity   *same*   *different*
8. operate   consider   *same*   *different*
9. practical   expensive   *same*   *different*
10. diploma   examine   *same*   *different*
11. majority   intelligent *same*   *different*
12. solution   vitamin   *same*   *different*
13. invitation celebration *same*   *different*
14. equipment   confusing   *same*   *different*
15. appointment devotion   *same*   *different*
16. planet   closet   *same*   *different*
17. danger   pleasure   *same*   *different*
18. people   city   *same*   *different*
19. building   swimming   *same*   *different*
20. washing   machine   *same*   *different*

E. Cross It Off the List

In each group of words below, cross out the words that do not have the same stress pattern as the underlined word. Remember, in order for words to have the same stress pattern, they must also have the same number of syllables.

succeed	**principle**	**migrate**	**activity**	**selection**
disagree	medicine	insult (n)	community	umbrella
command	grotesque	control	intelligent	surprise
construct	engineer	religion	independent	solution
deny	unique	weekend	democracy	decision
believe	vitamin	decade	credibility	cathedral
development	**celebrate**	**arithmetic**	**community**	**crisis**
entertainment	telegram	electrical	universally	vicious
philosophy	volunteer	pollution	nationality	another
available	degree	energetic	cooperation	present (n)
mathematics	realize	critical	biology	supplies
political	merciful	identity	decisively	perfect (v)

F. A White House or the White House?

When a noun or adjective modifies a noun, usually both words are stressed equally. But in some cases, the two words are used together so often that they become like a single word, called a *compound noun*. In that case, the first word is stressed more strongly and the second word is stressed less.

Modified Noun (equal stress)	**Compound Noun** (stress the first word)
a hot day	a hot dog
my best friend	my boyfriend
a good friend	a girlfriend
a white house	the White House
the green house	the greenhouse effect
a black board	a blackboard
a bad ache	a backache
ice tea	ice cream
a red ball	a football
the soft sweater	the software
a hard problem	a hardware problem
my older brother	my stepbrother
a large pot	a teapot
an empty box	a shoebox
a shiny knob	a doorknob

Modified Noun *(equal stress)*	Compound Noun *(stress the first word)*

Write the following words in the correct boxes above:

- bluebird
- bookmark
- pencil case
- old shoes
- grapefruit
- stop sign
- chocolate pie
- blackberry
- black jacket
- sweet berries
- sweetheart
- pocketbook
- favorite book
- high school
- good school
- keyboard
- lost key
- roommate
- good player

G. I Can Handle the Stress!

Circle the syllable that has the primary stress.

1. **dan** cer
2. phi **los** o phy
3. con **nec** tion
4. **pro** blem
5. de **light** ful
6. **hon** es tly
7. re **call** (v)
8. Ja **pan**
9. en th u si **as** tic
10. ar **riv** al
11. Ja pan **ese**
12. **ear** nest
13. re **mem** ber
14. de **fin** i tion
15. dec or **a** tion
16. pi **a** no
17. com **pe** ti tive
18. na **tion** al
19. **gar** age
20. pu **bli** city
21. **mes** sage
22. **or** gan
23. **pub** lic
24. **ex** er cise
25. pro **fes** sor
26. **cir** cul ate
27. vo **ca** tion
28. e **lec** tion
29. cir cu **la** tion
30. mu **se** um
31. **won** der ful
32. **re** cord (n)
33. **A** sia
34. **beau** ti ful
35. con **vict** (v)
36. **te** le phone
37. de **lay**
38. **re** bel (n)
39. **pho** to graph
40. **dif** fi cult
41. ob **ject** (v)
42. **al** pha bet
43. a **round**
44. **mam** mal
45. **hap** pi ness
46. es **tab** lish ment
47. **per** fect
48. pro nun ci **a** tion

CHAPTER 5
Don't Stress the Small Stuff

In the last chapter, we looked at how syllables within a word are stressed. In addition to word stress, in each sentence some words are stressed more than others. When we stress a word, we pronounce it more clearly. The pitch (like a musical note) may be higher. Our voice may be louder. The word may be pronounced more slowly and there will be less tendency to drop any sounds. Unstressed words will be pronounced quickly, and the vowel sounds may be "reduced" (that is, they may change to /ə/).

A. Listen Up

Listen to your instructor read the following phrases. Notice the words that are strongly stressed (in bold print letters), the words with neutral stress (in ordinary letters), and the words that are unstressed (in italic print.)

1. **Who wants** *to* **go**?
2. She **told** me *who* **went**.
3. I want **that** one.
4. I **knew** *that* I would **pass** the **test**.
5. I **read** *the* **whole book**.
6. **Kim stood** *at the* **bus** stop *for an* **hour**.
7. We **ate peaches** *and* **cream**.
8. **When** *is the* **movie** *going to* **start**?
9. I go *to* **bed** *when* I'm **tired**.
10. I **knew** *that* I *should have* gone *to* **bed earlier**.

B. Content or Function?

In general, content words are stressed and function words are unstressed.

Content Words	Function Words
nouns (John, book)	pronouns (I, him, who, that)
main verbs (run, think)	auxiliary verbs (has, will)
adjectives (big, pretty)	articles (the, some)
adverbs (quickly, already)	prepositions (in, under)
question words (Who? Why?)	conjunctions (and, while)

In each sentence, circle the content words. Then read the sentences and stress the content words. Pronounce the function words more quickly and lightly.

1. The big dog barked at the tiny kitten.
2. Because of the storm, school was cancelled for the day.
3. When we arrived, the party had already started.
4. I was afraid that she would miss the flight.
5. We enjoyed the movie because it had an exciting plot.
6. The only thing we have to fear is fear itself.
7. I believe that a solution to the problem will be found soon.
8. Who do you think will win the election?
9. I decided where to live after I got a new job.
10. She never expected to win any money in the lottery.

C. That's Old News

In general, new information is stressed more than old information. Also, if you ask a question about what someone just said, the repeated word is usually strongly stressed. Listen as your teacher reads the following dialogue. Then practice it with a partner.

Kimiko:	Hi, Young Hee. How **are** you?
Young Hee:	Fine thanks. How are **you**?
Kimiko:	**Great**. Did you **do** anything last **weekend**?
Young Hee:	I didn't do **much**, but I have big plans for **next** weekend.
Kimiko:	**Really**? What are you planning to **do**?
Young Hee:	My **husband** and I plan to **drive** up the **coast** to **San Francisco**.
Kimiko:	**San Francisco**? That sounds **great**! Have you ever **been** to San Francisco before?
Young Hee:	No, we haven't. **Last** month we went to **Las Vegas**, but that's the **only trip** we've taken since we **moved** here.
Kimiko:	San Francisco is **beautiful**. But be **sure** to take a **warm jacket**. It can be really **cold** there.
Young Hee:	In **July**?
Kimiko:	Yup, even in **July** you might need a jacket.
Young Hee:	Well, we sure didn't need one in **Las Vegas**. It was so **hot** there in **June**.

Kimiko: The weather can **really** change when you take a weekend trip. Have you been up in the local **mountains**?

Young Hee: No, I haven't. How's the weather **there**?

Kimiko: Well, in the **winter**, it might be warm enough to **swim** at the **coast**, but when you drive two hours up into the mountains, there is enough **snow** to **ski**.

Young Hee: Wow, I can see that we have a lot to **explore**! I wish we had more time to **travel**!

D. Stress for Emphasis

In addition to using stress to emphasize the content words, and to contrast new and old information, stressing one word in a sentence can change the focus of the meaning.

Listen as your teacher reads each sentence. Then practice saying them with a partner:

1. John Smith might get a new job in New York City next month.
   (neutral)
2. JOHN Smith might get a new job in New York City next month.
   (not Sam Smith)
3. John SMITH might get a new job in New York City next month.
   (not John Jones)
4. John Smith MIGHT get a new job in New York City next month.
   (or he might not!)
5. John Smith might get a NEW job in New York City next month.
   (not his old job)
6. John Smith might get a new JOB in New York City next month.
   (not a new apartment)
7. John Smith might get a new job in NEW YORK City next month.
   (not Oklahoma City!)
8. John Smith might get a new job in New York CITY next month.
   (not New York state)
9. John Smith might get a new job in New York City NEXT month.
   (not this month)
10. John Smith might get a new job in New York City next MONTH.
    (not next week)

26 Part 1 The Big Picture

Now you try it. Circle the word that you would stress in each sentence to make your meaning clear. Then practice saying the sentences with a partner.

1. <u>I</u> heard that the new English teacher has six children. (no one else heard it)
2. I <u>heard</u> that the new English teacher has six children. (I didn't read it in the <u>newspaper</u>.)
3. I heard that the <u>new</u> English teacher has six children. (not the old one)
4. I heard that the new <u>English</u> teacher has six children. (not the math teacher)
5. I heard that the new English teacher has <u>six</u> children. (not three)
6. I heard that the new English teacher has six <u>children</u>. (not cats!)

E. Stress for Contrast

When we are contrasting two or more things, the word that is different is usually stressed. Listen and repeat the following sentences:

1. Government OF the people, BY the people, and FOR the people shall not perish from this earth.
2. We can't go OVER it, we can't go UNDER it, we can't go AROUND it, so we'll have to go THROUGH it.
3. If you THINK you can, you CAN. If you think you CAN'T, you WON'T.
4. I looked for it ON the desk and IN the desk and AROUND the desk, but I forgot to look UNDER the desk.

F. Those Stressful Phrasal Verbs!

We mentioned above that prepositions such as *in*, *on*, and *of* are not stressed. However, the particles in phrasal (or two-word) verbs are an exception to this rule. These particles may look like prepositions (*in*, *over*) or adverbs (*away*, *after*).

Listen to the following sentences:

1. If you don't know what the word means, you can <u>look it UP</u>.
2. I wonder why his girlfriend <u>broke UP</u> with him.
3. He was shocked when she <u>called</u> the wedding <u>OFF</u>.
4. I told him to <u>calm DOWN</u> and <u>start OVER</u> again.
5. We took her to a movie to try to <u>cheer her UP</u>.
6. I asked the teacher to let me <u>do the test OVER</u>.
7. Most of the time I cook dinner, but sometimes I like to <u>eat OUT</u>.

8. If you want to <u>find OUT</u> the answer, ask him yourself.

9. We made plans to <u>get TOGETHER</u> after class.

10. I didn't want to <u>let him DOWN</u> again, so I worked even harder.

G. Correct the Stress

In each of the following sentences, the wrong word or words have been stressed. Cross out the incorrect words and circle the words that should be stressed. Then practice saying the sentences with a partner.

1. I explained THAT he needs to show his driver's LICENSE.
2. She asked me WHEN I expect to graduate.
3. They ate three pieces OF pie.
4. If you take a hike IN the mountains, BE sure to LOOK out for snakes.
5. Put it under the BED, not on the BED.
6. I don't HAVE an air conditioner, but at least I HAVE a fan.
7. I don't know WHERE the post office is.
8. I don't LIKE that song, but I LIKE this one.
9. I have ENOUGH money for a vacation, but I don't have ENOUGH time.
10. The teacher CALLED me James, BUT my name IS actually Jamil.
11. She's STUDYING accounting BECAUSE she is interested in business.
12. He was upset THAT he couldn't do IT over.

CHAPTER 6
Can I Ask You a Question?

If a language were music, its intonation patterns would be its melodies. Intonation is one of the first aspects of language that babies learn. They can make themselves understood before they learn actual words. This is why we can understand what a baby wants when she babbles. For instance:

Ana: Na na naaa? ↗

Mother: It's a ball. ↘

Ana: Na! ↘ *[reaches for the ball]*

Mother: OK, here you go. ↘ *[gives the ball to Ana]*

English intonation patterns feature a rising (↗) tone and a falling (↘) tone used in various combinations based on the speaker's intentions. Although Ana may not have the words to tell her mother what she wants, Ana's mother can understand Ana's intonation.

Later, when Ana is able to talk, she can give sentences different meanings based on the intonation she uses:

Kim: The test! ↘

Ana: The test? ↗ It's today? ↗

Kim: I think so, but I'm not sure. ↘

Ana: I'll check. ↘ Yup, it's today. ↘

A. The Meanings of Rising and Falling Intonation

As in many other languages, in English:

- **Falling intonation** usually means that the speaker is making a statement or commanding someone to do something.
- **Rising intonation** usually means that the speaker has questions.

Compare these short conversations:

Mike: That was your boyfriend. ↘

Gabi: Thanks. ↘ If he calls again, tell him I'll call him back later. ↘

In this conversation, Mike is making a statement, so he uses falling intonation. Gabi wants Mike to give her boyfriend a message from her, so she uses falling intonation, too.

Mike: That was your boyfriend? ↗

Gabi: Yes, it was. ↘ That was my Julio. ↘

This time, Mike doesn't know Gabi's boyfriend, Julio, so Mike asks Gabi about him. Because Mike is asking a question, he uses rising intonation.

B. Yes–No Questions

A Yes–No Question is a question that can be answered "Yes" or "No." We use rising intonation with these questions. For example:

Sunhee: Are you going home now? ↗

Rashid: Yes, I am. ↘ Are you leaving soon, too? ↗

Sunhee: No, but hopefully I can leave before 7:00. ↘ Have a good evening, Rashid. ↘

Rashid: Same to you. ↘ See you tomorrow. ↘

In this conversation, the rising intonation indicates a question.

C. WH–Questions

Not all questions use rising intonation. WH–Questions (Who? What? When? Where? Why? How?) end with falling intonation. For example:

Dad: Where are you going? ↘

Lisa: I'm going to the library. ↘

Dad: Why? ↘ Who's going to be there? ↘

Lisa: I have to study for a test with Remy and Marisol. ↘

Dad: When is this test? ↘

Lisa: Friday. ↘ Dad, why are you asking me so many questions? ↘

Dad: I just want to know what my little girl is doing. ↘

Notice that unlike the Yes–No Question, the WH–Question uses a falling intonation. This is because a WH–Question begins with a question word, so using a rising intonation isn't necessary.

D. Tag Questions

A Tag Question is a short question that follows a statement. It can have rising or falling intonation depending on the speaker's intention. For example:

Thu: It's going to rain, isn't it? ↗

Rick: Sorry, I don't know. ↘ I didn't see the weather report. ↘

In this conversation, Thu isn't sure if it will rain later, so she asks Rick if he knows.

Thu: It's going to rain, isn't it? ↘

Rick: I think so, too. ↘ I hope we get home before it starts. ↘

But in this conversation, Thu is pretty sure that it will rain, and she wants to find out if Rick agrees with her.

Lani: You went to the movies with Derek, didn't you? ↗

Dora: No, I went with my brother. ↘

In this conversation, Lani thought that Dora saw a movie with Derek, but she wasn't completely sure if that was true.

Lani: You went to the movies with Derek, didn't you? ↘

Dora: Who told you that? ↘

In this conversation, Lani knows Dora saw a movie with Derek, and she wants Dora to add to this information. But Dora thinks that Lani is being nosy.

But notice what happens if Dora changes the intonation in her response:

Lani: You went to the movies with Derek, didn't you? ↘

Dora: Who told you that? ↗ ↘

Now instead of simply asking a WH–Question, Dora is implying that what Lani heard is wrong. This sounds like the beginning of an argument!

As you can see, when using a Tag Question, it's important to use the correct intonation, or you can get a very different response from the one you expect.

E. Asked and Answered—Using What We've Learned So Far

Work with a partner and choose one of the situations below. Create a conversation for this situation. Be sure to use the correct rising and falling intonation patterns in your conversation. Present your conversation to the rest of the class.

Situation 1

Your neighbors have a son, Alex, who is very mischievous and who sometimes does things that annoy you. One day when you come home, your front window is broken. Alex is bouncing a ball against his garage door. When he sees you, he starts to walk away. But you want to talk to him.

Situation 2

You left a package of new USB drives on your desk. But when you return from a meeting, the package is open, and one USB drive is missing. Zelda, your co-worker, is typing on her computer, and you see a USB drive sticking out of it. This USB drive looks like one of your new USB drives. You want to find out where she got it.

Situation 3

Your friend has been acting a little strange. Usually she is happy and talkative, but these days she doesn't return your phone calls, and her e-mails to you are very short. Last month, she told you that her husband may lose his job and that she was worried about it. You want to talk to her and to offer to help her if she needs your help.

F. Alternatives

When we talk about two alternatives (choices), we use a combination of rising and falling intonation. For example:

Bibi: What's your schedule like? ↘ Are you taking biology ↗ or chemistry? ↘

Amir: Chemistry. ↘ Do you have math in the morning ↗ or in the afternoon? ↘

Bibi: I have it in the morning. ↘

Amir: Me too. ↘ Do you have Dr. Wolde ↗ or Dr. Brown? ↘

Bibi: Dr. Wolde. ↘ She's really nice. ↘

Amir: Great! ↘ We're in the same class! ↘

As Bibi and Amir talk about their schedules, they use rising and falling intonation to show that they are asking about pairs of possible choices that can be made. The rising intonation after the first alternative shows that another alternative is coming, and the falling intonation shows that the speaker has finished talking.

G. Snap Decisions—Apples or Oranges?

When they have trouble finding a topic to talk about, American men may play a game where they ask each other to make a snap decision between two alternatives until they find a topic that they can discuss. For instance:

Carl: Batman ↗ or Superman? ↘

Ben: Superman. ↘ Led Zeppelin ↗ or Metallica? ↘

Carl: Led Zeppelin. ↘ Steak ↗ or ribs? ↘

Ben: Ribs. ↘ The Lakers ↗ or the Celtics? ↘

Carl: The Celtics. ↘ Angelina Jolie or . . . →

Ben: *[interrupts Carl]* Wait, the Celtics? ↗ Are you crazy? ↗ The Lakers are way better than the Celtics! ↘

Carl: Hold on. ↘ Look at all the championships when the Celtics beat the Lakers! ↘ *[they keep arguing]*

Now You Try It

- Form 2 teams and line up on opposite sides of the room.
- Flip a coin to see which team will go first.
- Think as fast as you can, and try to stump the people on the other team.
- The first person in the Team 1 line gives a pair of alternatives to the person across from him or her in the Team 2 line. For example:

    Team 1, Person 1: Apples ↗ or oranges? ↘ (meaning: Do you prefer apples or oranges?)

    Team 2, Person 1: Oranges. ↘ Rain ↗ or snow? ↘

    Team 1, Person 2: Rain. ↘ Swimming ↗ or running? ↘

    Team 2, Person 2: Running. ↘ *[and so on]*

- When a person can't make a choice or come up with a new set of alternatives, the other team gets a point. For example, if a Team 1 person can't come up with a pair of alternatives, Team 2 gets a point.
- At the end of the 5 minutes, the team with the most points wins.

H. Lists

When we talk about a list of 3 or more items, we also use a combination of rising and falling intonation. Compare these sentences:

You can have coffee ↗ or tea. ↘
You can have coffee, ↗ tea, ↗ or juice. ↘
You can have coffee, ↗ tea, ↗ juice, ↗ or water. ↘

The rising and falling intonation pattern is almost the same as the one used for alternatives. The only difference is that we have more than 2 choices in a list, so there are more times that we will need to use rising intonation before we get to the end of the list.

I. Practicing Lists: The Go-to Person Scavenger Hunt

A **go-to person** is someone we go to whenever we need something because he or she always has what we need.

Directions

- Form a group of 4 or 5 people.
- Take your "stuff" out of your bookbag.
- Mark each item on the checklist below.
- Add up the points for the items you have. Two erasers, etc., only count as 1 item.
- Read your list to the group and add up your total points. Be sure to use rising intonation for each item until you get to the last one.
- Check to see who has the highest total points in the group. That person is the go-to person in your group!

The Go-to Person Checklist—(1 point per item)

_____ an eraser

_____ a new Scantron™ sheet

_____ a piece of gum

_____ a pen with red ink

_____ a dictionary

_____ a roll of tape

_____ a paper clip

_____ correction fluid (like Liquid Paper™)

_____ a class schedule book

_____ a bandage (like a Band-Aid™)

_____ a ruler

_____ a mirror

_____ a clean tissue

_____ a lunchbox or lunch bag

_____ a calculator

Bonus Items—(3 points per item)

_____ a fast-food coupon

_____ a Post-It™ note

_____ a rubber band or hair band

_____ a granola bar or Power Bar™

_____ a Golden Dollar coin or a foreign coin

_____ a postage stamp

_____ a staple puller

_____ an iPod™ or other music player

_____ a plastic fork or spoon

_____ a pink or blue highlighter

_____ a flashlight

_____ a lottery ticket or "scratch-off" ticket

_____ a flash (USB) drive

_____ a fresh fruit or vegetable

_____ a sheet of graph paper

_____ **YOUR TOTAL POINTS**

_____ **IS THE GO–TO PERSON IN OUR GROUP.**

J. Intonation Drama: A Tale of Passion and Betrayal

With a partner, read the play below. Mark each sentence with ↘ or ↗ to show a falling or rising intonation.

"Conversation Piece"

From *Ellery Queen Mystery Magazine* (1950) by Ned Guymon. Copyright © 1950 by Kathryn Guymon. Reprinted by permission.

Bob: No!
Tim: Yes.
Bob: You didn't!
Tim: I did.
Bob: When?
Tim: Just now.
Bob: Where?
Tim: Bedroom.
Bob: Dead?
Tim: Yes.
Bob: Why?
Tim: You know.
Bob: I don't!
Tim: You do.
Bob: Unfaithful?
Tim: Yes.
Bob: With whom?
Tim: With you.
Bob: No!
Tim: Yes.
Bob: She didn't . . .
Tim: She did.
Bob: We didn't . . .
Tim: You did.
Bob: You knew?
Tim: I knew.

Bob:	How long?
Tim:	Long enough.
Bob:	What now?
Tim:	Guess.
Bob:	Police?
Tim:	Later.
Bob:	Why later?
Tim:	Guess again.
Bob:	Tell me!
Tim:	Look.
Bob:	Oh, no!
Tim:	Oh, yes!
Bob:	You can't!
Tim:	I can.
Bob:	Please!
Tim:	Don't beg.
Bob:	Forgive me!
Tim:	Too late.
Bob:	Good God!
Tim:	Good-bye.
Tim:	911?

Can you explain what is happening in this story?

PART 2

A Mouthful of Vowels

CHAPTER 7
The Real Cheese Deal (/iy/)

A. Sound It Out

This is the sound American students know as "long e" and its symbol in American dictionaries is ē. To pronounce it, think of the word *cheese*. Why do people tell you to "Say cheese" before they take your picture? It's because you have to smile in order to pronounce the /iy/ sound in *cheese*. When you pronounce /iy/, your muscles are tense and your lips are in the smiling position, your tongue is in the front of your mouth and very high, almost touching the roof of your mouth, and your jaw is high and almost closed.

Like all vowels in English, /iy/ sounds a little bit different depending on the sound that comes after it. Vowels followed by unvoiced sounds are always pronounced quickly, while vowels followed by voiced sounds are stretched out. Vowel sounds at the end of a word are also stretched out.

First just listen carefully to the sound /iy/

Quick (unvoiced)	Stretched (voiced)	Stretched (final)
keep	leave	me
leaf	need	we
neat	these*	he
seek	breathe	she
piece/peace	seem	see/sea
teach	cheese*	be/bee
beneath	please*	tea
leash	eagle	flee/flea
teeth	even	fee
sleep	easy*	key

*The s in these words is pronounced /z/.

Compare these pairs of words. Both words have the sound /iy/, but the first /iy/ is quick and the second /iy/ is stretched:

piece	peas
niece	knees
leaf	leave

Listen as your instructor reads one word in each row and circle the word you hear:

1. cease   seize
2. thief   thieves
3. seat   seed
4. heat   heed
5. neat   need
6. grief   grieve
7. teeth   teethe

B. Spell It Out

When American children are learning to read, they sometimes learn a little rhyme to help them remember how to pronounce the vowel sounds:

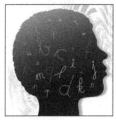

When two vowels go walking,
The first one does the talking.
What does he say?
He says his name.

This means that when you see two vowels together, like EE or EA, the first one will be pronounced and the second one will be silent, and the pronunciation of the first one will be the name of that letter in English. English speakers pronounce the name of the letter E /iy/. So it doesn't matter whether we see EE or EA; they are both pronounced the same. The most common spellings in English for the sound /iy/ are EE or EA:

EE	EA
sleep	neat
feel	leap
need	leave
tree	reach
free	leak
seem	reading
seen	tea
beef	cream

How do you know whether a word will be spelled EE or EA? Unfortunately, there is no rule for that. In fact, some words, called homonyms, have different spellings but are pronounced exactly the same, like *see* and *sea* or *week* and *weak*.

Like most spelling patterns in English, there are exceptions as well. Sometimes /iy/ is spelled IE or EI:

niece
piece
belief
either
neither

When the /iy/ sound comes at the end of a word it is often spelled Y

    key
    funny
    lucky
    happy
    funny

The word *people* has an unusual spelling for the /iy/ sound.

C. Silly Sentences

Circle all the /iy/ sounds in these sentences. Then practice saying them.

1. Three fleas leap on a sheep.
2. She keeps seizing pieces of my beef.
3. The thief reached for the cheese.
4. Please read each piece in three weeks.
5. He feels a need for free cheese.
6. Each teacher believes in sleep.
7. Neither niece eats beef.
8. He dreams of Jeanie each week.
9. A sailor went to sea to see what he could see.
10. I scream, you scream, we all scream for ice cream.

D. A Fable from Aesop: The Tree and the Reed

Take turns reading this story with a partner. Pay attention to the sound /iy/ in the words in bold.

Once a strong **tree** looked at a slender **reed** and asked, "**Dear Reed,** how can you **be** so **weak?** You should **reach** your **feet** down **deep** into the ground as I do, and grow beautiful **leaves.**" The **reed** had no answer and began to **feel** ashamed of his **weakness.** But soon a great storm arose. The **tree** was uprooted from the ground and came crashing down. But the **weak reed** bent his head in the wind, and when the storm passed, **he** stood up straight and tall again.

Moral: **Even** a **weak reed** may **be** stronger than it **seems.**

E. Dialogue

Practice saying this dialogue with a partner.

Lee: Hi, my name is **Lee.**

Jean: **Pleased** to **meet** you, **Lee.** My name is **Jean.** Haven't I **seen** you somewhere **before**?

Lee: Well, let's **see.** You might have **seen me** at the **beach.**

Jean: No, I don't **believe** so. I never go to the **beach.** I like to hang out at **Dean's Coffee Bean** and **read.**

Lee: Do you **mean** the one on **Peachtree Street**?

Jean: Yes, I go there every **week**!

Lee: So do I! We should **meet** there next **week** for **coffee** or **tea.**

Jean: I **agree**! When are you **free**?

Lee: Hmmm, let's **see** . . . .

F. Talk It Over

1. "A friend in **need** is a friend **indeed.**" Like many proverbs, the words to this one are a little puzzling at first. "A friend in **need**" doesn't **mean** a friend who **needs** your help. In fact, you are the one "in **need.**" And "indeed" **means** something like "for sure" or "in truth." Can you explain the **meaning** of this proverb? Can you think of a time when you found out who was "a friend **indeed**"?

2. What does a person really **need** in order to be **happy**? Is there a difference between a want and a **need**?

3. Do you **believe** that your **dreams** have a **meaning**? Did you ever have a **dream** that **seemed** to you to **mean** something important? Do you think your **dreams** can **predict** the future?

G. Speak Your Mind

1. Some **people believe** in **lucky** or **unlucky** numbers. For example, lots of Americans **believe** that the number **thirteen** is **unlucky.** Do you **believe** in **lucky** or **unlucky** numbers? How would you **feel** about taking Flight **13** on your next trip? Are there **lucky** or **unlucky** numbers in your **country**?

2. Is it hard to make friends in the United States? Where is a good place to **meet** new **people**? What advice would you give a young person who wanted to **meet** a boyfriend or girlfriend?

H. Can You Guess it?

The answer to each clue will be a word that has the sound /iy/.

1. Coffee or _____
2. The back of a shoe
3. We eat three of them a day
4. A gentle wind
5. The opposite of *those*
6. The farmer planted corn in his _____
7. The opposite of *strong*
8. Winter, spring, summer, and fall are the four _____
9. You wear your shoes on your _____
10. Beef and pork are types of _____
11. The dentist checks your _____
12. Another word for *myself*
13. A body of salt water
14. Pine, palm, and maple are three types of _____
15. The number after two
16. An insect that makes honey
17. The opposite of *expensive*
18. A fish that resembles a snake
19. A bicycle has two; a car has four
20. The opposite of *sour*
21. The opposite of *messy*
22. When you're tired, you want to _____
23. A hill that's very hard to climb is _____
24. The opposite of *shallow*
25. You say this to be polite

I. Not to Be Confused With . . . .

Most students don't have a hard time with the sound /iy./ The trouble arises when they hear the English sound /ɪ/ and confuse it with /iy/. We will study the sound /ɪ/ in the next chapter, but for now, notice that words spelled with two vowels have the sound /iy/ and words with just one vowel have the sound /ɪ/.

/iy/	/ɪ/
sheep	ship
sleep	slip
heap	hip
leave	live
heat	hit
beat	bit
weak	wick

J. 13 or 30

It's sometimes difficult to be sure whether someone is saying 13 or 30, 14 or 40, and so on, because both words contain the /iy/ sound. Here's a trick to help you pronounce these words so that everyone will understand what you mean:

Pronounce these words with a clear /t/ sound and a rising ↗ intonation at the end:	Pronounce these words with a /d/ sound and a falling ↘ intonation at the end:
13↗	30↘
14↗	40↘
15↗	50↘
16↗	60↘
17↗	70↘
18↗	80↘
19↗	90↘

Listen to your instructor and write the number you hear:

1. She was born in 19____.
2. Her friend is _____ years old.
3. There were _____ questions on the test.
4. The class is in room ____.
5. She invited ___ people to her party.
6. His address is ____ Main Street.

Now You Try It

Student A: Write any number from 13–19 or 30, 40, 50, etc., in each sentence. Then read your sentences to your partner and see if he or she can understand you correctly.

1. I have _____ dollars in my pocket.
2. The population of that country is _____ million people.
3. I want to make $ _____ an hour some day.
4. There were _____ people in the room.
5. She watched _____ movies last year.
6. The company plans to hire _____ people.
7. The answer to the math problem was _____.
8. She lives in Apartment _____.
9. That famous writer was born in 19_____.
10. I think humans will go to Mars in 20 _____ (two thousand _____)

Student B: Write any number from 13–19 or 30, 40, 50, etc., in each sentence. Then read your sentences to your partner and see if he or she can understand you correctly.

11. I spent _____ dollars at that restaurant.
12. There are _____ million people in that state.
13. He earns _____ thousand dollars a year.
14. That class has _____ students in it.
15. Can a person read _____ books in one month?
16. That company employs _____ workers.
17. I need to borrow _____ dollars.
18. The class meets in room _____.
19. That invention was created in 19_____.
20. Humans will probably find a cure for the common cold in 20_____ (two thousand _____).

CHAPTER 8
The Big Pig Jig (/ɪ/)

A. Sound It Out

American students call this sound "short i" and its symbol in American dictionaries is ĭ. When you pronounce /ɪ/, your muscles are relaxed and your lips are only slightly open. Your tongue is high (but not as high as /iy/), and your jaw is high (but not as high as /iy/). The sound /ɪ/ is a very quick sound.

First, just listen carefully to the sound /ɪ/:

Quick (unvoiced)	Stretched (voiced)	Stretched (final)
hip	bib	Note: the sound /ɪ/ never comes at the end of a word in English.
sit	hid	
pick	big	
kiss	whiz	
stiff	live	
pitch	rim	
fish	tin	
with	fill	

The following pairs of words have the same vowel sound, but the first one is quick and the second one stretched. Listen and circle the word you hear:

1. pick   pig
2. bit   bid
3. kit   kid
4. lit   lid
5. rip   rib
6. Miss   Ms.
7. Rich   ridge

B. Spell It Out

The most common spelling for the sound /ɪ/ is the vowel I alone.

        is   bin   finish   infinite

All of the following words have the /ɪ/ sound and regular spelling. Listen to your instructor and write each word.

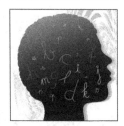

1.
2.
3.
4.
5.
6.

There are also some unusual ways to spell /ɪ/:

Y as in:

    g**y**m   Eg**y**pt   s**y**llable   m**y**stery

O as in:

    w**o**men (pronounced /wɪmɪn/)

U as in:

    min**u**te (pronounced /mɪnɪt/)

Finally, there are two words that can be confusing when you write:

been (pronounced /bɪn/ in American English)

    Tim has **been** to Mississippi.

being (pronounced /biyɪŋ/)

    Tim is **being** silly.

C. Silly Sentences

Circle all the /ɪ/ sounds in these silly sentences. Then practice saying the sentences.

1. It took fifteen minutes for him to list all his issues and six minutes to fix them.
2. Mickey and Minnie live in Disneyland.
3. Phillip's kitten bit him on the shin.
4. Will Cindy ever sing this song without hiccupping?
5. Little kids like trick or treating, but big kids should quit it.
6. Come quick! There's a pig in a bikini swimming in the pool!
7. It's a mystery why Izzy calls a violin a "fiddle."
8. Can you find India, Indonesia, and Indiana on a map?
9. The Wicked Witch of the West scares Mindy out of her wits.
10. Men and women often misunderstand each other, but in the end, they find some middle ground.

D. Limerick

There once was a **big billfish**
Who had one **little wish:**
To **live** to be **sixty,**
By being **shifty,**
And not to end up **in** a **dish.**

E. Dizzy Dialogue—Dessert: It'll Fill You or Kill You

Practice this dialogue with a partner.

Liz: Have some pie. **It's filled with vanilla pudding.** I'll put some **whipped** cream on **it,** too. Oh, and here's some **milk** to go **with it.**

Kim: Thanks, but **if** you don't mind, I **think I**'ll pass. All of those **delicious Indian dishes** really **filled** me up.

Liz: Come on, a **little** piece of pie and some **milk** really **hits** the spot, even after a **big dinner.**

Kim: **It** sounds **tempting,** but I'm lactose **intolerant. In** other words, **if** I have **anything with** dairy products **in it, it will** make me **physically ill.** Sorry.

Liz: That's the **silliest thing** I've ever heard! **Little kids drink milk** all the time, and they never get **sick. Dig in!**

Kim: If it's OK, I'd **still** rather pass. I don't want to **ruin** our **evening.**

Liz: Well, **if** you **insist.** How about a nice **dish** of **chilled** fruit **instead**?

F. Poetry Corner

Work with a partner and circle all the words in the following poem that contain the sound /ɪ/. Then practice reading it.

Don't Quit!

When things go wrong, as they sometimes will
And the road you're traveling seems all uphill
When worry is getting you down a bit
Rest for a while, but don't you quit.

Life is strange with its twists and turns
As every one of us finally learns
And many people who think they've failed
Might have won if they had not quit.

Success is failure turned inside out
The silver tint of the cloud of doubt
So stick to the fight when you're hardest hit
Though things seem bad, you must not quit.

Do you agree with the message of this poem? Are there times when you *should* quit?

G. Talk It Over

1. **If** you had three **wishes,** what would you **wish** for? Why are these **things important** to you?
2. **Which inventions** would you like to see **in** the future? Why?
3. **Which hidden abilities** (or talents) do you have?

H. Speak Your Mind

1. Has the **Internet** helped or hurt **interactions** between people? Why?
2. **In which situations** would you let your **children** make their own **decisions?** About their hobbies and **interests?** About their friends and **romantic** partners? About the **direction** of their education?
3. Some people say that you should never **discuss religion** or **politics.** Do you agree or **disagree?** When **is it** OK to **discuss** these **things?**

I. Can You Guess It?

1. A cover is a ____
2. A bag of potato ____
3. Your house is the place where you ____
4. My clothes are too tight. They don't ____
5. Not healthy
6. Before you go shopping, you make a ____ of what to buy
7. A large boat
8. Quiet and unmoving
9. A big smile
10. A mosquito bite makes you ____
11. A hug and a ____
12. To choose
13. Another word for *hog*
14. A very strong breeze
15. The opposite of *stand*
16. The person who throws a baseball is the ____
17. The opposite of *out*
18. The opposite of *thick*
19. You cross the ____ line at the end of a race
20. Coffee, beer, and water are all ____
21. To make a hole
22. The opposite of *small*
23. Some people like gold jewelry; others like ____
24. He, she, and ____
25. Cows give us ____ to drink

Chapter 8 Answers to B: Spell It Out

1. kid
2. rip
3. brim
4. pink
5. dig
6. tin

CHAPTER 9
The Red Hen's Dead End (/ɛ/)

A. Sound It Out

American students call this sound "short e," symbolized ĕ in American dictionaries. When you pronounce /ɛ/, your muscles are relaxed and your lips are slightly spread, your tongue is in the middle of your mouth and your jaw is in medium position.

First just listen carefully to /ɛ/ in the following words:

Quick (unvoiced)	Stretched (voiced)	Stretched (final)
bet	bed	Note: the sound /ɛ/ never comes at the end of a word in English.
neck	web	
Pepsi	egg	
mess	edge	
next	fell	
met	them	
left	men	
yes	send	
sketch	says	
breath	when	
nephew	end	

The following pairs of words have the same vowel sound, but the first one is quick and the second one stretched. Listen and circle the word you hear:

1. let   led
2. peck   peg
3. set   said
4. wept   webbed
5. etch   edge

B. Spell It Out

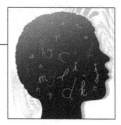

The most common spelling for /ɛ/ is the letter E alone:

       bell   leg   men   felt   bench   press

Spellcheck

All of the following words have the /ɛ/ sound and regular spelling. Write the word that you hear:

1.

2.

3.

4.

5.

6.

There are several common words that have the sound /ɛ/ with an unusual spelling:

any /ɛniy/ anyone, anywhere, anything, anyhow
many /mɛniy/ (notice that this word rhymes with *penny*.) Say: many pennies.
says /sɛz/
said /sɛd/ (notice that this word rhymes with *bed*.) Say: I said it's a bed.
friend /frɛnd/

Can you make a sentence that includes at least 5 of the words on this list?

Another common spelling of the sound /ɛ/ is EA. Listen and draw a line lightly through the letter A.

head	death
read (past tense)	meant
bread	heavy
dead	heaven
deaf	leather
breath	health

C. Rhyme Time

Fill in a word from the list above that will make a rhyme:

He sat down on his bed

Holding his hands to his _____.

I read the letter you sent

But I didn't know what it _____.

There once was a man named Seth

Who constantly held his _____.

It finally caused his _____!

The book was red, but never _____.

D. Silly Sentences

Circle all the /ɛ/ sounds in these sentences. Then practice saying them.

1. Fred said his hen is dead.
2. Ben wept when he left the deck.
3. Ed said many men have red necks.
4. Yesterday Betty read every website on the net.
5. The mess was left to them.
6. You said you'd confess, more or less.
7. He says many friends left.

E. Can You Guess It?

1. You sleep in a _____
2. Don't turn right, turn _____
3. More than one man
4. Birds lay these
5. It rings, at a school or church
6. Past tense of *feel*
7. You catch butterflies in a _____
8. Past tense of *say*
9. It's not alive, it's _____
10. The color of fire trucks
11. A penny is worth one _____
12. You write with a _____
13. The opposite of *borrow*
14. When you go camping, you sleep in a _____

15. In school, students sit at a _____
16. The opposite of *more*
17. Birds build these
18. If you're tired you should _____
19. Another name for an exam
20. The opposite of *east*
21. The opposite of *worst*
22. You see with your eyes and _____ with your nose
23. The past tense of *fall*
24. A sandwich is made with two slices of _____
25. A spider weaves a _____

F. Speak Your Mind

1. **Men** and women are not **exactly** the same, even though they are equal. What are some things that **many men** do that women don't usually do?

2. Think of jobs that are **messy.** Can you imagine an **invention** that would allow you to do the same job with **less mess?**

3. Write a short dialogue between a man and a woman. Start each line with "He **said**" or "She **said.**"

4. Who is your **best friend?** What makes a person a good **friend?** Do you know any famous sayings about **friends** or **friendship?**

5. Who is the most famous person you've **ever met?** Can you **remember** what you **said?** You could play a game called "I doubt it!" Give a short description of how you **met** a famous person and what you **said.** Your story can either be true or false. **Tell** your story to your group. They will try to **guess** if your story is true or not.

G. Not to Be Confused With: /ɪ/ vs. /ɛ/

Notice that your mouth is a little more open when you pronounce /ɛ/.

1. It's the opposite of *borrowed*	lent	lint
2. It's the fuzzy stuff that collects in a clothes dryer	lent	lint
3. It's like a needle without a hole	pen	pin
4. It's a type of writing tool with ink inside it	pen	pin
5. It's the number that comes after nine	ten	tin
6. It's a type of metal	ten	tin
7. It's a deep hole	pet	pit
8. It's a dog or cat that is a family member	pet	pit
9. It's a baseball glove	met	mitt
10. It's the past tense of *meet*	met	mitt
11. It's on top of your neck	head	hid
12. It's the past tense of *hide*	head	hid
13. It's the opposite of *alive*	dead	did
14. It's the past tense of *do*	dead	did

Chapter 9 Answers to B: Spellcheck

1. fed
2. less
3. spend
4. tell
5. deck
6. get

CHAPTER 10
The Whale's Tail (/ey/)

A. Sound It Out

American students call this the "long a" sound, and in American dictionaries the symbol is ā. When you pronounce /ey/, your muscles are tense and there is a gliding movement of your lips from a relaxed to a spread position; your tongue is in the mid-front position but glides up toward /iy/.

First just listen carefully to the /ey/ sounds in the following words:

Quick (unvoiced)	Stretched (voiced)	Stretched (final)
brake	plain	play
lace	tail	away
shape	Jane	May
place	scale	today
waist	game	delay
faith	save	holiday
take	sane	gray
fate	pale	Friday
ape	cage	say
hate	name	yesterday

The following pairs of words have the /ey/ sound, but the first one is quick and the second one stretched. Listen and circle the word you hear:

1. place   plays
2. mate   made
3. waif   wave
4. safe   save
5. cake   cage
6. great   grade
7. lace   lays

B. Spell It Out

The most common spelling for the sound /ey/ is the letter A plus another vowel.

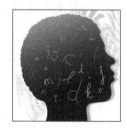

A (with silent E)	AI	AY
face	straight	maybe
lace	paint	away
Jane	sailor	tray
taste	wait	play
ape	aim	today

Other spellings of the /ey/ sound:

EI	EA
weight	break
sleigh	steak
reindeer	great
eight	
reign	
neighbor	

Because /ey/ can have several spellings, there are many homonyms—words pronounced the same but spelled differently:

1. I **ate eight** cupcakes.
2. Don't stomp on the **brake!** You'll **break** it!
3. You'll have to **wait** to find out your **weight.**
4. It **rained** while the king **reigned.**
5. They grilled **steaks** on **stakes** at the barbecue.
6. This pizza will taste **great** if you **grate** some cheese on it.

C. Silly Sentences

Circle all the words with the sound /ey/. Then practice saying these sentences.

1. Two space aliens swam in the bay in April and May.
2. The ape skated across the lake looking for Jake.
3. Tracy is spacey and sometimes a little lazy.
4. The frog in the lake ate an eight-pound steak.
5. The lady in Spain ate cake in the train.
6. Rain, rain, go away, come again another day.

7. Larry and Tracy were acting like babies and driving me crazy.

8. May can't wait to see her date who's always late.

9. Shane ate the cake that turned out to be fake.

D. Story: A Beautiful Day

Circle all the words in this story that have the sound /ey/. Then read the story out loud to your partner.

One sunny day early in May, a lady named Grace went out to wade in Lake James. The sky was so blue, that it seemed that someone had decorated it with crayons or paints. Clouds looked like patches of lace. Blue jays flew around the lake, and cranes stood still on their long, thin legs. Grace could have stayed at the lake till half past eight. Suddenly, her sister April came by with her basket full of raisin cake. Grace did not complain. She got out of the lake even though she wanted to stay. They sat under a maple tree and ate their cake quietly. They enjoyed the shade and the cool breeze as the leaves were swaying playfully. The day was done, the sky grew gray, and the sisters walked home as the sun's wavy rays paved the way.

E. Dialogue: A Day for Play

Practice reading this dialogue with a partner.

Jake: Hi, **May!** Do you want to **play** with **Kate** and me?

May: **Okay, Jake.** Is **April** also coming with us to **play games** at the park?

Jake: No, let's go to my house. I have a **Play Station**™ and lots of **games.**

May: Did your mother **make** any of her delicious **cakes?**

Jake: Yes, she **baked** all **day yesterday.**

May: That's **great!** What a fun **day!**

Jake: Let's go right **away** and enjoy this beautiful **day.**

May: **Great!** I'll get ready, and we'll be on our **way.**

F. Talk It Over

"An apple a day keeps the doctor away."

Do you eat fruit every day? Why is fruit good for your health? What is your favorite fruit? Is it true that a healthy diet can keep the doctor away?

"No pain, no gain."

How does this saying apply to exercise or fitness? What other aspects of life does it apply to? Can you give examples of times in your life when you had to accept some "pain" in order to get some "gain"?

G. Can You Guess It?

The answer to each clue will be a word that has the sound /ey/.

1. Better than good
2. Another word for *dish*
3. To cook bread in an oven
4. Your nose is on your _____
5. It travels on rails or tracks
6. Astronauts travel through _____
7. You feel this when you get hurt
8. The opposite of *love*
9. On vacation we _____ in a hotel
10. A+ is the best _____
11. The largest sea animal
12. You wear your belt around your _____
13. The opposite of *night*
14. If you drop a glass, it will _____
15. The number that comes before nine
16. Wine is made from _____
17. The Spanish language comes from _____
18. A time when things in a store are cheaper
19. We eat this at a birthday party
20. A child's favorite thing to do
21. Water that falls from the sky

22. An animal with a long, thin body and no legs

23. A contest to see who can run the fastest

24. The opposite of *early*

25. The month after April

H. Speak Your Mind

1. Do you believe that every person has a certain **fate** or destiny? Do you believe that the person you marry or the **place** where you now live is **related** to your **fate**?
2. What do you need to do to **obtain** good **grades** in your classes? Is it realistic to expect students to receive **straight A's**? Do parents put too much pressure on children to get good **grades**?

3. **Lately,** most people are using computers on a **daily basis.** Can you mention some important uses of the computer in your **everyday** life?

4. "Don't put off till tomorrow what you can do **today**" reminds us not to **delay** doing things we should do right **away.** Are you a **procrastinator?** What things do you often leave for tomorrow that you should have done right **away?**

I. Can You Match These?

____ 1. My mother's   a. ape
____ 2. Spring   b. cake
____ 3. A lion's   c. mane
____ 4. Up, up, and   d. angel
____ 5. A blue   e. ladybug
____ 6. Falling snow   f. rain
____ 7. A polka-dotted insect   g. apron
____ 8. Bake a   h. flakes
____ 9. The wings of an   i. away
____ 10. A chimp is an   j. whale

J. Backward Crossword Puzzle

The answer to each clue is a word that has the **opposite** meaning.

Across:	Down:
2. wild	1. work day
4. asleep	2. give
6. crooked	3. love
7. early	5. yesterday
8. night	6. waste

K. Not to Be Confused With . . . .

The /ɛ/ sound was introduced in Chapter 9. Compare the /ɛ/ and the /ey/ sounds. Notice that the /ɛ/ sound is shorter that the /ey/ sound.

/ɛ/	/ey/
wet	wait
letter	later
bet	bait
debt	date
pen	pain
when	Wayne

Mark the word you hear:

	/ɛ/	/ey/
1.	less	lace
2.	west	waste
3.	tech	take
4.	tell	tail
5.	sent	saint
6.	men	main

CHAPTER 11
The Rat Pack Attack (/æ/)

A. Sound It Out

American students know this sound as "short a" and the symbol in American dictionaries is ă. When you pronounce /æ/, your muscles are relaxed and your lips are open; your tongue is low (but not as low as /a/) and your jaw is low. If you use the A sound of your native language, English speakers will probably think you are saying /ə/ or /a/ instead of /æ/. So when you say you have a *cat*, they might think you have a *cut* or a *cot*.

First just listen carefully to /æ/ in the following words:

Quick (unvoiced)	Stretched (voiced)	Stretched (final)
bat	bad	Note: the sound /æ/ never comes at the end of a word in English.
last	man	
mask	can	
path	has	
map	cab	
flat	as	
cash	sand	
staff	badge	
back	am	
fax	ankle	
bath	and	
that	shall	

The following pairs of words have the same sound, but the first one is quick and the second one stretched. Listen and circle the word you hear.

1. bad   bat
2. sad   sat
3. bag   back
4. sag   sack
5. have   half
6. badge   batch

B. Spell It Out

The most common spelling for the sound /æ/ is the letter A alone.

Spell Check: All of the following words have the /æ/ sound and regular spelling. Listen and write each word.

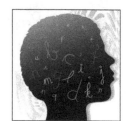

1.

2.

3.

4.

5.

6.

C. Silly Sentences

Circle all the /æ/ sounds in these sentences. Then practice saying them.

1. That fat black cat sat back on the mat at last.
2. Al had half a bad ham sandwich.
3. Stand and hand that man a fan.
4. That masked man can't laugh back.
5. He who laughs last laughs best.
6. I can't understand Stan.
7. We'll eat what we can, and can what we can't.

(Can you understand the last sentence? "To can" is a verb that means "to prepare vegetables in cans or glass jars so that they will last a long time." So the speaker might be a gardener with too many tomatoes.)

> See appendix on page 350 at the end of the book for more practice with *can* and *can't*.

D. Tongue Twister

How many yaks can a yak pack pack if a yack pack can pack yaks?

E. Poet's Corner

Listen to this poem and underline all the /æ/ sounds you hear. You might enjoy memorizing the poem and reciting it for the class.

The Cat of Cats

by William Brighty Rands

I am the cat of cats. I am
The everlasting cat!
Cunning*, and old, and sleek* as jam,
The everlasting cat!
I hunt the vermin* in the night—
The everlasting cat!
For I see best without the light—
The everlasting cat!

*cunning = smart and tricky, sleek = smooth, vermin=rats and mice, for example.
(from *Favorite Poems of Childhood*. ed. Philip Smith. New York: Dover Publications, 1992.)

F. Palindromes

Do you know what a palindrome is? It's a word or sentence that is the same when you read it forward or backward. For example, look at the name "Hannah." It's a one-word palindrome.

Here's a famous palindrome with several /æ/ sounds:

   "Madam, I'm Adam."

Ignore the spaces and read it backward. Can you figure out who the speaker is? Who he is introducing himself to?

Here's another famous palindrome that has a lot of /æ/ sounds:

   "A man, a plan, a canal—Panama!"

This sentence refers to the man who had a plan to build a canal through Panama so that ships traveling from New York to San Francisco wouldn't have to travel all the way around South America. President Teddy Roosevelt was the "man" who made this bold plan work—though he didn't care whose land he had to take to do it.

Notice that when English speakers say the word *Panama*, they pronounce each A differently. The first A in Panama sounds like /æ/. And only the second A in canal sounds like /æ/.

G. Can You Guess It?

The answer to each of the following clues is a word that contains the sound /æ/.

1. The opposite of *white*
2. You wear it on your head
3. The opposite of *front*
4. The subject you study when you learn about numbers
5. The opposite of *future*
6. The opposite of *good*
7. The opposite of *happy*
8. An animal that meows
9. Another name for *father*
10. The past tense of *have*
11. The opposite of *woman*
12. When you're dirty, you take a _____
13. The opposite of *slow*
14. You hit a baseball with a _____
15. The opposite of *first*
16. What you put in your car to make it go
17. When someone does a favor for you, you say _____
18. You carry books to school in a _____
19. What you do to a gift to make it look pretty
20. You need one to mail a letter
21. When you're tired in the afternoon, you take a _____
22. Campbell's soup comes in a _____
23. You build castles out of this at the beach
24. A train runs on a _____
25. You catch a rat in a _____

H. Speak Your Mind

1. "**I can't stand** it" is an idiom that means "I dislike it strongly." For **example,** you could say, "I like coffee, but I **can't stand** tea." It's often used to complain about things people do: "I **can't stand** people who talk on the cell phone while they're driving" or "I **can't stand** it when drivers don't use their turn signals." What are some things that you **can't stand?**

2. Are there some places where you **can't laugh?** Did you ever feel like **laughing** when you were in **class** or some other place where you should be quiet? Make a list of times and places where you **can't laugh.**

3. Did you ever try to do something that turned out to be a **bad plan?**

4. What are some things that a **cat can't** do?

5. If you could talk to anyone in the world, and **ask** them any question you want, who would you talk to and what would you **ask?** Can you make a guess what they would **answer?**

I. Not to Be Confused With....

Notice that when you pronounce the sound /æ/, your mouth is more open than for the sound /ɛ/.

Circle the word that you hear:

	/ɛ/	/æ/
1.	bed	bad
2.	said	sad
3.	men	man
4.	set	sat
5.	X	axe
6.	lend	land
7.	bet	bad

Chapter 11 Answers to B: Spell It Out

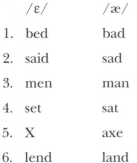

1. hand
2. fast
3. cat
4. ran
5. cash
6. tap

CHAPTER 12
All Together Now: Review of Chapters 7–11

A. Vowel Symbol Identification

Match the vowel sound with the correct IPA symbol.

1. mate _____   A. /ɪ/
2. meat _____   B. /ey/
3. met _____   C. /iy/
4. mitt _____   D. /æ/
5. mat _____   E. /ɛ/

Write the IPA symbol for the vowel sound in each word.

6. peel   _____
7. pail   _____
8. bell   _____
9. pill   _____
10. pal   _____

B. Listening Practice

Listen and circle the word you hear.

1. miss   mess   mass
2. hid   head   had
3. knit   net   gnat
4. lanes   lens   leans
5. him   hem   ham
6. feel   fail   fell   fill
7. take   tech   tack   tick
8. lid   lead   led   laid
9. sill   sail   sell   seal
10. teen   ten   tin   tan

C. Vowel Sorter

Work with a partner. One of you will be Student A and one will be Student B.

Student A: Read these words to your partner. Your partner will write the answers in the box below.

cave	kit	can
man	end	ink
pill	tack	tray
steak	wheat	head

Then, Student A: Listen and write the words your partner says in the correct box.

/iy/	/ɪ/	/ey/	/æ/	/ɛ/

Student B: Listen and write the words your partner says in the correct box.

/iy/	/ɪ/	/ey/	/æ/	/ɛ/

Then, change roles: Student B: Read these words to your partner.

thin	peas	great
brand	case	pick
name	chain	ask
shell	bread	egg

D. Sentence Practice

1. **Can** you **knit** a **net** to **catch** a **gnat?**
2. **We had** to **beg** for **bigger bags** of lemons **and** figs.
3. **Will Bren**da **tell** about the **trea**sure's **se**cret lo**ca**tion?
4. **Ask** him to **hem** a pair of **pants** or to **bake** a **ham.**
5. The **cam**era **lens** is **leaning** against Mr. **Lane's** hat.
6. **She missed seeing** that **massive mess in** the **mid**dle of the **street.**
7. **Betty felt happy when** she **did well** on the **tricky English test.**
8. **Sidney** always **brings** a home**made cheesecake** to **class** on Fri**days.**
9. **Is** the **end** of the movie worth **seeing,** or **is it** a **let**down?
10. **Al**an **is getting** a **ba**con, **let**tuce, and to**ma**to **sandwich.**

E. Contrast Practice /ɪ/ /iy/ /ɛ/ /æ/ or /ey/?

Read the sentence and circle the correct word.

1. It's where you store underground water	will	well	wheel
2. It helps bikes, cars, etc., roll	well	wheel	will
3. It's the present tense form of *would*	wheel	well	will
4. It's used to catch fish	bait	bit	bet
5. It's what people do at the racetrack	bet	bait	bit
6. It's a tiny amount of something	bit	bet	bait
7. It's another word for *friend*	pal	pail	peel
8. It's the skin of an orange	pail	peel	pal
9. It's the same thing as a bucket	peel	pal	pail
10. It's the back of your foot	hill	heel	hail
11. It's frozen rain	heel	hail	hill
12. It's a small mountain	hail	heel	hill
13. It's where you go to exercise	jam	gem	gym
14. It's similar to jelly	gem	gym	jam
15. It's another word for *jewel*	gym	jam	gem
16. It's a bird bite	peek	peck	pick
17. It's another word for *choose*	pick	peck	peek
18. It's a quick look at something	peek	pick	peck

Chapter 12 All Together Now *(Review of Chapters 7–11)* **69**

19. It's a group of related items — seat · set · sit
20. It's the present tense form of *sat* — set · sit · seat
21. It's the place where you sit — sit · seat · set
22. It's a kind of grain — wet · wait · wheat
23. It's how you feel when water spills on you — wheat · wait · wet
24. It's what you do if you arrive too early — wait · wet · wheat
25. It's the opposite of *good* — bed · bead · bad
26. It has a hole in it — bead · bad · bed
27. It's where you lie down to sleep — bad · bead · bed
28. It's another word for *husband* or *wife* — mate · met · meat
29. It's the past tense of *meet* — met · mate · meat
30. It's a food that comes from animals — met · meat · mate
31. It's the past tense of *light* — lit · let · late
32. It's the opposite of *early* — let · late · lit
33. It's another word for *allow* — late · let · lit
34. It's another word for *crash* — wreck · rake · rack
35. It's where you can find magazines — rake · rack · wreck
36. It's a tool for putting leaves in a pile — rack · wreck · rake

Now try the same sentences again, this time in a different order.

1. It's where you store underground water — will · well · wheel
2. It's a small mountain — hail · heel · hill
3. It's what people do at the racetrack — bet · bait · bit
4. It's another word for *friend* — pal · pail · peel
5. It's a food that comes from animals — met · meat · mate
6. It's the past tense of *light* — lit · let · late
7. It's a type of grain — wet · wheat · wait
8. It's the opposite of *good* — bed · bead · bad
9. It's where you can find magazines — rake · rack · wreck
10. It's similar to jelly — gem · gym · jam
11. It's another word for *choose* — pick · peck · peek
12. It's frozen rain — heel · hail · hill
13. It's a group of related items — seat · set · sit

14. It's where you go to exercise	jam	gem	gym
15. It's another word for *husband* or *wife*	met	mate	meat
16. It's the skin of an orange	pail	peel	pal
17. It's another word for *allow*	late	let	lit
18. It's used to catch fish	bait	bit	bet
19. It's how you feel if water spills on you	wheat	wait	wet
20. It's the place where you sit	sit	seat	set
21. It's a quick look at something	peek	pick	peck
22. It's the present tense form of *would*	wheel	well	will
23. It's another word for *crash*	wreck	rake	rack
24. It has a hole in it	bead	bed	bad
25. It's another word for *jewel*	gym	jam	gem
26. It's a bird bite	peek	peck	pick
27. It's the past tense of *meet*	met	mate	meat
28. It's a tiny amount of something	bit	bet	bait
29. It's the present tense form of *sat*	set	sit	seat
30. It's the same thing as a bucket	peel	pal	pail
31. It's what you do if you arrive too early	wait	wet	wheat
32. It's where you lie down to sleep	bad	bead	bed
33. It's the back of your foot	hill	heel	hail
34. It's a tool for putting leaves in a pile	rack	wreck	rake
35. It's the opposite of *early*	let	late	lit
36. It helps bikes, cars, etc., roll	well	wheel	will

CHAPTER 13
Love a Lucky Duck (/ʌ/)

A. Sound It Out

American students know this sound as "short u" and its symbol in American dictionaries is ŭ. When you pronounce /ʌ/, everything is relaxed. Your muscles are relaxed, your lips are relaxed and slightly parted, your tongue is relaxed and in mid-position, and your jaw is relaxed. This is the sound you would make if you suddenly bumped into something with your stomach and the air just got pushed out.

Listen carefully to the sound of /ʌ/:

Quick (unvoiced)	Stretched (voiced)	Stretched (final)
pup	cub	/ʌ/ does not occur at the end of words. Instead, the unstressed sound /ə/ is used at the end of words.
cuff	rub	
cut	sub	
but	tub	
us	bud	
must	mud	
just	mug	
dust	dull	
hush	gull	
much	run	
luck	fuzz	
stuck	buzz	

Compare these pairs of words. Both words have the sound /ʌ/, but the first /ʌ/ is quick and the second /ʌ/ is stretched:

1. cup   cub
2. mutt   mud
3. but   bud
4. fuss   fuzz
5. luck   lug

B. Spell It Out

The most common spelling for the sound /ʌ/ is the letter U, as seen in the examples on page 71. But notice that there are some words spelled with the letter U that do not have the /ʌ/ sound.

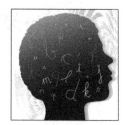

Listen to the following words and cross out the ones that are NOT pronounced /ʌ/:

1. but
2. cut
3. put
4. much
5. rush
6. push
7. bunch
8. bush
9. dull
10. pull

Another common spelling for the sound /ʌ/ is the letter O. Listen carefully to the pronunciation of the following words. All of them have the sound /ʌ/. Mark the /ʌ/ sound in each word.

blood	glove	shovel
brother	governor	some
color	honey	son
come	love	sponge
comfort	money	stomach
country	monkey	ton
cousin	month	tongue
cover	mother	touch
does	nothing	tough
doesn't	one	trouble
dozen	onion	won
flood	other	wonder
from	oven	young
front	rough	

Two other very common words with the sound /ʌ/ are *was* and *what*.

C. Silly Sentences

Circle all the /ʌ/ sounds in these sentences and then practice saying them:

1. Some lucky ducks must love the floods.
2. An unlucky dump truck was stuck in the mud.
3. Some brothers are nothing but trouble.
4. If you've got the money, honey, I've got the time.
5. The onion was rough on my stomach.
6. One cousin won a dozen shovels last month.
7. I wonder how much fun my other son had in the sun.
8. One governor comes from another country.
9. The cover was the color of mud.
10. My mother and my brother touched the monk for good luck.

D. Tongue Twisters

Can you say these sentences three times fast?

- Rubber baby buggy bumpers.

- Double bubble gum is double trouble.

E. Poetry Corner

How many /ʌ/ sounds can you find in this poem?

Only One Mother

By George Cooper

Hundreds of stars in the pretty sky,
Hundreds of shells on the shore together,
Hundreds of birds that go singing by,
Hundreds of lambs in the sunny weather,

Hundreds of dewdrops to greet the dawn,
Hundreds of bees in the purple clover,
Hundreds of butterflies on the lawn,
But only one mother the wide world over.

from *Favorite Poems of Childhood*, ed. Philip Smith, Dover Pub.

F. Dizzy Dialogues

Mark all the /ʌ/ sounds in each dialogue. Then practice saying the dialogue with a partner.

Son:	I want a puppy!
Mother:	Son, puppies cost too much money.
Son:	But mom, I saw a wonderful puppy that's doesn't cost much.
Mother:	A puppy is too much trouble. Puppies are rough on the furniture. They munch on shoes.
Son:	A puppy would be fun. My cousin has a puppy.
Mother:	Your cousin is much older. You're too young to have a puppy.
Son:	Mom, I'll be 21 next month!

Husband:	Honey, there's a bug in my coffee cup.
Wife:	Sorry, love. I'll get you another cup.
Husband:	Don't forget, two lumps of sugar.
Wife:	Coming right up.
Husband:	And could you give me another cinnamon bun with butter?
Wife:	Oh dear, that was the last one.
Husband:	What? I thought you made a dozen?
Wife:	That was last month!
Husband:	Last month? But the one I had tasted so fresh!
Wife:	Well, I keep them in the freezer, and then I put one in the oven for you each morning before you wake up.
Husband:	What a wonderful wife you are!

G. Talk It Over

1. In choosing a career, would you rather do **what** you **love,** even if the pay is low, or do you want a career that pays a lot of **money?** If you had to choose only **one—money** or **love**—in your career, which one would you choose?

2. How many **cousins** do you have? Are you close to your **cousins?** In **some cultures, cousins sometimes** marry each **other.** Is that **something** you would feel **comfortable** with?

3. Do you have a favorite **color**? Do you think a person's favorite **color** says **something** about his or her personality?

4. "You can't **judge** a book by its **cover**." Is this proverb true of books? Does it apply in **other** situations?

5. "**Some** people have all the **luck**." Is success in life a matter of **luck**? Benjamin Franklin said, "Diligence is the **mother** of **luck**" and a famous film producer, Samuel Goldwyn, said, "The harder I work, the **luckier** I get." What do these two sayings mean?

H. Speak Your Mind

1. **One** of the hardest things about moving to a new **country** is dealing with **culture** shock. In addition to the language, the **customs** are also different. What **customs** surprised you when you moved here? What **customs from** your home **country** did you miss? Can you offer **some** advice to people **from** your **country** who plan to **come** to this **country** to help prepare them for the new **culture**? Are there **some** American **customs** that you still find hard to **understand?** Is there a difference between being bilingual and being **bicultural?**

2. Every **culture** has important celebrations at certain times of the year. What is the biggest celebration in your **culture** or **country**? Are there special family celebrations as well?

I. Can You Guess It?

1. The opposite of *aunt*
2. Pecans and almonds are types of _____
3. A baby dog
4. The opposite of *down*
5. It says "quack"
6. You drink tea from a _____
7. You drink coffee from a _____
8. When you hope someone passes a test, you say "Good _____"
9. At an art museum, there are signs that say, "Please don't _____"

10. The person in charge in a court
11. When the ground gets wet it turns to _____
12. A small carpet
13. At noontime, you eat _____
14. You bake bread in an _____
15. 12 eggs is one _____
16. Every year has 12 _____
17. We didn't lose the game, we _____
18. When you chop this vegetable, it makes you cry
19. Red, green, and blue are _____
20. A city has a mayor, a country has a president, a state has a _____
21. To dig a hole you need a _____
22. A bird that is a symbol of peace
23. The children of your aunt and uncle are your _____
24. Bees make _____
25. The opposite of *old*

J. Not to Be Confused With...

If you do not use the correct pronunciation for /æ/ and /ʌ/, Americans might misunderstand what you are saying. Listen to the difference between these pairs of words:

	/æ/	/ʌ/
1.	cap	cup
2.	sadden	sudden
3.	mad	mud
4.	cat	cut
5.	fan	fun
6.	Dan	done
7.	stamp	stump

Now listen to the words your instructor says and write the number and the word in the correct column:

/æ/	/ʌ/

Chapter 13 Answers to J: Not to Be Confused With . . .

1. hat
2. hut
3. ban
4. bun
5. stand
6. stunned
7. Manny
8. money
9. Sam
10. sum/some
11. lump
12. lamp

CHAPTER 14
Banana Extravaganza (/ə/)

A. Sound It Out

The sound /ə/ is one of the most common sounds in English. In fact, it is so common, it has its own name—schwa. The sound /ə/ is the same as the sound /ʌ/, but /ə/ occurs in unstressed syllables and is quicker and lighter than /ʌ/. When you pronounce /ə/ your muscles are relaxed, your lips are relaxed and slightly parted, your tongue is relaxed and in mid-position, and your jaw is relaxed.

Compare the sound of the word *banana* (/bə næ: nə/) with the spelling. The middle syllable has the sound /æ/ because it is stressed. But the first and last syllables are unstressed, so the sound becomes /ə/. In fact, the vowel sound in almost every unstressed syllable is pronounced /ə/.

B. Spell It Out

It may be hard to believe, but /ə/ can be spelled with any one of the five vowels in English. If a vowel is unstressed, it will probably sound like /ə/ (or sometimes like /ɪ/). The underlined syllables below are unstressed and should be pronounced /ə/.

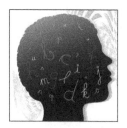

A	E	I	O	U
away	believe	cousin	lemon	circus
awake	before	pencil	lesson	minute
above	rely	punish	photograph	census
buffalo	revive	original	purpose	virus
Canada	predict	medicine	innocent	minus
banana	prevent	individual	confess	
relative	select		memorize	
			today	

Note: These examples are not bad pronunciation or even informal pronunciation. They are the normal pronunciation of these words.

78

C. Don't Stress Out!

Picture a person standing on stage with a spotlight shining down on her. In English, the stressed syllable is the only thing in the spotlight and the only one whose vowel sound is clear. The other vowels are in the shadow and are pronounced /ə/. In each word below, circle the stressed syllable. Draw a line through the other vowels to show that they are reduced to /ə/.

1. plea sant
2. moun tain
3. fa shion
4. sel dom
5. sig nal
6. de cide
7. me thod
8. prob lem
9. se cond
10. de ci mal

D. Attention Please!

The ending –TION is always pronounced /ʃən/ and is always unstressed. The syllable just before the –TION ending always receives primary stress. Circle the sound /ʃən/ and mark the stressed syllable in each word. Notice the reduced vowels in the other syllables.

1. pro nun ci a tion
2. in vi ta tion
3. re lax a tion
4. in ves ti ga tion
5. ce le bra tion
6. in tro duc tion
7. in ven tion
8. pre ven tion
9. de fi ni tion
10. ed u ca tion
11. lo ca tion

12. con tri bu tion

13. con nec tion

14. de co ra tion

15. de ter mi na tion

E. Silly Sentences

Mark the stressed syllables and draw a line through the unstressed syllables. Be sure to pronounce the unstressed syllables with /ə/.

1. The way to pronounce English is to relax.
2. The original purpose of the legal profession is to protect the innocent and to punish the guilty.
3. The American Constitution promises life, liberty, and the pursuit of happiness.
4. His determination to receive an education filled me with admiration.

F. State Secrets

Like other multi-syllable words, many of the names of the U.S. States have the vowel /ə/ (schwa) in unstressed syllables. Listen as your instructor pronounces the name of each state. The states marked with a * have at least one /ə/ (schwa) sound. Underline the vowels that sound like /ə/ (schwa). You might find as many as 50 /ə/ (schwa) sounds in the list.

*Alabama	*Florida	*Kentucky
*Alaska	*Georgia	*Louisiana
*Arizona	*Hawaii	Maine
Arkansas	*Idaho	*Maryland
*California	*Illinois	*Massachusetts
*Colorado	*Indiana	*Michigan
*Connecticut	*Iowa	*Minnesota
*Delaware	*Kansas	*Mississippi

*Missouri	*North Dakota	*Texas
*Montana	Ohio	Utah
*Nebraska	*Oklahoma	Vermont
*Nevada	*Oregon	*Virginia
New Hampshire	*Pennsylvania	Washington
New Jersey	*Rhode Island	*West Virginia
*New Mexico	*South Carolina	*Wisconsin
New York	*South Dakota	Wyoming
*North Carolina	*Tennessee	

G. Extreme Reductions

You've heard of extreme sports, but have you ever heard of extreme reductions? When people are talking casually or informally, they reduce many sounds to /ə/ and may omit some syllables completely. For example, *you* changes to /yə/ and *to* changes to /tə/. The helping verb *have* changes to /əv/ or even just /ə/.

Read each sentence below as it would be said by an American in a very casual situation. Then write the sentence the way it would be written or said in a more formal situation. (Notice that stressed words or words that come at the end of the sentence are not reduced.)

1. I woulda done it the way I usta if I'd (a) known ya wanted me to.

2. Whaddya wanna do?

   I dunno, whadda *you* wanna do?

3. When are ya gonna do it?

   I dunno. I'm supposta do it təmorrow.

4. You shoulda done it sooner.

   I woulda done it sooner if I hadna gotten sick!

5. I coulda had a V-8™! (a kind of vegetable juice)

   It mighta tasted better than this lukewarm tea!

6. Whacha doin?

   Watchin' tv. Wanna go somewhere?

   Sure, whereda ya wanna go?

H. Dizzy Dialogue

When we are talking about things we regret, we usually use the perfect modals: "I should have gone," or "I would have gone if. . . ," or "I could have gone, but. . . ." The word "have" often gets shortened to 've, pronounced /əv/, as in *I should've, I would've, I could've*. When people are speaking very casually, they often shorten these verbs even more, and it sounds like they are saying *shoulda woulda coulda*. This has become an expression that means that there's no sense talking about things you can't change.

Practice the following dialogue:

Jackie: Oh man, I can't believe I failed that class! Now I have to repeat it next semester. I shoulda studied harder!

Alex: Well, why didn't you?

Jackie: I woulda passed if I hadn't missed three weeks of class.

Alex: You missed three weeks of class? How come?

Jackie: It wasn't really my fault! My friends all had spring break at different times, and I wanted to go to Florida with them and party, and, well, I stayed there a little longer than I planned to.

Alex: You stayed there for three weeks?

Jackie: Yeah, but I coulda passed if the teacher had let me make up the work I missed. I woulda come back sooner if I had known she was so strict. She shoulda given me a break!

Alex: Are you kidding? Never mind all this shoulda, woulda, coulda! You were partying on the beach while everyone else was studying. Now you have to take the class again during the summer when the rest of us are relaxing.

Jackie: I guess you're right. I shoulda known better.

I. Talk It Over

1. Think of situations from your own life when you regretted a decision you made. What did you do? What should you have done? What would you have done if you had known better? What could you have done differently? (Use the informal pronunciation of *shoulda, woulda, coulda*.)

2. The word *of* is often reduced to /ə/ in ordinary conversation. So the phrase *a lot of* usually sounds like *alotta* (/əlɔdə/ or /əladə/. (Notice that in writing, *a lot* is two words!) What are some things that cost **a lot of** money? What are some projects that take **a lot of** time? What are some careers that pay **a lot of** money? Would you rather have **a lot of** money or **a lot of** free time?

3. "A piece of cake" is an idiom that means that something is very simple and easy. Notice that the word *of* is pronounced /ə/ in this idiom. Have you taken any classes that were "a piece of cake" for you? What is something you expected to be hard that turned out to be "a piece of cake"?

J. Speak Your Mind

There are **several amendments** to the United States **Constitution** that **concern** the rights of a **citizen**. Some of the **amendments** are still the subject of **discussion** and **controversy**. Work in groups to explain the meaning of each of the following **amendments** and how it **concerns** us **today**. Your instructor may choose to use this topic for a **panel discussion** (see Chapter 51).

First Amendment:

Congress shall make no law respecting an **establishment** of **religion,** or prohibiting the free exercise thereof; or **abridging** the **freedom** of speech, or of the press; or the right of the **people peaceably** to **assemble,** and to **petition** the **Government** for a redress of **grievances.**

Fourth Amendment:

The right of the **people** to be secure in their **persons,** houses, papers, and effects, **against unreasonable** searches and seizures, shall not be **violated,** and no **Warrants** shall issue, but **upon probable** cause, **supported** by Oath or **affirmation,** and particularly describing the place to be searched, and the **persons** or things to be seized.

Fourteenth Amendment:

All **persons** born or **naturalized** in the United States, and subject to the **jurisdiction** thereof, are **citizens** of the United States and of the State wherein they reside. No State shall make or enforce any law which shall **abridge** the **privileges** or **immunities** of **citizens** of the United States; nor shall any State deprive any **person** of life, liberty, or property, without due process of law; nor deny to any **person** within its **jurisdiction** the **equal protection** of the laws.

(Note: Perhaps the most controversial amendment of all is the Second Amendment, which will be discussed in Chapter 40. However, your instructor may choose to include that discussion here as well.)

CHAPTER 15
Watch that Octopus (/a/)

A. Sound It Out

American students call this the "short o" sound, and in an American dictionary the symbol is ŏ. The sound /a/ is the sound the doctor asks you to make when she wants to look at your throat. When you pronounce /a/, your lips are open as wide as a yawn, your jaw is open wide, and your tongue is at its lowest position, flat at the bottom of your mouth (so the doctor can see your tonsils). It sounds like the relaxing sound, Ahhh! but actually your muscles are tight when you pronounce it. Listen carefully to the /a/ sound in the following words.

Quick (unvoiced)	Stretched (voiced)
stop	father
pot	dodge
mop	tomorrow
clock	dollar
cop	problem
want	holiday
shop	possible
cot	hobby
fox	collar
hop	lobster

The following pairs of words have the /a/ sound, but the first one is quick and the second one is stretched. Listen and circle the words you hear:

1. lock   log
2. ox   odd
3. cod   cob
4. not   nod
5. mop   mob

B. Spell It Out

The most common spellings for the sound /a/ are A and O.

A	O
yacht drama mama papa	content comic toddler

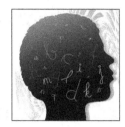

A less common spelling is OW:

> knowledge

Complete each sentence below with one of the following words:

> pond, dollars, doll, wallet, box, novels, holidays, shop, problem

1. Art sold his car to the dealer for five hundred _____.
2. Mark had a _____ with his truck so he took it to the repair _____.
3. For Christmas, I want to buy a _____ for my little niece.
4. The ducks swim in the _____.
5. I always spend the _____ with my family.
6. We are going to read two _____ this semester in my intermediate reading class.
7. For Valentine's Day, I gave my girlfriend a _____ of chocolates.
8. I always put my money in my _____ before leaving the store.

C. Silly Sentences

Circle all the words that have the /a/ sound. Then practice saying them.

1. Pop told Dot to cover the pot before it got hot.
2. I went to the shop to buy cough drops.
3. The robber stopped when the cop entered the shop.
4. The ox was on the cot eating corn on the cob.
5. Pa told Ma to stock up on popsicles and soda pop.

D. Story

Mark all the /a/ sounds in the following story. Then read it with a partner.

Oscar and Oliver are brothers. Their dream has always been to climb the Rocky Mountains. They have been planning a trip since October. They think this would be a very good time for bonding, since Oliver has been busy boxing and Oscar has been busy golfing. With proper training, they will reach the mountain top promptly. When they reach the top, they hope to find a great spot to watch the rocky scenery and enjoy a frosty drink.

E. Can You Guess It?

The answer to each clue is a word that has the sound /a/.

1. Another word for a police officer
2. You go to see this person when you are sick
3. To run at a slow pace
4. You need a key to open a door if it's _____
5. The opposite of *old-fashioned*
6. The tenth month of the year
7. The opposite of *bottom*
8. You wear it on your wrist to tell time
9. To pound or tap on a door
10. To buy things
11. A toy for girls that looks like a baby
12. A sea creature with eight arms
13. You wear them on your feet inside your shoes
14. To tie tightly, you make a _____.

F. Talk It Over

1. Do you have a **job?** What do you like about your **job** and what don't you like? What kind of **job** would you like to have in the future?

2. What kind of music do you like? Do you like to listen to **pop** music, hard **rock,** classic **rock** 'n' roll, rhythm and blues, classical, **electronic,** or some other style of music?

3. Are you an **optimistic** person? How do you show your **optimism?**

4. Do you like to go **shopping?** What kind of **shops** do you most frequently visit? What kind of bargains do you like to **shop** for?

CHAPTER 16

I Thought I Saw a Hawk (/ɔ/)

A. Sound It Out

When you pronounce /ɔ/, your muscles are tense and your lips are oval, your tongue is low and back, and your jaw is slightly closed. The pronunciation of this sound varies in the United States. Some Americans have a very strong /ɔ/ sound as part of their dialect. Other Americans may replace the /ɔ/ sound with /a/. And some Americans use /ɔ/ instead of /a/ in words like *doll* and *odd*. The examples in this chapter are words pronounced /ɔ/ by most Americans. In American dictionaries, the sound /ɔ/ is often symbolized ô.

First just listen carefully to the sound /ɔ/.

Quick (unvoiced)	Stretched (voiced)	Stretched (final)
thought	August	awe
taught	audio	law
caught	audience	saw
fought	all	thaw
bought	altar	flaw
ought	ball	jaw
hawk	fall	claw
awful	tall	paw
awesome	long	raw
awkward	strong	straw
author	wrong	draw

Listen and cross out the words that do NOT have the /ɔ/ sound.

1. thought   cough   bought   though
2. blow   law   draw   slow
3. daughter   father   aunt   mother
4. ladder   slaughter   laughter   lawyer

B. Spell It Out

The most common spellings for the sound /ɔ/ are AL, AU, and AW. There is a small group of past tense verbs with the sound /ɔt/, but there are two different spellings: -OUGHT and -AUGHT.

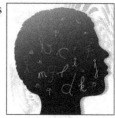

Ghost letters!

You probably noticed that the letters GH are not pronounced in words like *caught* and *thought*. Actually, hundreds of years ago, these letters were pronounced with a sound that we no longer have in English—the sound at the end of B*ach* in German and the beginning of *H*anukkah in Hebrew. The sound died out in English, and all that is left is the silent, ghostly letters GH. If you think of the word *ghost,* which starts with GH, you will remember how to spell these words more easily.

Listen and write each word. Don't forget the ghost letters!

1.
2.
3.
4.
5.
6.
7.
8.

C. Silly Sentences

Underline the words that contain the sound /ɔ/. Then practice saying the sentences.

1. That naughty daughter sought an audience.
2. I thought you bought them all at the mall.
3. Tall Paul ought not to fall.
4. All hawks have long strong claws.
5. I called the mall and bought an awesome ball.

6. I saw a hawk with a straw in its jaw.

7. You ought to applaud your strong daughter.

8. The law sought to stop the author.

9. The flaw in the law is wrong.

10. She taught the wrong way to draw.

D.   Awful or Awesome?

The words *awful* and *awesome* both come from the word *awe*. *Awe* refers to a feeling of amazement, wonder, respect, and even fear. You might say, "Seeing the birth of a baby filled me with awe" or "I was awed by the beauty of Mount Everest." The word *awesome* still has the meaning of something that fills you with awe: "The Grand Canyon is an awesome sight." But nowadays, people use *awesome* to mean anything that is good: an awesome meal or an awesome party.

The word *awful* originally meant *full of awe*, but it came to focus on the idea of fear rather than amazement. Nowadays, it means the opposite of awesome—terrible, bad, not good at all!

Take a minute to think of something good or bad that happened to you. Tell the class your story, and the class will say either "That's awful!" or "That's awesome!"

For example:

When I went out this morning, my car was gone! Someone stole it!

That's _____!

But when I called the police, they called me back in 30 minutes to tell me that they found my car!

That's _____!

Unfortunately, I left my laptop in the car, and it was gone.

That's _____!

But there was no damage to the car.

That's _____!

E.   Talk It Over

1. Another name for UFOs is "flying **saucers**." Do you believe that flying **saucers** or UFOs exist? Are they from another planet, or is there another explanation? Do you know anyone who has ever seen a flying **saucer**? What would you do if you saw a flying **saucer**?

2. Do you have a favorite **author**? Have you ever met a famous **author**? Which **author,** from the present or past, would you like to meet?

3. Do you think parents **ought** to treat their **daughters** differently than they treat their sons?

4. Recently in the United States, many schools have been focusing on what they call "the basics" and eliminating "extras" like art, music, drama, and even physical education or recess. What subjects **ought** to be **taught** in elementary school? Is it important for every child to learn to **draw** and to play a musical instrument?

F. Speak Your Mind

People often say "There **ought** to be a **law!**" when they are complaining about something that **bothers** them. Sometimes they are serious, and sometimes they are joking. For example, if you are in a restaurant with a friend and the person behind you is talking loudly on his cell phone, you might shake your head and say sarcastically, "There **ought** to be a **law**. . . ."

Or if the person next to you on a crowded airplane is eating a smelly sandwich of tuna and onion, you might think to yourself, "There **ought** to be a **law**. . . ." (Notice that *ought to* is usually pronounced *oughta*.)

What suggestions do you have, silly or serious, for **laws** that **ought** to exist?

G. Can You Guess it?

1. The past tense of *catch*
2. The eighth month of the year
3. Another word for the fall season
4. A person who writes a book
5. Another word for *car*
6. A small dish under a teacup
7. The past tense of *teach*
8. The grass in front of your house
9. An indoor place to go shopping

10. The opposite of *true*

11. The opposite of *short*

12. The past tense of *see*

13. Something uncooked

14. Another word for *should*

15. The opposite of *big*

16. When a man loses his hair, he becomes _____

17. You shake it on food to make it taste better

18. The past tense of *fight*

19. H_2O

20. A cat's feet

21. The past tense of *buy*

22. You do this with your mouth when you're tired

23. The opposite of *weak*

24. To stop briefly

25. Santa _____

Chapter 16 Answers to B: Spell It Out

1. thought
2. bought
3. ought
4. daughter
5. slaughter
6. caught
7. sought
8. naughty

CHAPTER 17
Together Again: Review of Chapters 13–16

A. Listening Practice

Listen and circle the word that you hear.

1. done   Don   dawn
2. fawn   fun   fan
3. stuck   stock   stalk
4. cup   cop   cape
5. cot   caught   cut
6. tell   tale   tall
7. shop   shape   sheep
8. doll   dull   dell
9. bottom   button   bitten
10. won   wind   wand

B. Say What?

Circle the word that you hear. The sounds are /ə/, /ʌ/, /a/, /æ/, and /ɔ/.

1. The lady wanted to buy a (cat/cot).
2. That's my bad (luck/lock).
3. The (rubber/robber) was not easy to find.
4. You need to (come/calm) down.
5. Does Jerry have a (cut/cot)?
6. Is that a (hat/hut)?
7. Please hang up the (cup/cap).

8. Don't step on the (bag/bug).

9. My sister brought me several (rags/rugs).

10. We saw (Sal/Saul) at the park yesterday.

11. Joe keeps his money in a (sack/sock).

12. I'm waiting here for my (bus/boss).

13. The (sun/sand) was very hot.

C. Minute Madness

Write as many words as you can for each of the following sounds before you hear your instructor say STOP.

/ʌ/	/ə/	/ɑ/	/ɔ/
(but)	(ago)	(cot)	(bought)
_____	_____	_____	_____
_____	_____	_____	_____
_____	_____	_____	_____
_____	_____	_____	_____
_____	_____	_____	_____
_____	_____	_____	_____
_____	_____	_____	_____
_____	_____	_____	_____
_____	_____	_____	_____
_____	_____	_____	_____

96 Part 2 A Mouthful of Vowels

D. My Crazy Cousins

The following words begin with the letter A but have different sounds. Listen to these words and put them in the correct list according to the sound you hear.

/æ/	/ey/	/a/	/ɔ/	/ə/
_____	_____	_____	_____	_____
_____	_____	_____	_____	_____
_____	_____	_____	_____	_____
_____	_____	_____	_____	_____
_____	_____	_____	_____	_____
_____	_____	_____	_____	_____
_____	_____	_____	_____	_____
_____	_____	_____	_____	_____
_____	_____	_____	_____	_____
_____	_____	_____	_____	_____
_____	_____	_____	_____	_____
_____	_____	_____	_____	_____

answer	angel	April	awesome	automobile	alien
art	always	artery	age	artist	although
abdomen	arcade	after	along	attic	arch
Arnold	am	apple	attitude	asleep	ask
astronaut	August	ape	athlete	acorn	agree
able	among	afraid	above	add	after
all	also	arm	ago	across	alternate
anger	aim	awful	army	agent	around
auburn	awake	about	away		

E. Winner!

Listen to the words that your instructor reads and write them under the correct symbol. When you have filled all the spaces, call out Winner!

/ʌ/	/ə/	/a/	/ɔ/

F. Vowel Symbol Matching

Match the underlined sound in each of the words in Column A with the correct symbol in Column B.

    A   **B**

_____ 1. b<u>o</u>ttle   a. /iy/
_____ 2. m<u>y</u>stery   b. /a/
_____ 3. s<u>a</u>lt   c. /ə/
_____ 4. <u>e</u>lephant   d. /ey/
_____ 5. <u>a</u>way   e. /ʌ/
_____ 6. ch<u>ee</u>se   f. /æ/
_____ 7. s<u>ai</u>lor   g. /ɛ/
_____ 8. d<u>u</u>ck   h. /ɔ/
_____ 9. m<u>a</u>th   i. /ɪ/

98 Part 2 A Mouthful of Vowels

G. Listening Practice

Listen to the words below and cross out the one word in each line that does **not** have the same vowel sound as the others.

1. but   son   club   ball   tub
2. month   love   some   stood   rough
3. cop   maze   block   drop   rock
4. cough   spot   box   stop   pot
5. sauce   draw   pause   strong   taught
6. raw   fault   mop   straw   cross
7. <u>a</u>go   <u>au</u>tumn   <u>a</u>gainst   <u>a</u>mong   <u>a</u>head
8. <u>o</u>ppose   <u>o</u>pen   <u>u</u>pon   <u>a</u>ppear   <u>o</u>ccur

H. Tongue Twisters

1. /a/ The doctoring doctor doctors the doctor. Why? The doctoring doctor wants to doctor the doctor, but not the way the doctored doctor wants to be doctored

2. /ɔ/ I thought a thought. But the thought I thought wasn't the thought I thought I thought. If the thought I thought had been the thought I thought I thought, I wouldn't have thought so much.

3. /ʌ/ Rubber baby buggy bumpers. (say three times fast!)
   Don't trouble about trouble until trouble troubles you.

I. Sentence Practice

Read the sentences below to practice the sounds /ʌ/, /a/, /ɔ/, and /ə/.

/ʌ/

1. Bud put the buns in the oven.
2. Here's your cup of coffee and your cupcake.
3. The truck got stuck in the mud.
4. Let's run and have fun in the sun.

/a/

5. My father is as strong as an ox.
6. Birds of a feather flock together.
7. My friend is as sly as a fox.
8. Dolly and Molly went to a holiday party.
9. I like to shop until I drop.

/ɔ/

10. My girlfriend is the talk of the town.
11. Paul went to the store to buy a saw to cut the door.
12. The author of this book is awesome.
13. I felt awful because I caught a cold at the football game yesterday.

/ə/

14. A balloon floated upon the wind.
15. We didn't appreciate having him around until he went away.

Instructor's List of Words for Activity E. (Choose words at random from different categories)

/ʌ/	/ə/	/a/	/ɔ/
month	ago	clock	broad
club	ahead	top	caught
fun	aside	flock	call
truck	upon	spot	auto
brush	applause	Bob	chalk
mother	afraid	shop	long
bunch	around	father	tall
son	away	stop	strong
run	above	lock	wrong
brother	approve	block	law
but	afford	box	draw
duck	attend	dot	hawk
pump	arrive	not	cough
bunch	agree	drop	saw
bus	among	mop	straw

CHAPTER 18
Go Rope a Goat (/ow/)

A. Sound It Out

American students know this sound as "long o" and in an American dictionary, it is represented by the symbol ō. When you pronounce /ow/, you begin with round, open lips which close up like a camera shutter. Your muscles are tense, and your tongue moves from mid-back and glides toward /uw/.

If you compare the English sound /ow/ to the Spanish or Japanese sound /o/, you will notice the movement in the English sound. Listen to an American try to pronounce "Yo no hablo Español" and you will hear the movement that makes an English /ow/ different from Spanish /o/.

Listen carefully to the sound of /ow/:

Quick (unvoiced)	Stretched (voiced)	Stretched (final)
rope	robe	oh
goat	load	go
spoke	vogue	no
loaf	stove	low
host	hose	grow
both	loathe	toe
coach	roll	foe
	foam	though
	phone	

B. Spell It Out

The /ow/ sound can be spelled in many different ways.

O	OW	OE	OA	OU(GH)
OK	**ow**e	t**oe**nail	b**oa**t	sh**ou**lder
oh	**ow**n	f**oe**	**oa**tmeal	b**ou**lder
ocean	bl**ow**er	d**oe**	t**oa**d	d**ough**
over	kn**ow**n	ob**oe**	r**oa**d	alth**ough**
ph**o**ne	sh**ow**		s**oa**k	thor**ough**
h**o**pe	borr**ow**		wh**oa**	
g**o**	bel**ow**			
als**o**				

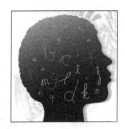

One unusual spelling of the sound /ow/ is EW in the word *sew*.

C. Silly Sentences

Practice saying these sentences with a partner.

1. The **owner poked** a **hole** in his **Picasso.**
2. Thanksgiving is in **November, so go** on a diet.
3. There's a **crow** chasing a little **sparrow,** and the **sparrow** is **going** to win!
4. **Joe** was on a TV **show** where his **own** friends played **jokes** on him.
5. If silence is **golden,** then **Joan** and **Toby** are **broke.**
6. When you **roller** skate **over** a **pothole,** just **go** with the **flow.**
7. If you **throw those moldy potatoes** into the **compost** bin, they'll **grow.**
8. **Lola bowled** a **whole** game with her eyes **closed** and still won a **trophy.**
9. **Otto rode** the **pony slowly.**
10. When **Sonia** plays **old folksongs** on the **saxophone,** she gets a sore **throat,** and we get sore ears.

D. Tongue Twisters

1. If you **go** toward a **gopher,** the **gopher** will **go** for a **gopher hole.**
2. If you **notice** this **notice,** you'll **notice** this **notice** is not worth **noticing.**
3. There are **old soldiers,** and there are **bold soldiers,** but there are **no old bold soldiers.**

E. Dizzy Dialogue: To Snowboard or Not to Snowboard?

Practice this dialogue with a partner.

Owen: Where do you want to **go?**

Nola: Let's **go** to Lake **Tahoe.** We could hit the **slopes.**

Owen: **OK.** It's been **so cold** there, **so** there's lots of **snow.**

Nola: You **know,** I'd like to try **snowboarding.** It seems **so** much easier than skiing—**no** heavy boots, **no poles** . . . just you and the **snowboard,** and you're good to **go.**

Owen: I **hope** you're **joking.** I've seen **so** many **snowboarders moaning** and **groaning** while they try to **roll** themselves out of the **snow. Also,** the Ski **Patrol** is always **towing snowboarders** with **broken bones** down the mountain. I **don't** want one of them to be you.

Nola: Well, I'm not **going** to **show** off. I learned to ski in **no** time, **so** I **don't** think **snowboarding** will be hard to learn.

Owen: **I don't know.** You may be a **pro** skier, but you're too **old** to risk **blowing** out your knee or **throwing** your back out. I **don't** want to **load** you into the car and **go home** early.

Nola: That may be **so,** but I still want to give **snowboarding** a **go.** I promise I'll take it **slow.**

F. Talk It Over

1. Tell about the **moment** that you knew that you had **grown** up (become an adult). What happened?

2. What is a good way to **cope** with **nosy** people? Why does your method work?

3. What should you do if you **don't** want to **show** your **homework** to your friend?

4. Have you ever been on a **road** trip in the U.S.? Where did you **go?** What did you see? If you haven't been on a **road** trip, where would you like to **go?**

5. When you catch a **cold** and can't **go** to the doctor, which **home** remedy do you use to help yourself feel better?

6. Some people say, "You can't teach an **old** dog new tricks." Are you ever too **old** to learn new things?

G. You're a Poet, and You Don't Even Know It

Work with a partner or small group and write your **own poem** together. Try to see how many words with the /ow/ sound you can use in your **poem.** When you finish your **poem,** read it to the class.

Here are a few topics to get you started:

Family or friends
Love
School or work
Goals or dreams for the future
Fun activities (sports, hobbies, interests)
Food
Holidays or other special days
Your **own** topic

Here are two examples of **poems:**

Growing Old

Oh no! I'm **growing old!**
I'm always **cold.**
My hair is gray, not **gold.**
I can't see my **own toes.**
My ears **don't** work.
My **shoulders** hurt.
My knees **won't fold.**
Oh no! I'm too young
to be **so old!**

My Hometown

My **hometown** is **close** to my **home** today.
In fact, it's **only** a **stone's throw** away
My **whole** family lives there.
And **most** of my friends are just down the **road.**
Everywhere I **go,** I see people I **know.**
So you can say I'm never **alone**
In my **hometown,** I'm always at **home!**

H. Can You Guess it?

1. You have 5 of these on each foot
2. The wind _____
3. When children get bigger, they _____
4. The opposite of *yes*
5. You use a needle and thread to _____
6. The opposite of *high*
7. Before you bake it, bread is called _____
8. The past tense of *ride*
9. An expensive and beautiful metal that jewelry is made of
10. The past tense of *sell*
11. The past tense of *tell*
12. The opposite of *young*
13. You cook on top of a _____
14. In soccer, you try to kick the ball into the _____
15. The capital of Italy
16. The place where you live
17. To make your hair look neat, you use a brush and a _____
18. You can eat soup in a _____
19. You call people on the _____
20. A beautiful red flower
21. A small ship
22. How we choose the president
23. The past tense of *write*
24. The past tense of *speak*
25. A skeleton is made of many _____

CHAPTER 19
Cute Cuckoo's Clues (/uw/ and /yuw/)

A. Sound It Out

American students know this sound as "long u," symbolized ū in American dictionaries. The English sound /uw/ is similar to the sound /u/ in many languages, but there is some movement in the English sound. When you pronounce /uw/, your muscles are tense, your lips are closed and rounded like you are going to whistle, your tongue is in its highest position, with the back of your tongue pushed up, and your jaw is high and closed. Americans make this sound when they are surprised in a good way—"Oooh."

First just listen carefully to the /uw/ sounds in the following words:

Quick (unvoiced)	Stretched (voiced)	Stretched (final)
loot	rude	grew
fruit	soon	glue
shoot	food	who
group	pool	new
hoop	fool	through
truth	rule	threw
booth	school	blue
tooth	bloom	stew
roof	room	zoo
proof	tube	flew
moose	news	do
goose	cruise	two

Compare the sound /uw/ before unvoiced and voiced sounds. Listen and circle the word that you hear:

1. root   rude
2. hoot   who'd
3. proof   prove
4. loose   lose
5. suit   sued

B. Spell It Out

There are five spelling patterns that are pronounced /uw/ or /yuw/.

U	OO	OU	EW	UI
cube	tool	soup	chew	fruit
cute	fool	group	few	suit
lute	school	youth	flew	juice
rude	broom	wounded	drew	bruise
dude	groom	through	grew	cruise
flute	moon	routine	blew	
huge	food		jewel	
tune	zoo		nephew	
uniform	too		view	
rule	choose		review	
tuna	tooth		threw	
student	loop			
plural	mood			
true	soon			
	spoon			

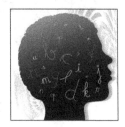

Note: The spelling OO can also have another common pronunciation /ʊ/ in words such as *book* and *foot*. See Chapter 20.

C. Y or Y Not?

Many words that have the sound /uw/ add the sound /y/ before it. No words in English begin with the sound /uw/; the /y/ sound is always added at the beginning of words with the sound /uw/. The sound /yuw/ also occurs in other situations when /uw/ is spelled with the letter U. If you speak Spanish, compare the Spanish pronunciation of *Cuba* /kuba/ with the way Americans pronounce /kyuwbə/. Americans are adding a /y/ sound, probably because they are thinking of the English word *cube* /kyuwb/.

Listen and repeat the following words. Mark the place where you hear the /y/ sound.

union	cute	cucumber
uniform	music	coupon
United States	beauty	view
university	museum	few
unity	human	huge
unique	humor	pure
cube	bugle	future

D. Silly Sentences

Underline the words that contain the sound /uw/. Then practice saying the sentences.

1. A loose tooth flew into his soup.
2. Who threw the fruit through the hoop?
3. The students will choose new uniforms soon.
4. Ruth made beautiful music on her flute.
5. Two dudes are shooting hoops.
6. The truth about the news made her blue.
7. You knew the student who was rude at school.
8. Do you swear to tell the truth, the whole truth, and nothing but the truth? I do.

E. The Zoo or Hoops?

Mark the words that contain the sound /uw/. Then practice the dialogue with a partner.

Ruth: Tell me the truth, Luke. Do you want to go to the zoo?

Luke: I don't mean to be rude, Aunt Ruth, but the truth is that I've been to the zoo too many times.

Ruth: But they have some new animals. Have you ever seen a trained baboon?

Luke: A trained baboon? What does it do?

Ruth: It plays the flute and eats soup with a spoon.

Luke: Is that really true?

Ruth: Okay, maybe not, but I just wanted to take my favorite nephew to the zoo.

Luke: I'd rather hang out and shoot some hoops in the schoolyard.

Ruth: I think I would too. I'll go with you.

Luke: Cool!

F. Talk It Over

1. The expression "once in a **blue moon**" means "not often, very seldom," probably because it refers to a month that has **two** full **moons,** which doesn't happen very often. What is something **you** only **do** once in a **blue moon?** For example, **do you** go out for dinner often, or is that something **you do** only once in a **blue moon?**

2. Some people are always in a good **mood,** but other people are more **moody.** When a person feels mildly depressed, we say they are feeling **blue.** Are you a **moody** person? What causes you to feel **blue? Do you** have any suggestions for how to **improve** your **mood?** (Notice the difference in the pronunciation of *good* and *mood*. Only *mood* has the sound /uw/.)

3. Most people believe that the **United** States put the first man on the **moon** in 1969, but a **few** people believe that they have **proof** that the **moon** landing wasn't **true;** they say it was a hoax. What evidence would **you** accept as **proof** that man has really walked on the **moon?** Do **you** think **humans** should return to the **moon soon?** In the **future,** will ordinary people travel to the **moon** and other planets?

4. What's your favorite **food? Do you** have a favorite **fruit?** How about a favorite **soup?**

5. What would life be like without **music?** What are some of the **uses of music?** For example, most stores play **music.** Why?

G. Speak Your Mind

Students in most countries wear **uniforms** in elementary **school** and even in high **school,** but in the **United** States, only a **few students,** mostly in private **schools,** wear **uniforms.** Did **you** wear a **uniform** in high **school?** What did it look like? What are the advantages and disadvantages of **school uniforms?** In recent years, some American **school** districts have **argued** that requiring **uniforms** could **improve** test scores and cut down on conflict in their **schools.** But many parents and **students** disagreed with requiring **uniforms. You** might like to conduct a survey or have a debate about the benefits of requiring **school uniforms.**

H. Can You Guess it?

1. It shines in the sky at night
2. The color of the sky
3. You wear them on your feet
4. You wear them on your feet when the weather is cold or wet
5. It helps you solve a puzzle or mystery
6. Apples, pears, and plums are _____
7. Hammers, screwdrivers, and wrenches are _____
8. The opposite of *warm*
9. The liquid that comes from a fruit
10. Another word for *impolite*
11. You use this to draw a straight line
12. Sticky stuff used to fix broken things
13. A matching jacket and pants
14. The number after *one*
15. The opposite of *me*
16. You go here to look at animals
17. The opposite of *rough*
18. The place where students go every day
19. A short time from now
20. Past, present, and _____
21. The opposite of *false*
22. The past tense of *fly*
23. The past tense of *blow*
24. An illness like a cold, but worse
25. The part of a plant that grows underground

I. Not to Be Confused With....

The letter U is used to spell both the sound /uw/ that we have been studying in this chapter, and the sound /ʌ/ that we studied in Chapter 13. The sounds are not confusing, but you may be confused by the spelling and be unsure whether a word has the sound /uw/ or /ʌ/.

Listen as your instructor reads the following words and write them in the correct place in the chart.

/uw/	/ʌ/

1. custom
2. culture
3. cut
4. cute
5. cub
6. cube
7. stuck
8. student
9. public
10. pupil
11. punish
12. studio
13. tunnel
14. tune

CHAPTER 20
Look, a Wolf in the Bush! (/ʊ/)

A. Sound It Out

In an American dictionary, the sound /ʊ/ is represented by û or o͞o. When you pronounce /ʊ/, your lips are relaxed, slightly apart and weakly rounded, your muscles are relaxed, and your lips are relaxed but slightly rounded. Your tongue is high and back, and your jaw is in a medium position, higher than /ow/.

First, just listen carefully to the sound /ʊ/:

Quick (unvoiced)	Stretched (voiced)	Stretched (final)
book	good	Note: the sound /ʊ/ never comes at the end of a word in English.
cook	could	
look	should	
put	would/wood	
foot	hood	
push	full	
	pull	

B. Spell It Out

The sound /ʊ/ has several common spellings.

OO	OU	U	O
b**oo**k	w**ou**ld	p**u**ll	w**o**lf
st**oo**d	c**ou**ld	b**u**sh	w**o**man

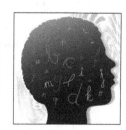

111

C. Silly Sentences

Circle all of the words with /ʊ/ sounds in them. Then practice saying these sentences.

1. If you pull a door that says "Push" or push a door that says "Pull," you could be there for a good long time.
2. Should you use sugar to cook a wolf?
3. Looking for some goodies, Mr. Goodwin put his hand in the cookie jar.
4. He understood how the woman felt when she gave him a left hook to the jaw.
5. Because the pulley was crooked, the tuna fell off the hook.
6. We couldn't sell the wooly cushion because it looked like a bushy octopus.

D. Tongue Twister

How much **wood would** a **woodchuck** chuck

If a **woodchuck could** chuck **wood**?

He **would** chuck, he **would,** as much **wood** as he **could**

And chuck as much **wood** as a **woodchuck would**

If a **woodchuck could** chuck **wood**

E. Dizzy Dialogue—Sugar Cookies?

Practice this dialogue with a partner.

Ann: **Could** you help me bake some **cookies**?

Ben: You **should** do it yourself. They're easy to make.

Ann: I don't know what I **should** do to start. I can't **cook**.

Ben: Everyone **should** know how to **cook**. Just **pull** out a c**oo**kb**oo**k, and **look** for an easy recipe.

Ann: Wow, **would** you **look** at all these **cookie** recipes! These **sugar cookies look good**. I'll try these!

[3 hours later]

Ann: **Look** at the **goodies** I made! They **should** be delicious! Try one!

Ben: They do **look good!** *[tastes one and makes a face]* Are you sure you **understood** the recipe? This **cookie** tastes like you **put** salt instead of **sugar** in it!

F. Talk It Over

1. Is there ever a **good** time to be **pushy**? When? Why?

2. **Should** you always tell the truth even if you can hurt the listener's feelings? Or **should** you **cushion** the blow? Why?

3. Have you ever felt **pushed** and **pulled** between two important choices (like going to college **full**-time or going to work **full**-time)? Tell about this time. What decision did you make? Why? Are you happy with this decision now? Why or why not?

4. To "**put** your **foot** in your mouth" means to accidentally say something rude or insulting to someone else. Have you ever **put** your **foot** in your mouth? Tell what happened and how you resolved this problem.

G. Speak Your Mind

How serious is the problem of **bullying** in schools? What is a good way to stop **bullying** in schools? Who **should** get involved—parents, teachers, or even the police? Why?

H. Advice to the Lovelorn

Read this letter and then tell Woody what he should do.

Dear **Brooke,**

I don't know what I **should** do. I'm in love, but my girlfriend **could** be a **crook.**

When we met four months ago, I fell in love with her at first sight, and I'm pretty sure she felt the same way. She **took** every opportunity to tell me that she **couldn't** live without me. She **would** make me feel so **good** about myself and about our future.

But I **looked** at my credit card statement, and I **shook** my head in disbelief. The payment is much, much higher than it **should** be, so I called the company. They said that I **took** out a lot of cash advances. I never **took** out that many!

My girlfriend has a **good** job, but she makes less money than I do. Yesterday, she drove up in a new car. She **looked** so happy, and she **cooked** me my favorite dinner to celebrate. I just **couldn't** spoil her **good** mood, so I didn't ask her any questions about the car.

114 Part 2 A Mouthful of Vowels

We don't have a joint credit card account, so I hope that she hasn't done anything **crooked** to **put** the down payment on her car. I know I **should** trust her, and it **would** be rude to ask her how she **could** afford the car and how she plans to make the payments later.

Help me, **Brooke!** I'm really **hooked** on my girlfriend, and I don't want to hurt her, but I can't help but think my girlfriend **could** have **pulled** the **wool** over my eyes. I don't want to **foot** the bill for the car, but I don't want to let money get in the way of our love. What **should** I do?

Woody in **Westwood**

I. Can You Guess It?

1. The opposite of *bad* good
2. Open your eyes and look
3. The opposite of *pull* push
4. The past tense of *can* could
5. The past tense of *take* took
6. A collection of recipes cookbook
7. The opposite of *push* pull
8. The opposite of *empty* full
9. The past tense of *stand* stood
10. Something you read book
11. A robber or a thief is a crooker
12. The past tense of *shake* shook
13. To check your car's engine, you have to open the hood
14. Another word for *ought to* should
15. To catch a fish, you put a worm on the hood
16. A small river or stream brook
17. The opposite of *man* woman
18. The opposite of *raw* cooked
19. The past tense of *will* would
20. The opposite of *straight* crooked
21. Pick it up, and put it away
22. The 43rd President of the United States was George W. Push
23. A chocolate chip cookie
24. You put it in your coffee or tea to make it sweet sugar
25. The trunk of a tree is made of wood

CHAPTER 21
Tiger, Tiger Smiling Bright (/ay/)

A. Sound It Out

American students call this sound "long i," symbolized ī in American dictionaries. When you pronounce /ay/, there is movement from one position to another. Your lips move from open to only slightly parted, your jaw also moves from open to closed, and your tongue moves from low central to high front position.

Listen carefully to the /ay/ sound in the following words:

Quick (unvoiced)	Stretched (voiced)	Stretched (final)
bite	hide	bye
light	provide	try
kite	aisle	pie
ice	iron	sky
sight	shine	my
night	guide	cry

Compare the following pairs of words and notice the difference between the vowel before unvoiced and voiced consonants:

1. right   ride
2. sight   side
3. light   lied
4. ice   eyes
5. spice   spies

B. Spell It Out

The most common spellings for the /ay/ sound are:

I...E	I	IGH	Y	IE
divine	kindness	light	my	lie
fine	find	bright	try	die
like	hi	fight	why	tried
mice	blind	sigh	cry	cried
time	Friday	night	deny	fried

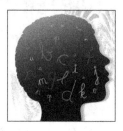

Some unusual spellings of /ay/:

EIGH as in *height*

AI as in *aisle*

UY as in *buy* and *guy*

C. Dialogue: I'm Confused

Mark all the words that contain the sound /ay/. Then practice the dialogue with a partner.

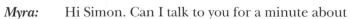

Myra: Hi Simon. Can I talk to you for a minute about something that's on my mind?

Simon: Sure. What's up?

Myra: I'm confused about greetings in the United States. Why do Americans say "Hi" and "Bye" all the time without even knowing you? They also smile and look at my eyes when they talk to me.

Simon: We're not trying to be rude or funny. And we are certainly not trying to make anyone feel shy. These expressions are as common as apple pie.

Myra: In many countries, people would think that Americans are trying to be funny. Others might think that Americans are rude or disrespectful.

Simon: Sorry to hear that. Americans are just trying to be friendly, especially with foreigners.

Myra: What other friendly expressions do Americans use?

Simon: "See you tonight." "Do you want a bite to eat?" "You're all right." "You're a nice guy." These expressions are usually said with a smile.

Myra: Thanks, Simon. Now I can smile back at Americans when they are trying to be friendly. Bye, bye, Simon. I'll see you tonight at Sky Dive in Anaheim.

Simon: Bye, Myra.

D. Can you Guess It?

1. Frozen water
2. You use this to get the wrinkles out of your clothes
3. The largest country in Asia
4. Land that is completely surrounded by water
5. The opposite of *hello*
6. To cook in oil
7. A person who is afraid to talk to other people is very _____
8. When you eat Asian food, you usually have a bowl of _____
9. The plural of *mouse*
10. This facial expression shows that you are happy
11. To make a sandwich you need two _____ of bread
12. A cold dessert you eat in a cone
13. The opposite of *wrong*
14. The opposite of *day*
15. A large cat-like animal with black stripes
16. An eight-legged creature that makes webs
17. The opposite of *dark*
18. A person who can't see is _____
19. Can you look at your watch and tell me the _____?
20. Words that end the same, such as *pat, cat, rat* are words that _____

E. Same but Different: Homophones

A homophone is a word that sounds the same as another word, but has a different spelling and different meaning. Practice saying the homophones below containing the /ay/ sound.

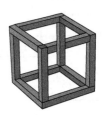

tie – Thai
dye – die
hi – high
I – eye
buy – bye – by
night – knight
time – thyme
aisle – I'll – isle

118 Part 2 A Mouthful of Vowels

F. Light My Fire

Practice saying these sentences several times until you can say them quickly without making any mistakes.

1. Star **light,** star **bright,** please let me meet someone special **tonight.**
2. **Ike** went with his **wife** to celebrate the Fourth of **July.**
3. **Mike** said that he'd **like** to go on a **hike** at **twilight.**
4. "**My** oh **my,**" said **Ivan** looking into **Eileen's eyes.**
5. You and **I** will **fly tonight** to a special place called **Paradise.**
6. **Eileen sighed** with **delight.**

G. A Travel Story: A Feast for the Eyes

Circle all the words with the sound /ay/. Then read this story to your partner.

Have you ever thought about what places in the world you would like to visit? How about visiting the islands of Hawaii to see all the beautiful sights? Or maybe you could go to Iceland to see the icebergs shining still in the night.  In Scotland, you could listen to the sounds of the bagpipes. Then travel to Ireland to admire the beautiful Emerald Isle. Cross the Atlantic to the Caribbean islands of Puerto Rico, Cuba, the Dominican Republic, and other surrounding isles. There you can see the crystal-clear waters and the beautiful romantic skies. There are so many places to visit, but so little time. Luckily we can always visit these places in our minds and enjoy these beautiful sights without paying a dime. Would you like to go on this imaginary flight? All aboard!

H. I Spy!

Write words that have the /ay/ sound following the spelling patterns.

I...E	IGH	I	Y
ice	sight	find	try

I. Talk it Over

Explain what the following sayings mean and give examples of situations when you would use these expressions.

1. You're the apple of **my eye.**

2. No man is an **island.**

3. A stitch in **time** saves **nine.**

4. You're as sweet as apple **pie.**

5. If at first you don't succeed, **try** and **try** again.

6. Let's break the **ice** between us.

7. He's **tied** to his mother's apron strings.

8. An **eye** for an **eye,** and a tooth for a tooth.

9. Are you a **night** owl or a morning lark?

10. **Wise** men think **alike.**

11. **Silence** is golden.

CHAPTER 22
A Noisy Oyster (/ɔy/)

A. Sound It Out

When you pronounce /ɔy/, there is a lot of movement from one position to another. This is known as a glide vowel or diphthong. Your lips begin in an oval position and move toward a smiling position, your jaw rises, and your tongue moves from low back to high front.

First just listen carefully to the /ɔy/ sound in the following words:

Quick (unvoiced)	Stretched (voiced)	Stretched (final)
voice	oil	joy
choice	boil	boy
moisture	soil	enjoy
oyster	loyal	soy
rejoice	royal	toy
	noise	annoy
	join	destroy
	coin	employ
	poison	
	avoid	

B. Spell It Out

There are only two spellings for the sound /ɔy/ in English: OI or OY. At the end of words, the spelling is always OY. In the middle of words, OI is the most common spelling. Listen and write the most likely spelling for each word:

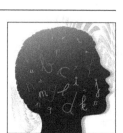

1.
2.
3.
4.
5.
6.
7.
8.

C. Silly Sentences

Underline the words that contain the sound /ɔy/. Then practice saying the sentences.

1. The scientists were paranoid about an asteroid poised to strike the earth.
2. We avoided the poisoned oysters.
3. Lloyd enjoyed the noise of his corduroy pants.
4. It's your choice: you can broil the sirloin or you can boil it, but if you boil it, you will certainly spoil it.
5. The royal family was loyal to its employees.

D. Dizzy Dialogue

Practice the dialogue with a partner.

Floyd: I am feeling a little **paranoid.**

Lloyd: Why, what's worrying you?

Floyd: I saw a report about an **asteroid** that **destroyed** the dinosaurs.

Lloyd: That happened a long time ago. Why are you **paranoid** now?

Floyd: Suppose another **asteroid** is **poised** to strike the earth?

Lloyd: I don't think you should worry about **unavoidable** events.

Floyd: Well, my cousin is **clairvoyant,** and she had a vision of people taking a **voyage** to Venus to **avoid** the **asteroid.**

Lloyd: I don't mean to **annoy** you, but what other visions has your **clairvoyant** cousin had?

Floyd: Hmm, well, she once told me that **boysenberries** were **poison.**

Lloyd: I hate to **disappoint** you, but I don't think she's really **clairvoyant.**

Floyd: **Boy,** I hope you're right. I read that Venus is so hot that our blood would **boil** and our skin would **broil!**

E. Talk It Over

1. What do you **enjoy** doing in your free time? Are you a person who likes to **join** clubs or other groups, or do you prefer spending your free time at home?

2. Can **noise** be harmful to our health? What kinds of jobs require working in a **noisy** environment? How can people **avoid** the consequences of working in a **noisy** environment?

3. Some people think that children were more creative when **toys** were simpler. Are children today **spoiled** by having too many fancy **toys**? What was your favorite **toy** when you were a child? Do you think that homemade **toys** are better for children than expensive modern **toys**?

4. Do you enjoy eating **oysters**? How do you like to eat them? Here's a simple recipe:

    Broiled Oysters
    - 1 large jar of **oysters**
    - flour, salt, and pepper
    - **oil** or melted butter

    Put **oil** or melted butter in a shallow pan. Drain and rinse a large jar of **oysters**. Roll the **oysters** in a mixture of flour, salt, and pepper. Place the **oysters** in the pan and turn to coat both sides with **oil** or butter. Place the pan under the **broiler**. When they are brown, turn and brown the other side. Serve with lemon juice.

F. Speak Your Mind

1. Immigrants, especially undocumented immigrants, may sometimes be **exploited** (cheated, taken advantage of) by their **employers**. Do you know of any cases in which workers are **exploited**? How can people protect themselves from being **exploited**?

2. Modern society depends on **oil** for much of our energy. Some people say that we need to limit our use of **oil**. What problems does **oil** cause in the world? Think about political and economic problems, as well as environmental problems. How can we **avoid** these problems? Are there alternatives to **oil**?

3. When the economy is slow, many people lose their jobs or can't find a job, so **unemployment** rises. What advice could you give **unemployed** people to help them find a new job? What would help them **avoid** becoming discouraged or depressed while they are **unemployed**?

G. Can You Guess It?

1. The opposite of *girl*
2. A child plays with this
3. A feeling of great happiness
4. You fry food in this
5. A bean used to make tofu and many other foods
6. The sharp tip of a pencil
7. Nickels, dimes, and quarters are _____
8. A thin piece of aluminum used to wrap food
9. To heat water until it bubbles
10. Another name for kings and queens
11. A long trip, especially by ship
12. Another word for faithful and trustworthy
13. A shellfish that makes pearls
14. The opposite of *quiet*
15. Chicago is in this state
16. Food that is too old to eat is . . .
17. To become a member of a club
18. That singer has a beautiful _____
19. Another name for dirt, especially in a garden
20. I have to do it; I have no _____

Chapter 22 Answers to B: Spell It Out

1. toy
2. enjoy
3. avoid
4. choice
5. coin
6. boil
7. foil
8. noise

CHAPTER 23
Mouthy Cow Sounds (/aw/)

A. Sound It Out

The /aw/ sound is a combination of /a/ and /u/ or /w/. When you pronounce /aw/, there is a lot of movement from one position to another. (This is known as a glide vowel or diphthong). Your lips move from open and relaxed to a round, closed position, your jaw rises and closes, and your tongue moves from low central to high back.

Listen carefully to the /aw/ sound in the following words:

Quick (unvoiced)	Stretched (voiced)	Stretched (final)
house	cloud	allow
blouse	down	how
couch	brown	eyebrow
out	ground	plow
spouse	town	now

B. Spell It Out

There are two common spellings for the /aw/ sound:

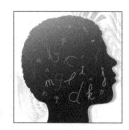

OU	OW
mouth	crown
south	now
around	down
proud	crowd
pronounce	clown
mouse	shower
shout	brown
found	town
hour	tower
our	flower

Chapter 23   Mouthy Cow Sounds (/aw/)   125

C. X Marks the Spot

Cross out the one word in each row that does **not** have the /aw/ sound.

1. bow down   tile   town   out   coward
2. mouth   owl   towel   throw   vow
3. found   south   flower   vowel   model
4. automobile brow   hour   outline   ground
5. our   powerful   also   mountain   loud
6. autumn   outcome   cowboy   down   outside
7. council   smile   sound   scout   down
8. round   Howard   outgoing   dollar   gown
9. chowder   rocket   mouth   blouse   frown

D. The /aw/ Sound Ladder

Work in small groups to climb the ladder to the top by writing words with the letters below that represent the /aw/ sound. The first team to reach the top of the ladder wins.

OW   OU
cow   out
____   ____
____   ____
____   ____
____   ____
____   ____
____   ____
____   ____
____   ____
____   ____

E. Can You Guess It

The answer to each clue will be a word that has the sound /aw/.

1. We get milk from this animal
2. I want to dance, but I don't know _____
3. The color of coffee
4. These circus performers make us laugh
5. The opposite of *up*
6. If you know how to swim, you won't _____
7. A small city
8. A large group of people
9. The sky is full of fluffy white _____
10. The past tense of *find*
11. Use your fingers to _____ from 1 to 10
12. I live in a _____
13. A small animal that cats chase
14. The opposite of *in*
15. A wise-looking bird that hunts at night
16. When he got an A, he felt _____
17. The opposite of *north*
18. Sixty minutes is one _____
19. A long wedding dress
20. After a concert, the performers _____
21. A woman's shirt
22. Another word for *sofa*
23. Another word for *yell*
24. Sixteen ounces equals one _____
25. Kings and queens wear these on their heads

F. Talk it Over

Discuss what each of these idioms mean and how you would use them in sentences.

1. Wise as an **owl**.
2. **Proud** as a peacock.
3. Quiet as a **mouse**.
4. **Out** of this world.
5. **Down** to earth.
6. Let the cat **out** of the bag.
7. Don't beat **around** the bush.
8. Make a monkey **out** of me.
9. The talk of the **town**.
10. By word of **mouth**.
11. Two is company, three is a **crowd**.
12. **Out** of the frying pan and into the fire.
13. **Out** of sight, out of mind.
14. Actions speak **louder** than words.
15. **Doubt** is the beginning of wisdom, but faith will move **mountains**.

G. A Famous Fable

Read the fable by Aesop and mark all the words that contain the sound /aw/. Then discuss what it means. Can you relate this fable to your own life?

The Town Mouse and the Country Mouse

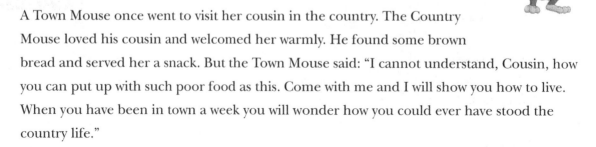

A Town Mouse once went to visit her cousin in the country. The Country Mouse loved his cousin and welcomed her warmly. He found some brown bread and served her a snack. But the Town Mouse said: "I cannot understand, Cousin, how you can put up with such poor food as this. Come with me and I will show you how to live. When you have been in town a week you will wonder how you could ever have stood the country life."

The Town Mouse and the Country Mouse set off for the town and arrived at the Town Mouse's house late at night. "Let me show you how we eat in town," the Town Mouse said proudly. They found the remains of a fine feast, and soon the two mice were eating a big round cake covered in ground nuts.

Suddenly they heard a loud sound. "What is that?" asked the Country Mouse.

"It is only the dogs of the house," answered the Town Mouse.

"I do not like that sound," said the Country Mouse.

Two large dogs ran into the house and began to chase the mice around and around. "Good-bye, Cousin," said the Country Mouse.

"What! Are you leaving so soon?" asked the City Mouse.

"Yes," he replied. "I have learned my lesson: A simple life lived in peace is better than a life of luxury lived in fear."

CHAPTER 24
Come Together: Review of Chapters 18–23

A. Mix and Match

Match the sound with the correct IPA symbol.

1. took _____   A. /ɔy/
2. toil _____   B. /aw/
3. tool _____   C. /ow/
4. toll _____   D. /ʊ/
5. down _____   E. /uw/
6. dial _____   F. /ay/

Write the correct IPA symbol for the vowel sound in each word.

7. stole _____
8. sour _____
9. stool _____
10. style _____
11. soil _____
12. stood _____

B. I Hear You!

Listen and circle the word you hear.

1. bowl   boil   bull
2. cool   coal   coil
3. whole   while   wool
4. noise   news   nose
5. sight   suit   soot
6. right   root   wrote

Part 2 A Mouthful of Vowels

7. tow   toy   tie   two
8. boos   boys   buys   bows (verb)
9. loud   loot   light lout
10. full foul   fool   foil

C. Vowel Sorter

Work with a partner and write each word in the correct box below.

foot	goal	smooth
wood	joke	hood
roll	food	tune
tool	stool	goof
full	rule	lone
goat	wool	cook
wrote	should	duty
cone	tube	wound

/ʊ/	/uw/	/ow/

Work with a partner and write each word in the correct box below.

coin	smile	sign
while	voice	count
owl	eye	boil
fine	south	style
flour	point	shout
how	sour	spoil
light	pie	dry
loud	try	round

/aw/	/ay/	/ɔy/

Chapter 24   Come Together *(Review of Chapters 18–23)*   **131**

D. Sentence Practice

Practice saying the sentences below

1. **South** America is **close to** the **South Pole; however,** some people think Australia is **closer.**
2. **Soap couldn't** get the **blood out** of his **trousers, so** the killer **tried using lighter fluid.**
3. To make beef **soup, boil** some **cow bones** in a **stockpot full** of water for a **whole hour.**
4. **Moe** is such a **sourpuss** that **cute** children and **tiny** puppies **annoy** him.
5. When I saw that **my brown** and **white** cat had been **dyed blue, I** didn't **know** if **I should smile** or **cry.**
6. Mr. and Mrs. **Powell** had a **fight about** whether **owls** and fish **close** their **eyes** when they sleep.
7. **While Julie** wasn't **looking,** the **boys climbed** the **side** of the **house** and walked **around** on the **roof.**
8. The baby **found** some **old coins** on the **ground, so** she **put** them **into** her **mouth.**
9. **Tyler** pretended **to drown so** that the **cute lifeguard would** come and **pull** him **out** of the **pool.**
10. If **you** have a **comb-over, you** shouldn't **go outside** on windy days.

E. Get a Clue /ow/ /uw/ /ʊ/ /aw/ /ay/ /ɔy/

Read the clue and circle the correct word.

1. Another word for *island*	owl	isle	oil
2. Another word for *street*	ride	road	rude
3. Another word for *fashion*	style	stole	stool
4. A relaxing ocean vacation	crows	cruise	cries
5. Cats chase _____	mouse	mice	moose
6. A mosquito _____	boat	boot	bite
7. A song without words	town	tune	tone
8. Another word for *performance*	show	shy	shoe
9. A heavy _____	loud	lied	load
10. You're in trouble and no one can help you	dome	doom	dime
11. A seat with three legs	stole	stool	style
12. You ride this on the water	bite	boat	boot
13. The opposite of *polite*	rude	ride	road
14. You fry food in _____	isle	owl	oil

15. You wear this on your foot — shy — shoe — show
16. The opposite of *quiet* — load — loud — lied
17. When a baby is hungry, she _____ — cruise — cries — crows
18. A very large animal with antlers — moose — mice — mouse
19. A musical note — tune — town — tone
20. A bird that comes out at night — oil — owl — isle
21. The past tense of *steal* — stool — stole — style
22. A 10¢ coin — doom — dime — dome
23. A flock of big, black birds — cries — crows — cruise
24. You _____ a bike or a horse — road — ride — rude
25. A community that is smaller than a city — tone — tune — town
26. The past tense of *lie* — lied — load — loud
27. A type of shoe that covers your ankles — bite — boot — boat
28. A round roof on a building — dime — dome — doom
29. Like a rat but smaller — mice — moose — mouse
30. The opposite of *friendly* — shoe — shy — show

CHAPTER 25
Nerdy Bird's Word Search (/ɜ/ and /ə/)

A. Sound It Out

The sound /ɜ/ is almost the same as the sound /r/, but used as a vowel. Think of the sound that a rooster makes! Your throat tightens while your tongue is curled or bunched as for /r/. The sound /ə/ is pronounced the same as /ɜ/ but with less stress.

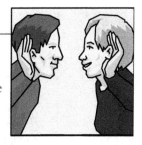

First just listen carefully to the /ɜ/ sound in the following words:

Quick (unvoiced) /ɜ/	Stretched (voiced) /ɜ/	Unstressed in final position (/ə/)
shirt	word	paper
first	third	teacher
worst	heard	worker
burst	curb	mother
worth	hers	cover
purple	burger	cleaner
surf	learn	taller
church	stern	actor
work	burn	doctor
nurse	turn	player
	curve	
	nerve	

(Note: Some texts consider /ɜ/ and /ə/ to be separate sounds, but in this text the stressed and unstressed sound will be practiced together.)

Compare the sound before unvoiced and voiced sounds. Listen and circle the word that you hear:

1. hurt   heard
2. Burke   berg
3. thirsty Thursday
4. hearse hers
5. surf   serve

B. Spell It Out

The sound /ɝ/ can be spelled in several ways. (Italics indicates unstressed /ɚ/.)

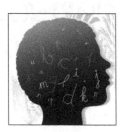

ER	AR	IR	OR	UR(E)	EAR
her	sug*ar*	bird	work	surf	heard
nervous	doll*ar*	third	world	turn	learn
serve	coll*ar*	shirt	worse	nurse	early
were	regu*lar*	birth	word	burger	earth
jerk	gramm*ar*	sir	worth	fur	pearl
certain	popu*lar*	dirt	worm	church	search
verb	alt*ar*	first	actor	hurt	
fing*er*	cell*ar*	girl	doctor	murder	
pap*er*	coug*ar*	quirk	profess*or*	purse	
fath*er*	pol*ar*		flav*or*	rural	
broth*er*	cellul*ar*		col*or*	turtle	
paint*er*	simil*ar*		raz*or*	turkey	
mak*er*	famili*ar*		sail*or*	fail*ure*	
dang*er*			senat*or*	fig*ure*	
loud*er*			instruct*or*	nat*ure*	
tall*er*			calculat*or*	pict*ure*	
			visit*or*	meas*ure*	

In a few words borrowed from French the sound /ɝ/ is spelled OUR:

courteous   courtesy   journal   journey

C. Silly Sentences

Circle all the words with the sound /ɝ/ or /ɚ/. Then practice these sentences with a partner.

1. The nervous nurses were the worst workers in the world.
2. Shirley's first birthday is on Thursday.
3. Her mother's thirty-third birthday came first.
4. This burger isn't worth a dollar.
5. The burglar searched for the pearl in her purse.
6. The girl measured the earthworm.
7. Professor Kirk used a calculator to figure out the answer.
8. Burke is taller than his brother, but his brother is heavier.

D. Dizzy Dialogue

Mark all the /ɜ/ and /ɚ/ sounds. Then work with a partner and practice the dialogue.

Mr. Turner: I want to learn to surf. Can you suggest a good teacher?

Ms. Lerner: Well, Mr. Turner, I am familiar with all the dangers of surfing.

Mr. Turner: The dangers? But surfing is very popular! Is it really that dangerous?

Ms. Lerner: Oh it certainly is! If you surf in an area where there are few doctors, what would you do in an emergency?

Mr. Turner: I don't know. I just want the pleasure of enjoying nature.

Ms. Lerner: But you could get hurt. If you fall off your surfboard, who will search for your body?

Mr. Turner: My body! Goodness, maybe it's not worth it to learn to surf after all.

E. Poetry Corner

Underline all the /ɜ/ or /ɚ/ sounds you find in the poem, and then practice saying it.

Hurt No Living Thing

By Christina Rossetti

Hurt no living thing:
Ladybird, nor butterfly,
Nor moth with dusty wing,
Nor cricket chirping cheerily,
Nor grasshopper so light of leap,
Nor dancing gnat, nor beetle fat,
Nor harmless worms that creep.

F. Can You Guess It?

1. The planet we live on
2. They have feathers and can fly
3. The cat has soft black _____
4. The opposite of *clean*
5. The opposite of *boy*
6. What you do at your job

7. The day you were born

8. First, second, _____

9. The opposite of *best*

10. Many people pray here on Sunday morning

11. My hair is so straight, but I wish it were _____

12. These beautiful jewels for making a necklace come from oysters

13. The past tense of *hear*

14. I don't know how to play the piano, but I want to _____

15. A polite title for a man (the opposite of *ma'am*)

16. The past tense of *are*

17. The early bird gets the _____

18. A doctor's assistant

19. You find thousands of these in a dictionary

20. To ride a board on ocean waves

21. What fire does

22. How you feel when you have to give a speech

23. These make you sick (another word for *bacteria*)

24. We eat this on Thanksgiving

25. Ouch, that _____!

G. Talk It Over

1. Have you ever kept a **personal journal** or diary? How about an online **journal?** What sorts of things would you write in a **journal?**

2. What are some situations that make you feel **nervous?** How can you keep yourself from being **nervous** in those situations?

3. Many parents try to warn their children about "**stranger danger**" by telling them not to talk to **strangers.** What **dangers** do you think parents need to teach their children about?

4. Are there any **birthdays** that are especially important in your **culture**? How do people usually celebrate their **birthday** in your **culture**?

5. What is the **worst** job in the **world**?

H. Speak Your Mind

1. Do you believe people should wear clothing made of **fur**? Is it possible for animals to be raised for their **fur** and killed in a humane way? Or is all **fur** cruel?

2. Is the **earth** becoming **over-populated**? If so, how should we deal with that problem? Is there a limit to how many people can sustainably live on the **earth**?

I. Not to Be Confused With. . . .

Because the /ɜ/ and /ɚ/ sound can be spelled several different ways, be sure not to confuse it with other r-colored vowels.

Listen as your instructor pronounces the following words and cross out the ones that are **not** pronounced /ɜ/ or /ɚ/.

1. farm   firm   first   fear   fur
2. heart   heard   hurt   herb   herd
3. nurse   nerve   near   narrow
4. thirsty   thirty   thorn   Thursday
5. birth   bird   burden   bark   burger   beer

CHAPTER 26
The Boring Boar (/ɔr/)

A. Sound It Out

The sound /ɔr/ is another r-colored vowel. You begin with a sound close to /ɔ/, but your lips are rounded and your tongue is curled or bunched for /r/.

Listen carefully to the /ɔr/ sound in the following words:

Quick (unvoiced)	Stretched (voiced)
fork	stored
stork	storm
pork	chord
fort	warmed
port	floor
cork	mourn

B. Spell It Out

The most common spellings for the /ɔr/ sound is OR:

more   torn   score   worn   forth   horse   dorm   corn   sort   bored

Other spellings are:

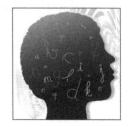

AR	OAR	OUR	OOR
warm	board	four	poor
ward	roar	fourth	floor
war	soar	pour	door
	coarse	court	
		course	

Chapter 26 The Boring Boar (/ɔr/) 139

C. Map Search

Look at the map of the United States and find eight states that have the /ɔr/ sound. Write these states on the lines provided and circle the sound.

OR
1. Oregon
2. California
3. Colorado
4. North Dakota
5. North Carolina
6. Georgia
7. New York
8. Florida

ER sound
1. Vermont
2. New Hampshire
3. New Jersey
4. Virginia
5. West Virginia
6. Missouri
7.
8.

140   Part 2   A Mouthful of Vowels

D. Silly Sentences

Circle all the /ɔr/ sounds in these sentences. Then practice them with a partner.

1. The lion roared when it hit the floor.
2. The bored boar ordered food at the store.
3. When you snore, I'm out the door.
4. George was born in the middle of the storm.
5. The orange orangutan played the organ in the orchestra.
6. Horace the Horse was eating corn.
7. There were forty swordfish swimming down the shore.
8. Orville the porter was an accordion performer.
9. Dora went to court to order mortgage forms.
10. Nora kept warm by blowing a horn.

E. Listening Comprehension

Circle the word that you hear.

1. shirt   short
2. burn   born
3. bird   board
4. worm   warm
5. were   wore
6. dare   door
7. scare   score
8. stir   store
9. perk   pork
10. curse   course

Circle the sentence that you hear.

1. a. I left my shorts at the laundromat.
   b. I left my shirts at the laundromat.
2. a. Did you say "turn"?
   b. Did you say "torn"?

3. a. The bird fell on the floor.
   b. The board fell on the floor.
4. a. The bookshelf was sturdy.
   b. The bookshelf was stored.
5. a. I saw Jerry at the mall.
   b. I saw Jordan at the mall.
6. a. That's a good firm.
   b. That's a good form.
7. a. Flora said she saw a boar at the zoo.
   b. Flora said she saw a bear at the zoo.
8. a. Are you worried about the curse?
   b. Are you worried about the course?

F. A Love Story

Read the following dialogue with a partner.

Orlando: What a beautiful **morning!**

Dora: Yes, look at the **orange** reflection of the sun on the **seashore.**

Orlando: Oh, and the **storm** we expected seems to have vanished.

Dora: Look, **Orlando,** there are **porpoises** playing in the water.

Orlando: They look like **performers** dancing to the beat of an **orchestra.**

Dora: We are certainly the spectators of an **extraordinary** view.

Orlando: This is a spectacular **Fourth** of July. Tonight we can look **forward** to fireworks under the glittering **northern** sky. What a romantic night it will be!

Dora: Let's **record** each scene in our **memory** as a reminder of our first date together.

G. Can You Guess It?

1. The opposite of *rich*
2. A place where you buy things
3. Not interested
4. You get into a house through the _____
5. The number after three

6. The opposite of *outdoor*

7. The opposite of *less*

8. A paddle used to move a rowboat

9. The sound that a lion makes

10. At the end of the game the _____ was 6 to 3

11. How your muscles feel after you exercise too much

12. Where you keep your socks

13. Disney World is in _____

14. A child whose parents have died

15. An animal that can pull a wagon

16. When you're driving, you beep this to warn someone

17. Your birthday is the day when you were _____

18. The opposite of *south*

19. The opposite of *tall*

20. A black and white killer whale is an _____

21. Place where ships dock

22. Soccer, baseball, and tennis are _____

23. Document needed to travel internationally

24. Rose bushes have _____

25. The opposite of *remember*

H. Story

Circle all the words that contain the sound /ɔr/. Then read this story with a partner.

Ordinary People, Extraordinary Feats

Have you ever thought about how many people who seemingly live ordinary lives are capable of doing extraordinary things? Think about the person who performed the first organ transplant or organized the first symphony orchestra. Look at the people that enforce law and order, investigate organized crime, explore outer space, establish orphanages and other similar institutions to deal with the needs of our society. There are also those men and women who join the armed forces and fight in wars that they hope will keep the world safe. Certainly, we must offer a tribute to these extraordinary people who make this world a better place to live. Do you know any extraordinary people? Tell their story.

I. Talk It Over

1. Do you consider yourself a **morning** person? Or do you **perform** better in the afternoon or evening?

2. If you had no children of your own, would you consider adopting one or **more orphans?**

3. Are you an **organized or disorganized** person? Give examples of your daily routine.

4. Do you prefer **ordering** products online or shopping in **stores?** What are the benefits of each? Are some products easier **or** harder to buy online?

J. Speak Your Mind

1. Do you think that women in the armed **forces** should go to **war?**

2. Do you think that undocumented immigrants should be **deported?** Should they be allowed to work with a restricted permit?

3. Are you **for or** against **organ** transplants? Should animal **organs** be transplanted into humans?

4. Do you think that teenagers should be allowed to have an **abortion** without parental consent? Should a woman be able to have an **abortion** without the consent of her partner?

CHAPTER 27
Park Your Car in the Yard (/ar/)

A. Sound It Out

The sound /ar/ is one of the r-colored vowels. The sound is similar to the sound /a/, but your lips are rounded and your tongue is curled or bunched for /r/ beginning with the vowel sound. In American dictionaries, this sound may be represented by är.

First just listen carefully to the sound /ar/:

Quick (unvoiced)	Stretched (voiced)	Stretched (final)
harp	barb	are
cart	hard	tar
dark	Mars	far
spark	carve	bar
scarf	charge	star
marsh	harm	jar
March	yarn	car

B. Spell It Out

The /ar/ sound is usually spelled AR as in:

art   army   bark   party   car   guitar

There are a few unusual spellings of the sound /ar/:

heart   bazaar   bizarre

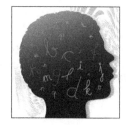

C. Silly Sentences

Practice these sentences with a partner.

1. Wear a **parka** if you go to **Antarctica!**
2. **Carla** made a **scarf** out of **yards** of **yarn**, but **Harvey's** neck was still too **large.**
3. Their house looks like a **barn,** but their **yard** looks like a **park.**
4. **Sharp** knives **are** less **harmful** than dull ones, but don't test either of them on your **arm!**

5. **Barney** threw **darts** at a **target,** but **hardly** any of them hit their **mark.**
6. What would happen if **Charles Darwin** saw Noah's **ark?**
7. Those **carnival** rides **are** fun but they **are far** from safe.
8. Mrs. **Carter** seems **harsh,** but her **bark** is worse than her bite.
9. She **carved** a **heart** out of **dark** chocolate for him, and he **carved** a **heart** out of **marshmallows** for her.
10. This **carton** of **lard** looks like **margarine,** so how do you tell them **apart?**

D. Tongue Twister

1. **Argyle gargoyle**
2. **Aardvarks aren't** in the **marsh.** The **sharks** in the **marsh** ate the **aardvarks.**
3. Pets **are** on **carpets,** but **are carpets** on pets?

E. Dizzy Dialogue—I'm Going to Be a Star!

Practice this dialogue with a partner.

Armando: I'm trying out for a **part** in a play. It's a **starring** role, and I'm perfect for the **part.**

Barbara: Great! What's the play called? **Are** there other people trying out for the **part,** too?

Armando: The play is called *The Heartbreaker.* If they were **smart,** the other actors would stay home because this **part** is off the **market!** It's already mine.

Barbara: You **are** tall, **dark,** and handsome, and you **are** very **charming** when you want to be. Yes, even though you've just **started** acting, the people in **charge** should do the **smart** thing and just give you the **part.**

Armando: Don't be so **sarcastic.** If anyone in the Industry sees me in *The Heartbreaker,* they'll see a true **artist** at work. Movie **parts** will **start** flooding in, and before I know it, I'll be a **superstar** strolling down the red **carpet** every **March.**

Barbara: Now, that's a little **farfetched.** Did you know that learning a **part** takes **hard** work and long hours? And, you'll have to **star** in lots of **larger** productions to get noticed. You can't just get by on good looks and **charm** alone. Besides that, you have to get this *Heartbreaker* **part** first.

Armando: So what if I'm just **starting** out? Why is it so **hard** for you to believe in my **star** power? And besides, what's wrong with a little **harmless** dreaming? You can't be a **star** until you reach for them first!

F. Talk It Over

1. What is the **hardest** problem you've ever solved by yourself?

2. Is it better to follow your **heart** and not your head? Give an example to support your opinion.

3. Have you ever had your palm or your **cards** read by a psychic? Do you believe that these things can foretell the future, or **are** they just **harmless** fun? Can fortune telling ever be **harmful**?

G. Speak Your Mind

1. A "domestic **partnership**" is a relationship like a marriage, but the people **are** not legally married. What is your opinion of domestic **partnerships**?

2. When is it a good idea to **start** over again and **carve** out a new life for yourself?

3. Some people prefer to **barter** their services instead of **charging** people money for them. For instance, you could wash your neighbor's **car** in exchange for her babysitting your child while you and your spouse **are** at a **party.** What is your opinion of **bartering**? Do you think **bartering** your services is a better **bargain** than **charging** money for them?

H. Can You Guess It?

1. The opposite of *near*
2. To fight with words
3. Painting, drawing, and sculpture are types of _____
4. Cooking food outside on a grill
5. Something you bought cheaply
6. A big red building for keeping animals
7. The loud sound made by a dog
8. You send these for Christmas or birthdays

9. The opposite of *light*
10. Land for growing crops
11. A person who protects a place
12. An area with flowers, plants, or vegetables
13. The opposite of *easy*
14. The organ that pumps blood through your body
15. Another word for *big*
16. The third month of the year
17. The fourth planet from the sun
18. A public playground
19. The opposite of *finish*
20. When you are late for class, you are _____
21. You aim an arrow at a _____
22. The area behind a house
23. Soft string for knitting a sweater
24. We see the moon and the _____ at night
25. Pickles and jam come in a _____

I. Now for the Hard Part . . .

Find all of the answers for Part H "Can You Guess It?" in the puzzle below. The words can be spelled horizontally (→ ←) vertically (↑↓), or diagonally (↘↗↙↖). Be careful! Some of these words are spelled backward, too. For example, the word, "ART," looks like "TRA" in the puzzle.

B	A	R	N	J	T	E	Q	O	W	H	M
L	A	K	H	E	K	R	M	I	T	R	A
H	C	R	A	M	D	N	K	U	T	P	R
A	S	A	B	S	C	R	T	R	A	T	S
R	T	D	M	E	A	A	O	L	A	W	
D	A	Y	H	P	Q	E	R	G	N	R	P
K	R	A	B	R	H	U	G	D	S	D	T
T	S	R	L	A	R	G	E	G	S	Y	H
E	R	N	F	Q	U	R	T	W	A	O	F
J	A	R	A	A	U	A	R	R	O	A	L
C	T	H	R	G	B	E	D	O	R	T	H
Y	S	D	M	N	B	A	R	G	A	I	N

J. Not to Be Confused With . . .

The /ar/ sound can easily be confused with the /a/ sound that we studied in Chapter 15 or the /ɔ/ sound that we studied in Chapter 16.

Directions

Listen as your instructor reads the sentences. Find the words with the /ar/, /a/, and /ɔ/ sounds in them. There are 8 words that contain the /ar/ sound, 12 words that contain the /a/ sound, and 5 words that contain the /ɔ/ sound. List these words in the chart below.

/ar/	/a/	/ɔ/

1. Andy **almost** had a **heart** attack when he **lost** his **wallet.**
2. I don't think you **ought** to tell **Mom** that you spent all your money.
3. They stayed at a very nice **lodge** in the mountains last June.
4. How much **farther** is the closest gas station?
5. **Donna** is a careful **shopper,** but she can't resist a good shoe sale.
6. She made several **jars** of blueberry jam for her friends and family.
7. The boat sailed back to the **dock** as the sun went down.
8. **Grandpa** and **Tommy** play **cards** every Saturday afternoon.
9. Randy's face gets red when he eats **hot,** spicy food.
10. At the **art** show, people have fun throwing paint at a **wall.**
11. The cake recipe asks for 3 **large** eggs and a pound of butter.
12. **Bob** says dumb things, but he's **sharper** than he seems.
13. It's healthier to have grilled **cod** instead of fried shrimp.
14. Nick was able to pull a bird out of his cat's **jaws.**
15. Lisa is afraid of the **dark,** so she sleeps with the lights on.
16. Let's get your **father** a new sweater for his birthday.

CHAPTER 28

Weird Deers and Bears There (/ɪr/ and /ɛr/)

A. Sound It Out

In addition to the r-colored vowels /ɝ/, /ɚ/, /ar/, and /ɔr/ that we practiced in the previous three chapters, two other vowels may combine with R to create distinctive vowel sounds.

The sound /ɪr/ is close to /iy/, but your lips are rounded and your tongue is curled or bunched as for /r/ beginning with the vowel sound.

The sound /ɛr/ is close to the sound /ey/, but your lips are rounded and your tongue is curled or bunched as for /r/ beginning with the vowel sound.

First just listen carefully to the vowel sounds in the following words:

/ɪr/	/ɛr/
beer	air
cheer	bear/bare
deer	care
ear	dare
fear	fair/fare
gear	glare
hear/here	hair
hero	mare
clear	snare
near	pair/pare/pear
peer	rare
queer	stare/stair
rear	tear
steer	there/they're/their
tear	wear/where
year	
we're	
zero	

B. Spell It Out

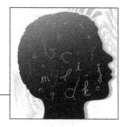

The two most common spellings for the sound /ɪr/ are EER or EAR:

EER	EAR
beer	ear
deer	clear
cheer	dear
jeer	fear
leer	gear
peer	hear
queer	near
steer	rear
veer	tear

The two most common spellings of the sound /ɛr/ are ARE and AIR.

ARE	AIR
bare	air
care	fair
dare	hair
fare	lair
hare	pair
mare	stair
pare	
square	
rare	
stare	
ware	

However, there are a few cases in which the same spelling is used for two different sounds: *tear* is pronounced /tɪr/ when it refers to crying, but it is pronounced /tɛr/ when it means *rip* (as in *tear, tore, torn*.) And notice the different pronunciation of *here* /hɪr/ and *there* /ðɛr/.

C. Silly Sentences

Circle all the words with the sound /ɪr/ or /ɛr/. Then practice these sentences with a partner.

1. With tears in their eyes, they cheered for the hero.
2. We have nothing to fear but fear itself.
3. Steer clear of the deer, dear!
4. Open your ears so you can hear if they jeer.

5. Near beer tastes weird.

6. A pair of fair-haired girls stared at the square.

7. The hare and the mare returned to their lair.

8. He pared the rare pear.

9. These are the stairs that lead to the fair.

10. We must take care of the air.

D. Dizzy Dialogue: A Scary Nightmare

Practice this dialogue with a partner.

Mary: I had a **terrible nightmare** last night.

Laird: What happened?

Mary: I walked up the **stairs** in my house, and an enormous **bear** was **staring** at me. I was afraid it was going to **tear** me to pieces.

Laird: No wonder you were **scared!** Then what happened?

Mary: The **bear reared** up on its hind legs, and then a **fairy appeared** and turned him into a handsome prince. But he still looked a bit like a **bear** because he had a big **beard.**

Laird: I can't wait to **hear** what happened next!

Mary: Well, it only seemed **fair** to marry the prince because everyone knows that **fairy** tales should end happily ever after. But then the prince turned into a **deer** and ran away from me. And finally the **deer disappeared** into thin **air.**

Laird: What a **weird** dream!

Mary: It really was **weird,** but when I woke up, there were **tears** on my pillow!

E. Can You Guess It?

/ɪr/

1. The opposite of *far*

2. How you turn a car

3. A popular drink in Germany

4. When you cry, these fall from your eyes

5. Santa Claus has one, and so does Abraham Lincoln

6. Another word for your job or profession

7. 365 days equals one _____

8. The opposite of *cloudy*

9. Bambi is a _____

10. What you do when your team scores

/ɛr/

11. It grows on your head

12. A bad dream

13. An extra tire for emergencies

14. Afraid, frightened

15. We breathe _____

16. To give some to everyone

17. A shape with 4 equal sides

18. The money you pay to ride the bus

19. Two shoes equals one _____

20. You walk up these to get to the top floor of a building

F. Talk It Over

1. Have you ever had a **nightmare** that really left you **scared?** What do you think causes **nightmares?**

2. What is your definition of a **hero?** Who are some **heroes** that you admire?

3. Some people have a **fear** (or phobia) of high places or spiders. Do you have any unusual or intense **fears?**

4. How would your life be changed if you could not **hear?**

G. Speak Your Mind

What is the best way for a society to make sure that everyone pays a **fair share** of taxes? Is it **fair** that wealthy people pay a higher percentage of their income in taxes than poor people? Some people say that a flat tax (in which everyone pays the same percentage of their income) or national sales tax would be **fairer** than an income tax. What do you think?

H. Not to Be Confused With. . . .

Listen as your instructor reads the following words. Write the number and the word in the correct box.

/ɑr/	/ɪr/	/ɛr/	/ɔr/	/ɝ/ or /ɚ/

1. bar
2. beer
3. bear
4. bore
5. bird
6. star
7. steer
8. stare
9. store
10. stir
11. wear
12. bored
13. storm
14. weird
15. farm
16. nurse
17. bark
18. here
19. there
20. warm
21. work
22. party
23. beard
24. care
25. word
26. swear
27. world
28. corn
29. clear
30. park

CHAPTER 29
Together We Can Make It
(Review of Chapters 25–28)

A. Listening Practice

Listen as your instructor reads one word from each row and circle the word that you hear.

/ar/	/ɛr/	/ɪr/	/ɔr/	/ɝ/
1. scar	scare		score	
2. tar	tear	tier	tore	
3. far	fair	fear	for	fur
4. are	air	ear	or	
5. star	stare	steer	store	stir
6. car	care		core	
7. bar	bare	beer	boar	burr
8. farm			form	firm
9. barn			born	burn
10. card	cared		cord	curd
11. park			pork	perk

B. Symbol Matching

Match the underlined sound in each of the words in **Column** A with the correct symbol in **Column** B.

A	B
_____ 1. p<u>or</u>t	a. /ɝ/
_____ 2. st<u>ar</u>	b. /ar/
_____ 3. <u>ear</u>	c. /ɔr/
_____ 4. b<u>ear</u>	d. /ɪr/
_____ 5. h<u>ear</u>d	e. /ɛr/

154

C. Minute Madness

Write as many words that rhyme with the cue words as you can in one minute.

jar /ar/	care /ɛr/	near /ɪr/	four /ɔr/	sir /ɝ/

D. Can You Guess It?

/ar/

1. The opposite of *light*
2. To disagree
3. The opposite of *dull*
4. The opposite of *easy*
5. The month after February
6. An area of flowers, plants, or vegetables
7. A public playground
8. Another word for *big*

/ɛr/

1. To look at someone for a long time
2. You use shampoo to wash your _____
3. An extra tire is called a _____
4. A yellow fruit similar to an apple
5. Clothes are things that you _____
6. Many children have a toy teddy _____
7. The opposite of well-done steak is _____

/ɪr/

1. The opposite of *far*
2. There are twelve months in a _____
3. When you cry these fall from your eyes
4. A feeling of danger
5. The opposite of *cloudy*
6. Another word for *profession*
7. They pull Santa's sleigh

/ɔr/

1. The opposite of *indoor*
2. The sound that a lion makes
3. Not less but _____
4. The opposite of *interesting*
5. An utensil to eat with
6. Roses have sharp _____
7. The past tense of *wear*
8. A dresser has several _____

/ɝ/

1. The number before *second*
2. You put it on a hook to catch fish
3. To mix with a spoon
4. The opposite of *best*
5. The edge of the sidewalk next to the street
6. The bag that women carry
7. To ride a board on ocean waves
8. Another word for salesperson

Chapter 29   Together We Can Make It *(Review of Chapters 25–28)*   **157**

E. Silly Sentences

Circle all the words that contain r-colored vowels. Then practice saying the sentences.

1. The doctor and nurse were nervous because it was their first open-heart surgery.
2. The art department at our university has many works by famous artists.
3. My family owns very fertile farmland.
4. The students are nervous because the test is hard.
5. Mary purchased these portraits at the bazaar.
6. The thirsty boys drank more water after the soccer game.
7. My sister got a ticket for driving alone in the carpool lane.
8. Martha has a big heart.
9. My father and I had a conversation about earning money in the future.
10. The lawyer defended the murderer in court.

F. Idioms

Circle all the r-colored vowels in the following idioms. Then explain what each idiom means and how you could use it.

1. Little pitchers have big ears.
2. Easier said than done.
3. Actions speak louder than words.
4. Beggars can't be choosers.
5. Neither a borrower nor a lender be.
6. Better late than never.
7. Two heads are better than one.
8. Here today, gone tomorrow.
9. First come, first served.
10. There's no place like home.

PART 3

Conquering Consonant Confusion

CHAPTER 30
Lucy Loves Robby Rabbit (/l/ and /r/)

A. Sound It Out

Many students have a hard time pronouncing the sounds /l/ and /r/. To pronounce the sound /l/, the tip of your tongue should touch the area just behind your teeth. Be sure to keep your lips relaxed.

To pronounce the American /r/ sound, your lips should be rounded and your tongue should be tense and slightly curled or bunched up, but your tongue must **not** touch the top of your mouth. Both /l/ and /r/ are continuants.

To help us remember which sound is which, picture the two letters like this:

$$l \quad R$$

The tall loop of the letter L looks like your tongue, touching the top of your mouth. And the round shape of the letter R looks like your round lips.

First just listen carefully to the /l/ sound in the following words:

Initial Position	Initial Blend	Middle Position	Final Position
lady	black	milk	tail
lamp	blue	melt	bell
lettuce	clue	bald	hill
lend	click	help	doll
little	flood	old	dull
link	glow	also	trial
long	please	fallen	apple
lost	slow	balloon	sample
lucky			single
lunch			travel
			local

B. Spell It Out

The sound /l/ is always spelled with the letter L.

For most English-speakers, the letter L is silent in a few words:

talk folks walk calf chalk yolk half
should would could palm calm salmon

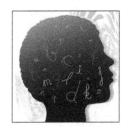

C. Silly Sentences

Circle all the words that contain the sound /l/. Then practice these sentences with a partner.

1. Lazy lizards are lying in the lane.
2. Little Linda likes licking lollipops.
3. Eleven elephants left the London zoo.
4. Leonard and Laura like living in Los Angeles.
5. The lady from Louisiana laughed at the law.
6. Lily lulled the baby to sleep with a long, low lullaby.
7. Louise lent Lakisha her lovely lipstick.
8. The Lakers lost their leader.
9. Lydia loves her laptop.
10. Lexie left her lover alone.

D. Dizzy Dialogue

Circle all the words that contain the sound /l/. Then practice the dialogue with a partner.

Lily: Let's go to that luxurious new restaurant that just opened!

Lloyd: All right. But I hope the food isn't too strange. I like familiar foods.

Lily: Oh look, they have lamb stew with lemons. That sounds lovely!

Lloyd: I like lamb, but I don't want it with lemons.

Lily: Well, how about the calf's liver with leeks?

Lloyd: Seriously?

Lily: Ok, well there's a vegetarian special: lima beans and lentils.

Lloyd: Maybe I'll just have a salad. And key lime pie for dessert.

Lily: Luckily, I like lemons, so I'll have the lamb stew.

E. Loony Limerick

The Flea and the Fly

A flea and a fly in a flue
Were imprisoned, so what could they do?
Said the fly, "Let us flee,"
Said the flea, "Let us fly,"
So they flew through a flaw in the flue.

(Note: Fleas and flies = insects, flue = a kind of tube or pipe, flaw = something like a crack.)

F. Can You Guess It?

The answers to each clue begin with the sound /l/.

1. The opposite of *big*
2. The opposite of *high*
3. The opposite of *short*
4. A very sour yellow fruit
5. A very sour green fruit
6. The opposite of *win*
7. The opposite of *die*
8. What you say to someone who is trying something difficult: Good _____!
9. The opposite of *hate*
10. It's dark in here. Turn on the _____
11. Don't turn right, turn _____
12. The opposite of *tight*
13. A dog has 4, a bird has 2, a snake has none
14. A baby sheep
15. A song to help a baby fall asleep

G. Sound It Out

Remember that when you pronounce /r/, your tongue must **not** touch the top of your mouth.

Now listen carefully to the /r/ sound in the following words:

Initial Position	Initial Blend	Middle Position	Final Position
rain	brand	arrow	car
rent	crab	borrow	hear
ripe	drive	carry	door
round	fry	direct	fire
run	grass	error	fur
red	prince	around	wonder
reason	scream	arrive	poor
rhyme	shrink	terrible	ogre
race	spring	argue	
rice	street	mirror	
rock	three	tomorrow	
right	trip	barrel	
wrong			

H. Spell It Out

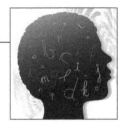

The sound /r/ is always spelled with the letter R in English. The letter R is never silent in English. The only unusual spellings of the sound /r/ are RH (silent H) in words borrowed from Greek, and WR (silent W) from Old English words.

RH	WR
rhyme	wrap
rhythm	wrist
rheumatism	wreck
rhinoceros	wrinkle
rhinestone	wrong
Rhode Island	write

I. Silly Sentences

Circle all the words that contain the sound /r/. Then practice these sentences with a partner.

1. Rabbits are running round and round.
2. Ronald reads and writes very well.
3. Rebecca ran right in front of a rhinoceros.
4. Red rover, red rover, send Robert right over.
5. Ripe red raspberries remain in the garden.
6. Rita remembered the road to Rome.
7. Rick regrets wrecking the room.
8. Red roses remind me of Rachel.
9. Ron is really wrinkled.
10. Right or wrong, Rick reported the result.

J. Tongue Twisters

1. Rolling red wagons rolled around.
2. Really weary, really weary, really weary.
3. A really weird rear wheel.

K. Dizzy Dialogue

Circle all the words that contain the sound /r/. Then practice the dialogue with a partner.

Rita: I am looking forward to my vacation—I want to really relax!

Richard: But I thought you were going to Rome!

Rita: I was, but I regretted that idea as soon as I made the reservation. So I got a refund, and I rebooked my trip. I'm going to rural Rhode Island.

Richard: Rural Rhode Island? You mean a farm?

Rita: Right! I'm going to ride a horse and read mystery stories and write in my journal.

Richard: Well, it sounds relaxing all right, but don't you think you might get bored?

Rita: Not at all, I think it will be romantic!

Richard: Romantic? Rome is romantic, not Rhode Island.

Rita: What could be more romantic than riding a horse through a field of roses?

L. Can You Guess It?

The answer to each clue begins with /r/.

1. The color of fire engines
2. You wear it on your finger to show that you're married
3. The opposite of *poor*
4. A male chicken
5. Like a mouse, but bigger
6. Water that falls from the sky
7. Beautiful colors that appear in the sky after a storm
8. Snakes, turtles, lizards, and alligators are this type of animal
9. Dried grapes
10. All the members of your extended family
11. You pay this to live in an apartment
12. Another word for *fix*
13. To say something again
14. The opposite of *fake*
15. A place you go to eat a nice meal

M. Not to Be Confused With. . . .

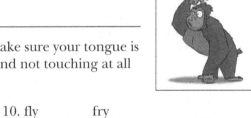

Listen to the contrast between each pair of words. Make sure your tongue is touching right behind your teeth when you say /l/ and not touching at all when you say /r/.

1. long — wrong
2. lock — rock
3. lane — rain
4. low — row
5. led — red
6. light — right
7. liver — river
8. lace — race
9. loyal — royal
10. fly — fry
11. flee — free
12. glass — grass
13. clown — crown
14. climb — crime
15. collect — correct
16. alive — arrive
17. little — riddle
18. pilot — pirate

N. Listen Up!

Circle the word that your instructor says.

1. The answer was long/wrong.
2. I need a lock/rock.
3. I walked in the lane/rain.
4. Turn to the light/right.
5. I don't like that liver/river.
6. She finished the lace/race.
7. The prince is loyal/royal.
8. I don't like to fly/fry.
9. Don't walk on the glass/grass!
10. The teacher will collect/correct the tests.
11. He wants to be a pilot/pirate.

O. Talk It Over (/l/ and /r/ combined)

1. Would you **rather live** in an **urban area or** a **rural area?** What **are** the advantages and disadvantages of each?

2. What's the most **relaxing place** you've ever gone for vacation? The most **romantic?** The most **luxurious?** What kind of vacation do you enjoy the most?

3. Many companies **work hard** at creating "**brand loyalty.**" **For** example, they want you to be **loyal** to Coke™ and never switch to Pepsi™. Do you pay attention to **brands** when you shop? **Are there** any **brands** that you **are very loyal** to?

P. Speak Your Mind

There's a famous saying about **loyalty** to one's country that says, "**My country, right or wrong.**" Is it good to be so **loyal** to **your country** that you will defend it **whether** it is **right or wrong?** If a citizen thinks that his or **her country** is doing something **wrong,** what should he or she do?

Q. Poetry Corner

Underline the sounds /l / and /r/. Practice saying the poem.

The Eagle
by Alfred Lord Tennyson

He clasps the crag with crooked hands;
Close to the sun in lonely lands,
Ringed with the azure world he stands.
The wrinkled sea beneath him crawls;
He watches from his mountain walls,
And like a thunderbolt he falls.

(crag = mountain, azure=blue, thunderbolt=lightning)

CHAPTER 31
Ed's Endings (/t/, /d/, and –ED endings)

A. Sound It Out

The /t/ and the /d/ sounds are produced the same way. When you pronounce /t/ or /d/, your tongue touches the ridge behind your top teeth. You stop the air for a moment and then move your tongue and let the air out. The difference between /t/ and /d/ is that /t/ is unvoiced and /d/ is voiced. There is a puff of air when /t/ is at the beginning of a word. Compare the sounds in the words below.

Beginning		Middle*		End	
tip	dip	liter	leader	beat/beet	bead
ten	den	matter	madder	lit	lid
tall	doll	petal	pedal	great/grate	grade
to/two/too	do/due/dew	written	ridden	height	hide
tore	door	seating	seeding	sent	send
time	dime	rating	raiding	bolt	bold
town	down	hearty	hardy	court	cord

*****Note:** When /t/ is in the middle of a word, it is generally pronounced the same as /d/. Both /t/ and /d/ in the middle of a word sound like the "r" sound in the Spanish word, *pero*, (*but*) or in the Japanese word, *kara* (*from*). The IPA symbol for this sound is /ɾ/.

B. Warm up: Tongue Twisters

1. **Two tiny tigers take two taxis to town.**
2. **Did Dick dig Doug's ditch,** or **did Doug dig Dick's ditch?**
3. **Betty Botter bought** some **butter, but, she said,** the **butter's bitter.**
   If I **put it** in my **batter, it'll** make my **batter bitter.**
   But a **bit** of **better butter** will make my **bitter batter better.**
   So she **bought** some **better butter, better** than the **bitter butter,**
   Put it in the **bitter batter,** and the **bitter batter's better.**

C. Pronouncing -ED Endings

The pronunciation of the past tense -ED ending changes depending on the sound before it.

If a verb ends in an unvoiced consonant sound, -ED sounds like /t/:
wrap → wrapped
look → looked
stuff → stuffed
pass → passed
wish → wished
reach → reached

If a verb ends in a voiced consonant sound or a vowel, -ED sounds like /d/:	
rob → robbed	free → freed
sag → sagged	play → played
wave → waved	thaw → thawed
raise → raised	glue → glued
breathe → breathed	sew → sewed
loan → loaned	annoy → annoyed
seem → seemed	try → tried
fill → filled	vow → vowed
budge → budged	care → cared

If a verb ends in a /t/ or /d/ sound, -ED sounds like /ɪd/:	
greet → greeted	need → needed
shift → shifted	scold → scolded
hint → hinted	blend → blended
start → started	guard → guarded
list → listed	

Note: In some adjectives, -ED also sounds like /ɪd/:

naked   crooked   wicked   wretched   learned   blessed

D. Spell It Out: -ED Endings

- Words that end with **one** vowel followed by **one** consonant—double the consonant before adding –ED.

    grip → gripped   wag → wagged
    plot → plotted   star → starred
    pad → padded

    Exceptions:
        Don't double W or X.
        snow → snowed
        fix → fixed

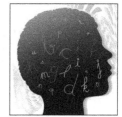

Don't double the consonant in words of more than one syllable unless the word is stressed on the last syllable.

    happen → happened
    open → opened
    visit → visited
    commit → committed

- Words that end in a consonant + Y—change the Y to I and add ED.
    try → tried
    cry → cried
    deny → denied
    reply → replied

- Words that end in a vowel + Y—just add ED.
    play → played
    obey → obeyed
    delay → delayed

(Hint: If you end up with three vowels together, you made a mistake.)

- Words that end in silent E—add just D after the silent E.
    tape → taped
    like → liked
    stage → staged
    lie → lied
    rate → rated
    fade → faded

E. Spellbound

Work with a partner. For each verb, write the correct spelling of the past tense. Explain why your answer is correct. These are all regular (-ED) verbs.

1. stop _____
2. hop _____
3. hope _____
4. tap _____
5. tape _____
6. pretend _____
7. invent _____
8. plan _____
9. plan t_____
10. fasten _____
11. plow _____
12. tax _____
13. remember _____
14. lick _____
15. spy _____
16. stay _____
17. imply _____
18. rely _____

19. fry _____

20. relax _____

21. submit _____

22. permit _____

23. destroy _____

24. rob _____

25. beg _____

F. Sounds from the Past

Listen to the word. Mark the sound you hear at the end of the word.

	/t/	/d/	/ɪd/
1. pulled			
2. fished			
3. clapped			
4. visited			
5. jammed			
6. fixed			
7. hugged			
8. mashed			
9. stored			
10. closed			
11. planted			
12. sighed			
13. stirred			
14. coated			
15. needed			
16. played			
17. flashed			
18. coughed			
19. started			
20. passed			

G. Silly Sentences

Practice the following sentences with a partner.

1. Dorothy and Toto **traveled** to the wonderful land of Oz, but they **missed** Kansas after two days.
2. We **stuffed** a chicken into a duck, **stuffed** the duck into a turkey, **roasted** them all together, and we **enjoyed** a tasty turducken.
3. Todd **dreamed** that he **skated** to Tahiti and almost **drowned.**
4. Tito was too **embarrassed** to admit that he **watched** dumb videos on the Internet.
5. Don's white underwear **turned** pink after Dad **tossed** his red t-shirt into the washer, too.
6. The cats and dogs **lived** together because they **stayed** on opposite sides of the house.
7. Trinh **dusted** her dollhouse with a tiny feather duster.
8. Donatella **paired** a polka-**dotted** skirt with a **striped** top and a butter-**colored** coat.
9. The tide **rocked** the little boat so hard that it **tipped** over and **bobbed** back up again.
10. Dylan **wanted** to tell Tanya he **loved** her, but he **changed** his mind.

H. Dizzy Dialogue: I Should Have Stayed Home

Practice this dialogue with a partner.

Tara: So, how was your vacation? I know you **looked** forward to it for a long time.

Dean: Well, it wasn't what I **expected** at all.

Tara: But you were so **excited** about going. What **happened?**

Dean: Well, when I **arrived** at the hotel, I asked for a non-smoking room, but my room **smelled** like a dirty ashtray. I **tried** to change rooms, but the hotel was **booked** up, so I was stuck with the room I had. But the room **overlooked** the beach.

Tara: Wow, you must have **loved** that!

Dean: I did! I **opened** the window and **enjoyed** the view while I **dreamed** of all the surfing and diving I **planned** to do. But the next day, as I **walked** down the beach, I **stepped** on a little jellyfish hidden in the sand. I **wondered** how that jellyfish **washed** up on the shore. I thought they **stayed** in the water. My foot **swelled** up, so I **rested** in my room until my foot got better.

Tara: That sounds terrible!

Dean: Yeah, it was. I got so **bored!** I **stared** out the window all day and **watched** TV all night. Then I **realized** that I could do that at home, so I **rescheduled** my flight and came home early.

Tara: How awful! I'm sorry that your trip didn't work out for you.

Dean: Actually, it **turned** out great! I got **bumped** from the flight home, and the airline **passed** out ticket vouchers to us. I've already **started** planning my next vacation!

booked up—full

get bumped—lose your seat on an airplane

ticket voucher—a coupon for a discount on a plane ticket

I. Talk It Over

Write /t/, /d/, or /ɪd/ over each –ED ending to indicate the correct pronunciation. Then take turns reading the story aloud.

My Mother Never Worked

Abridged version of "My Morther Never Worked" by Bonnie J. Smith-Yackel, © 1974, 2011, reprinted by permission.

My mother and father got **married** in 1921 and began farming. They had two babies in two years. They didn't have enough money to buy a farm, so they **rented** one. My father also **worked** for two other farmers. He **worked** from early morning until late at night. My mother was not a farm girl, but she **learned** quickly. She **learned** how to raise chickens and pigs. She **milked** cows and **planted** and **harvested** a garden. She **canned** fruits and vegetables. She **carried** water from a well and **washed** the clothes by hand with a scrub board. They **saved** as much money as they could.

She **shucked** grain and **cooked** for the farm workers. After a third and fourth child were born, my mother and father finally had enough money to buy a farm of their own. They **moved** all their animals and furniture 55 miles over **rutted** and muddy roads.

They **started** working to make the farm better. My mother **chopped** out weeds with a hoe. She **walked** through the fields every day and **pulled** out smaller weeds. She **raised** chickens, and she **planted, hoed,** and **harvested** a large garden.

When there was a drought, my mother and father **carried** water from the well to the animals and **watered** the fields as well as they could. When they finally **harvested** the corn, they couldn't afford to take it to town to sell because the price was so low. So they **burned** it in the furnace to stay warm that winter.

My father **hunted** rabbits, and my mother **cooked stewed** rabbit and **fried** rabbit, but she **wished** she could eat hamburger again. My father **hunted** ducks and other wild birds. My mother **plucked** the feathers and **cooked** the birds and **saved** the feathers to make pillows.

In the winter, my mother **sewed** every night to make clothes for her children. Sometimes, she **begged** neighbors for old clothes that she could use to make new clothes for her children.

Every day, my mother **milked** cows, **tended** pigs and calves, **cared** for chickens, **picked** up eggs, **cooked** meals, **washed** clothes, **scrubbed** floors, **cleaned** the house, and **minded** her children.

She also **sewed** and **quilted** beautiful quilts. She **saved** every scrap of cloth and **braided** rugs as well. She had eight children. After her last child **graduated** from high school, she **continued** to work hard. She **baked** her own bread and **sewed** her own clothes.

One day, my mother and father **started** to drive to town to do some shopping. The car **crashed** in a ditch, and my mother was **injured.** She was **paralyzed** from the waist down. The next year, my father **died.** Still, my mother kept working. She **learned** to live in a wheelchair. She still **canned** pickles and **baked** bread and **ironed** clothes and **sewed.**

Can you believe that after my mother **died,** the Social Security office told me, "Your mother never **worked**"?!

1. After reading the story, what is your opinion of Smith-Yackel's mother and the work that she did throughout her life?
2. When you were growing up, who took care of you? What did he or she do for you every day? What important lessons did this person's actions teach you?
3. Oprah Winfrey once said that raising a family is "the hardest job in the world." Is being a parent today as difficult as it was during the time that this story took place?
4. Some people have tried to pass a law saying that the government should pay stay-at-home parents for all of the work that they do. Should stay-at-home parents be paid?

J. Speak Your Mind

1. In many cultures, people have **arranged** marriages. In an **arranged** marriage, parents choose a spouse for their son or daughter. Sometimes, the son or daughter is already **acquainted** with the future spouse, and other times, the couple gets **married** soon after they are **introduced** to each other. Supporters of **arranged** marriage say that parents want the best for their children, so they will choose a spouse who is successful, **well-educated,** and kind. On the other hand, others believe that **arranged** marriages are **old-fashioned** and that people should be **allowed** to choose their own spouses. What do you think?

    spouse—husband or wife

2. While they are strong enough to make their own decisions, some terminally-ill people have **decided** to end their lives through **assisted** suicide. People choose **assisted** suicide because they have **suffered** terrible pain, completely **depended** on others to take care of them, and don't want machines to keep them alive. **Assisted** suicide is illegal in most states, but people have **argued** that they have the right to choose when and how they will die. What is your opinion of **assisted** suicide?

terminally-ill—having a disease, like cancer, that cannot be cured

assisted suicide—committing suicide with the help of a family member or friend who has agreed to help the terminally-ill person commit suicide

K. Can You Guess It?

What is the spelling and the pronunciation of the past tense of . . .

1. bake?
2. work?
3. lean?
4. glow?
5. knit?
6. spell?
7. stop?
8. watch?
9. chew?
10. jump?
11. seat?
12. stay?
13. walk?
14. clean?
15. show?
16. try?
17. open?
18. print?
19. copy?
20. vow?
21. type?
22. brew?
23. call?
24. shout?
25. laugh?

CHAPTER 32
Susan Saves the Zoo (/s/, /z/, and –S endings)

A. Sound It Out /s/ and /z/

To pronounce the /s/ sound, keep the tip of your tongue behind your top teeth and let air flow out. The /s/ sound is unvoiced; it sounds like the hiss of a snake.

The /z/ sound is produced exactly like the /s/ sound, but it is voiced, so you should feel a lot of vibration. It sounds like a buzzing bee or mosquito.

Listen to the contrast between these words:

/s/	/z/
Sue	zoo
see	Z
sack	Zack
sewn	zone
sane	Zane
sip	zip
bus	buzz
fuss	fuzz
race	raze
price	prize
face	faze
lacy	lazy

B. Spell It Out

Words that begin with the letter S always have the sound /s/ (exceptions: sugar, sure). Other spellings for the sound /s/:

C (before e, i, and y):
    century   nice   piece   slice   office   city   tricycle

SC:
    scene   scissors   scenery   scent

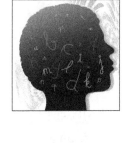

In a few words, the S is silent:
    island   aisle

Words that are spelled with the letter Z always have the sound /z/. But there are many words in which the letter S is pronounced /z/ in the middle or end of words. Listen to the following words and write /s/ or /z/ over each letter S.

Example: S u s a n
          /s/ /z/

1. p l e a s e
2. f e a s t
3. r e s u l t
4. m u s i c
5. s i s t e r
6. r e a s o n
7. c a u s e
8. r a i s e
9. c o u r s e
10. l e a s e
11. r a i s i n
12. c o u s i n
13. t h o u s a n d
14. c r u i s e
15. p h y s i c s

C. Those Puzzling –S Endings

English uses the -S ending for plural nouns, 3rd person singular verbs, possessives, and contractions. (For example, *books, thinks, John's,* and *let's*). These –S endings all follow the same pronunciation rules. The pronunciation of the –S ending depends on the sound that it comes after.

The -S ending is pronounced /s/ after unvoiced sounds /f/, /k/, /p/, /t/, and /θ/.

1. stops
2. tapes
3. sets
4. waits
5. that's
6. paths
7. baths
8. trucks
9. Jack's
10. Jeff's
11. coughs
12. cuffs

178 Part 3 *Conquering Consonant Confusion*

The -S ending is pronounced /z/ after voiced sounds /b/, /d/, /g/, /l/, /r/, /m/, /n/, /ŋ/, /ð/, /v/, and all vowel sounds.

1. cubs	11. hums	21. snows
2. Bob's	12. comes	22. blows
3. cards	13. pans	23. plays
4. Dad's	14. Stan's	24. bays
5. begs	15. rings	25. shoes
6. bugs	16. brings	26. clues
7. calls	17. breathes	27. bees
8. hills	18. bathes	28. radios
9. stars	19. loves	29. bananas
10. bars	20. wolves	30. potatoes

The -S ending is pronounced as a separate syllable /ɪz/ after the sounds /s/, /z/, /ʃ/, /tʃ/, /dʒ/, and /ʒ/. (Note that the letter X sounds like /ks/ so –S is pronounced like /ɪz/ in words ending in X.)

1. buses	10. reaches
2. kisses	11. peaches
3. pieces	12. George's
4. boxes	13. ages
5. fixes	14. pages
6. mazes	15. judges
7. buzzes	16. charges
8. washes	17. garages
9. dishes	18. massages

D. More than One

Plural nouns: Write the –S ending sound (/s/, /z/, /ɪz/)

1. a blue car—blue cars / /
2. a large package—large packages / /
3. a small town —small towns / /
4. a green kite—green kites / /

5. one language—two languages / /
6. an expensive watch—expensive watches / /
7. a chocolate chip cookie—chocolate chip cookies / /
8. a blue shirt—blue shirts / /
9. a fuzzy bear—fuzzy bears / /
10. a good time—good times / /

E. Feeling Possessive

Put a check mark under the correct -S ending sound.

	/s/	/z/	/ɪz/
1. Joey's umbrella			✗
2. Pete's car	✓		
3. Tess's glass			✗
4. Mother's kitchen	✗		
5. George's restaurant		✗	
6. The girls' bedroom		✗	
7. The cat's food	✓		

F. Verb to Go

Put a check mark under the correct -S ending sound.

	/s/	/z/	/ɪz/
1. walks			
2. loves			
3. arranges			
4. kicks			
5. finishes			
6. follows			
7. cuts			
8. brushes			
9. laughs			
10. commands			

G. Verb Squares

Write each word in the correct box.

invites	loves	washes	forgets	plays
dresses	speaks	breathes	faces	walks
grows	misses	eats	performs	rides
corrects	cheers	preaches	pleases	kicks
meets	teaches	manages	sings	gives
kisses	hopes			

/s/		

/z/		

/ɪz/		

H. Listen Up!

Circle the word that you hear. (Notice that the vowel sound is stretched before /z/ because /z/ is a voiced sound.)

/s/	/z/
1. place	plays
2. spice	spies
3. ice	eyes
4. race	raise
5. Sue	zoo
6. dice	dies
7. bus	buzz
8. close	clothes
9. price	prize
10. peace	peas
11. floss	flaws
12. since	sins
13. rice	rise
14. face	faze
15. sip	zip
16. hiss	his
17. niece	knees
18. dose	doze
19. fleece	fleas
20. fussy	fuzzy

I. Silly Sentences

Mark /s/ or /z/ over the letters S and Z. Remember that the letter S is often pronounced /z/. Then practice the sentences with a partner.

1. The busy bees flew away when the blizzard came their way.
2. Two horses and two cows danced to the music of the cat's meow.
3. Two furry bears were pleasantly chatting under the stairs.
4. My boyfriend's flair for dancing makes my toes go prancing.

5. Sally's silly dogs sought out the seven zany rats.
6. Sammy's six lizards smell like rusty, dusty boots.
7. The fleas agree that kittens flee too rapidly.
8. The rise in the price of rice brought tears to my grandmother's eyes.
9. My sister sneezes whenever she pats Fuzzy.
10. Stacy's dog likes to chew on Sally's six pairs of shoes.

J. Tongue Twisters

1. Six slimy snails slid silently.
2. Moses supposes his toeses are roses,
   but Moses supposes erroneously.
3. Six sleek swans swam swiftly southwards.
4. Denise sees the fleece.
   Bernice sees the fleas.
5. Sounding by sound is a sound method of sounding sounds.
6. Sally sells sea shells by the seashore.
   But if Sally sells seashells by the seashore, where are the seashells that Sally sells?
7. Six sick sea serpents swam the seven seas.

K. Can You Guess It?

1. There are seven in a week
2. They gallop at the race track
3. They have wings and feathers
4. Beautiful scented flowers with thorny stems
5. Some people live in houses, and others live in _____
6. These are published daily with articles, news, and entertainment
7. *The Three Bears*, *The Ugly Duckling*, and *Cinderella* are examples of children's _____
8. Very tall buildings in a city are _____
9. People taking classes are _____
10. Reptiles that have shells are _____
11. Pencils, rulers, notebooks, and erasers are examples of school _____
12. Beethoven, Mozart, and Verdi are examples of classical _____
13. Milk, butter, yogurt, and cheese are examples of dairy _____
14. Soccer and basketball are examples of _____

15. Poodles and beagles are kinds of _____
16. Children play with these
17. Brothers and sisters are called _____
18. Venice is famous for its _____
19. Happiness, sadness, and anger are examples of _____
20. Machines used for word processing and Internet access

L. Talk It Over

1. Do you have any favorite **sports teams** that you follow? Talk about the **names** of local **sports teams**—do you know why they have those names or what they **mean?**

2. Many people like to collect **things, such as stamps** or **coins.** Do you collect any **special items?** What would you collect if you had a lot of money?

3. **Suppose** you found out that you were about to become the parent of **twins.** If you have a car you would need to buy two car **seats** for sure. Would you need two **cribs?** Two **strollers? Discuss** how preparing for **twins** would be different from preparing for a **single** baby.

M. Speak Your Mind

1. For **hundreds** of **years,** most information was **stored** in **books,** but recently **devices** such as **computers** and **Kindles**™ are becoming common as a way to access information. Will **books** ever become **obsolete** (no longer **used**)? Do **books** have any **advantages** over electronic **storage devices?** Any **disadvantages?**

2. Many **governments** and other **groups** have **sometimes** tried to ban books that contained **ideas** that were considered **dangerous** or **offensive.** Should **books sometimes** be banned? Why or why not?

N. Story Time

Circle all the words that contain the sounds /s/ or /z/. Read the story out loud to your partner, paying attention to the pronunciation of /s/ and /z/.

Surprise Endings

On the first day of summer school, Professor Susan Casanovas was teaching an ESL conversation class when a student walked in late. He apologized for his tardiness and proceeded to find an empty seat. The professor noticed that he was very well dressed and extremely polite. His desire to improve his language skills was soon quite evident. Little did she know that this student's questions would drive her crazy by the end of the summer.

When Professor Casanovas asked him why he was taking the course, he said that he had been accepted to UCLA, and that he was taking this course to brush up on his English because Spanish was his first language. He was surprised to see a Hispanic instructor in the classroom as he expected an American professor. You could see his disappointment when he realized that English was not Professor Casanovas' first language.

The student continued to be late for class, but he explained that it was because he was a musician and he often worked late. By the end of the semester, he was so embarrassed by his tardiness that he invited Professor Casanovas and her sisters to a concert to hear him play. The performance was amazing! He invited Professor Casanovas to many more concerts and other events, and she eventually ended up marrying her former student. A year later, she was on her way to California with her spouse. Some stories have surprise endings.

CHAPTER 33
Three Thumbs Up (/θ/ and /ð/)

A. Sound It Out

The letters TH represent the unvoiced sound /θ/ as in *thought*, and the voiced sound /ð/ as in *these*. Both the voiced and unvoiced sounds can occur at the beginning, middle, or end of a word.

When you pronounce /θ/, the tip of your tongue should be between your teeth. The sound /θ/ is a very quiet sound, and you should not hear a lot of hissing. (If you hear hissing, you are probably saying /s/ by mistake.)

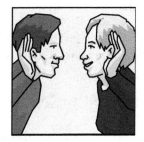

Unvoiced /θ/		
Beginning	*Middle*	*End*
thick	author	teeth
thoughtless	pathway	truth
theater	anthem	booth
think	authority	twelfth
thread	athlete	math

When you pronounce /ð/, the tip of your tongue should be between your teeth. This sound is voiced and you can continue the sound. (If you can't continue it, you are probably saying /d/ by mistake.)

Voiced /ð/		
Beginning	*Middle*	*End*
them	other	bathe
therefore	feather	teethe
these	soothing	clothe
though	lather	breathe
they	together	soothe

B. Spell It Out

The sounds /θ/ and /ð/ are always spelled with the letters TH.

/θ/	/ð/
thanks	them
thirty	there
birthday	feathers
healthy	clothing
month	brother
strength	weather

The letters TH are always pronounced either /θ/ or /ð/ except in the word *thyme* and a few proper names such as *Thomas, Thompson,* the *Thames River, Thai,* and *Thailand.*

C. Silly Sentences

Circle all the words that contain the sound /θ/ or /ð/. Then practice these sentences with a partner.

1. Thirteen thirsty thieves thought Thursday was theater night.
2. Think of three thin things; then think of three thick things.
3. I think that thinking thoughtful thoughts brings things we should be thankful for.
4. I thought that Thanksgiving was this Thursday, but thankfully Thanksgiving is the fourth Thursday of the month, not the third Thursday of the month.
5. The thoughtful thinker thought thankful thoughts, though I wonder how many thankful thoughts that thoughtful thinker thought.
6. He threw three free throws.
7. The thirty-year-old thug thought about things in the morning.
8. Thelma is throwing a party for her thirty-third birthday this Thursday.

D. Listen Up!

Circle the word that you hear.

1. thirty   dirty
2. mass   math
3. booth   boot
4. thorn   torn
5. bird   birth

6. pass   path
7. thaw   saw
8. ride   writhe
9. fort   forth
10. letter   leather
11. then   ten
12. tin   thin
13. bath   bass
14. wetter   whether
15. thought   taught
16. tree   three
17. mouse   mouth
18. teeth   teas
19. fate   faith
20. brought   broth

E. Can You Guess It?

1. If you have a lot of money you are _____
2. The opposite of *here*
3. Twenty plus ten is _____
4. The person who writes a book
5. You drink water when you are _____
6. The day that follows Wednesday
7. The number that comes after 999 is one _____
8. The sum of ten and three
9. Rose bushes have sharp _____
10. The day you were born is your _____
11. The opposite of *sick*
12. The opposite of *fat*
13. The opposite of *birth*
14. The opposite of *rough*
15. Number three in a line is the _____

16. Not north but _____

17. The name of our planet

18. Sunny and cloudy refer to the _____

19. A year has twelve _____

20. When you see lightning, you hear _____

F. Idioms

Circle all the TH sounds in the following idioms. Then explain the meaning of each idiom.

1. I heard it through the grapevine.
2. The boxer threw in the towel.
3. I'm all thumbs lately.
4. We live from hand to mouth.
5. That's the way the ball bounces.
6. I'll stand by you through thick and thin.

G. Story Time

Circle all the TH sounds in the following story. Then practice reading it.

Thankful Memories

Matthew and Beth Thornton saved for three years for their trip to Northern Ireland. They saved three thousand dollars, which would allow them to stay there for thirty thrilling days. They were very excited about traveling together. Beth learned from her friend Ruth that the weather in Ireland is very unpredictable. Beth and Matthew packed their leather boots and lots of thick, warm socks. They packed their thermal pajamas just in case the thermostat got too low for them to withstand and an umbrella in case of thunderstorms. They were thrilled about this trip. They were thinking about all the things they would do when they got to Ireland. They knew that they would have fond memories for many months to come.

H. The TH Word Search

```
T A B S C D E F G T H Y R O I D Q S V R B
H L M Q N O P Q R H S T U C S Q A H D T V
R A B R C D A T F A G H I W L W S R A H P
I N O T P Q S H S N T U Y Y K U D T T K O
L T H I C K V R F K G H I U R S C Y H T Y
L M N C O P B E R F S T T H J D D J E H C
E X Y M Z A N A C U D H T O S G V M M O Q
R K L M N O S T Q L R E S Q D H U V A U A
Y Z A B C O K E E T H O S E G V T T T G J
I J K L T M L N T H E R M O S N R H I H H
Q R S F T U V W X Y Z E A X R M O E C T B
H I E J K L M E N O P M Q D U L K O G A C
W H X Y Z A N B C D T H O R A X J R F T S
T G H I J O K L E M N O P T T A N Y A H E
V B H L R R V L Z D I N S Y E S Q Z M E D
W C I H O S T H E R M O S T A T B A J A X
X D T M P S H W A E J O T M X M A S Y T Q
Y E J N I T A X B F K P U V U Q Y F S E J
Z F K H Q U W Y C G L Q V H Q R T R G R H
A G T H E R A P Y H M R T H E S E G B F G
```

| THRUSH | THEATER | THORAX | THERMOS |

| THYROID | THICK | THEOREM | THEFT |

| THRONE | THEMATIC | THERAPY | THRILLER |

| THISTLE | THOSE | THANKFUL | THREATEN |

| THUMB | THERMOSTAT | THEFT | THESE |

| THAW | THOUGHT | THEORY | |

CHAPTER 34

Shop 'n' Chop (/ʃ/, /tʃ/, and CH)

A. Sound It Out

As you can see by looking at the symbols, the sounds /ʃ/ and /tʃ/ are related. The sound /ʃ/ is a continuous sound made with your lips in a rounded position. The sound /tʃ/ has a stop sound like /t/ at the beginning, followed by the sound /ʃ/. Both sounds are unvoiced. We will practice each sound individually first, and then contrast the two sounds.

First just listen carefully to the /ʃ/ sound in the following words:

Initial Position	Middle Position	Final Position
shape	ashtray	wash
shelf	fashion	wish
shirt	passion	hash
shoe	cushion	mesh
sheep	washer	dish
shack	pushup	fish
ship	bashful	leash
shy	mission	posh
sheet	technician	crush
share	politician	hush
shark	musician	brush
shell		
sugar		

[handwritten notes: tion, sion, cian = shun; French like SH: chef, chic, Machine, Chicago, Michigan]

Chapter 34   Shop 'n' Chop (/ʃ/, /tʃ/, and /CH/)   **191**

B. Spell It Out

At the beginning and end of words, the sound /ʃ/ is usually spelled SH, with the exception of words like *sure* and *sugar*. But there are many words in which the sound /ʃ/ in the middle of a word is spelled with the letters T, C, or S.

Underline the letter(s) that represent the sound /ʃ/ in the words below:

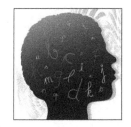

ocean	special	mission
presidential	possession	extension
physician	invention	addition
accommodation	artificial	delicious
impatience	expression	insurance
initial	quotation	assure
repetition	exclamation	pressure
fraction	affection	tension

C. Sound It Out

Now listen carefully to the /tʃ/ sound in the following words:

Initial Position	Middle Position	Final Position
change	catcher	church
child	archer	much
church	teacher	each
chapter	patchwork	sketch
check	grouchy	teach
chosen	butcher	watch
chest	bachelor	catch
cheese	kitchen	speech
chimney	pitcher	lunch
chat		bench
chew		hatch
chicken		coach

192 Part 3 Conquering Consonant Confusion

D. Spell It Out

The sound /tʃ/ is always spelled CH or TCH. However, the letters CH have two other common pronunciations. Study the chart below:

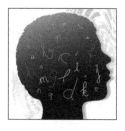

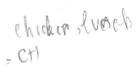

chicken, lunch
= CH

Words Borrowed from French: /ʃ/	Words Borrowed from Greek: /k/
chute	character
parachute	chorus
Chicago	chord
Cheyenne	cholesterol
champagne	stomach
chef	ache
chic	chemical
chaperone	anchor
chauffeur	mechanical
chandelier	monarch
chivalry	Michael
Charlotte	echo
chalet	chaos
charade	chlorine
chauvinist	technical
pistachio	technique
brochure	technology
Michigan	orchid
Michelle	mocha
crochet	Christmas
mustache	Christian
machine	psychology
	chrome
	chiropractor
	architect
	school
	schedule

E. Not to Be Confused With . . . .

Listen to the contrast between /ʃ/ and /tʃ/ in the following pairs of words:

/ʃ/	/tʃ/
ship	chip
sheep	cheap
share	chair
shoe	chew
sheer	cheer
sheet	cheat
shop	chop
wish	witch
wash	watch
cash	catch

F. Silly Sentences

Mark the /ʃ/ and /tʃ/ sounds in the following sentences. Then practice the sentences with a partner.

1. Sheila has a passion for fashion.
2. Shawn washed sheep in the shower.
3. Chuck watched the cheetahs and chimpanzees at the Chelsea Zoo.
4. Shannon's shoes are a shocking shade of fuschia.
5. Sharon shoveled sugar into her sherbet.
6. Charles showed us a shark in the shallow water.
7. Shaq's championship ring is shiny!
8. Michelle shops at Shaw's for shirts.
9. Sheldon shivered from the ocean breeze.
10. Sherman shipped a bushel of shrimp.
11. Charlotte assured us she would shelter the shepherd.
12. Mitchell mixed French champagne into a pitcher of cherry punch.

G. Dizzy Dialogue : Shop Till You Drop

Mark each bolded word as /ʃ/ and /tʃ/. Then practice the dialogue with a partner.

Shane: **I wish** I had a new **shirt** to wear to **Sheila's** baby **shower**. My old ones all look **shabby**.

Sharleen: Let's go **shopping**. I need some new **shoes**, too.

Shane: All right, **shall** we go to **Showalter's Shop**?

Sharleen: **Sure**! I can also look for some **sheets** while I'm there.

Shane: I hope it won't take all day! You know I get **impatient** with **shopping**.

Sharleen: Rest **assured**, we won't **shop** till we drop.

(at the **shopping** center)

Shane: Wow, look at those **sheepskin** boots! Those **sure** look **shaggy**.

Sharleen: And how about these **shiny shoes**—they **shimmer** when you move! And this **shawl** is a **luscious shade** called **Passionfruit**.

Shane: This is all very **chic**, but you need to help me **choose** a **shirt**!

H. A Challenging Show

Circle all the /ʃ/ sounds and underline all the /tʃ/ sounds you find in this story. Then read it with a partner.

One of my favorite TV shows is a Food Network show called *Chopped*. In each episode, four young chefs compete to cook a delicious appetizer, main course, and dessert for three judges. After each round, one of the contestants is "chopped," or eliminated. What makes the show challenging—and exciting—is that for each course, the chefs must include all the secret ingredients found in a basket, and they have a very short time to create their meal. The secret ingredients are sometimes very strange; for example, they may be challenged to create an appetizer out of cheese, cherries, and champagne, or a main course may have to include chicken, chestnuts, Chinese cabbage, and sherry. For dessert, they might find chocolate and Chablis wine in the basket, and they might choose to create a sherbet. The chef who manages to create the best meal is chosen as the *Chopped* champion.

I. Can You Guess It?

All the answers start with either /ʃ/ or /tʃ/

1. A large boat
2. To cut into small pieces
3. Not expensive
4. An animal that gives us wool
5. You wear these on your feet
6. We get eggs from them
7. Crunchy potato _____
8. You sit on a _____
9. To give an equal amount to everyone
10. You put these on a bed
11. Two games played on a board with small squares
12. Santa Claus comes down the _____
13. He doesn't play fair! He _____
14. A large, dangerous fish with big jaws
15. I don't want to sit in the sun. I prefer the cool _____
16. Pointed, like a knife or a pencil

17. You write on a blackboard with _____

18. If you touch an electric outlet, you'll get a _____

19. What you do with your teeth

20. Your heart is in your _____

21. A book is divided into _____

22. When the sun is behind you, you see this in front of you

23. Cheddar is a type of _____

24. I like all of them, so it's hard to _____ which one I want

25. The country with the largest population in the world

J. Talk It Over

1. In the past, families often had 5 or more **children**, but these days most families are smaller, and many families have only one **child**. How many **children** would you like to have, or would you **choose** to be **childless**? Are there advantages to having fewer **children**? Are there any disadvantages?

2. Some judges have tried to use a sense of **shame** to keep people from committing crimes. For example, a young woman who **shoplifted** from a store was required to stand in front of the store wearing a sign that said, "I am a **shoplifter**." Do you think **shaming** people is a good way to stop **shoplifting** and other minor crimes?

3. **Chicken** is one of the most popular foods around the world. Can you **share** your favorite **chicken** recipe? (If you don't eat **chicken**, **share** another recipe that you think your classmates would enjoy.)

K. Speak Your Mind

Many schools are concerned about students **cheating** on tests and papers. How has technology made the problem of **cheating** worse? What do you think that **teachers** or schools **should** do to deal with this problem?

CHAPTER 35
A Treasured National Vision (/ʃ/ and /ʒ/ -TION, -SION, -CIAN and -SURE)

A. Sound It Out

In Chapter 34, you studied the unvoiced sound /ʃ/ as in *show* and *rush*. The voiced partner of /ʃ/ is /ʒ/. You pronounce /ʒ/ the same way as /ʃ/, but it is voiced, like the letter J in the French words, *je* and *Jacques*. When you pronounce /ʒ/, your tongue tip is near but not touching your teeth, and the sides of your tongue press lightly against your teeth. Your lips should be a little tense.

There are not many words in English that include /ʒ/. Listen to these words:

Beginning*	Middle	End*
genre	treasure	corsage
	measure	mirage
	vision	beige
	explosion	sabotage
	usual	espionage
	casual	camouflage
	Asia	garage
	seizure	massage
	luxury	

*Note: When /ʒ/ is at the beginning or end of a word, some Americans pronounce it /dʒ/. But when /ʒ/ is in the middle of a word, they always pronounce it /ʒ/.

B. Spell It Out

Most of the time, /ʒ/ is spelled with an S.

    treasure   vision   casual

It can also be spelled with GE.

    rouge   mirage   genre

And /ʒ/ can have some unusual spellings:

    azure   seizure   luxury

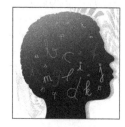

The suffixes -TION, and -SION both indicate nouns and both are usually pronounced (/ʃən/). However, in some words -SION is pronounced /ʒən/. Compare these words:

Words Ending in -TION (/ʃən/)	Words Ending in -SION /ʃən/	Words Ending in -SION /ʒən/
condition	confession	confusion
emotion	expression	explosion
motion	mission	illusion
addition	admission	invasion
perfection	permission	vision
direction	discussion	decision
section	session	occasion
position	passion	precision
commotion	commission	conclusion
tension	tension	revision

There is another suffix, -CIAN, that also sounds like /ʃən/. Like -TION and -SION, it indicates a noun, but it always refers to a person:

Words Ending in -CIAN /ʃən/
musician
physician
technician
mathematician
statistician
cosmetician
beautician
optician
dietician
politician

Like -SION, the suffix, -SURE indicates a noun, and it has two different pronunciations. It can sound like /ʃɚ/ or /ʒɚ/. Compare these words:

-SURE /ʃɚ/	-SURE /ʒɚ/
pressure	exposure
insure	closure
ensure	leisure
assure	measure
reassure	pleasure
	treasure

C. Silly Sentences

Decide whether each bolded word is pronounced /ʃ/ or /ʒ/. Then practice these sentences with a partner.

1. George **casually mentioned** the **explosion** in the **garage.**
2. **Sherman's solution** to the bee **invasion** was the **elimination** of all of the flowers in the yard.
3. In the **fashion** world, makeup artists are **cosmeticians,** hair stylists are **beauticians,** and skincare **technicians** are **aestheticians.**
4. Eating a live **crustacean** is a **noxious sensation.**
5. The **physician's conclusion** was that he got a **concussion** from **crashing** the **celebration.**
6. **Addition** and **multiplication** are no problem for me, but **subtraction** and **division** fill me with **trepidation.**
7. The **ocean** was **azure** blue and the **shore** was **beige,** but it was only a **mirage.**
8. The **visual distractions** at the mall cause **collisions** between **unconscious shoppers.**
9. **Mathematicians** can be **statisticians,** but can **statisticians** be **mathematicians?**
10. **Politicians** think the **precision** of **television** news is **questionable.**

D. Dizzy Dialogue: Congratulations!

Practice this dialogue with a partner.

Jan: Wow, you're all dressed up. What's the **occasion?**

Joe: I've come to the **realization** that I want to **share** my life with **Sasha.** I'm going to ask her to marry me.

Jan: **Congratulations!** When did you make this **decision?**

Joe: Well, I saw an **unusual** old couple at the train **station.** They were having a **casual conversation** about the people and **situations** around them and making each other laugh. And when they looked at each other, there was still some **passion** there! It seemed like their greatest **pleasure** was just being together. Suddenly I **envisioned Sasha** and me as a happy old couple. Our **relationship** is just like that old couple's, and I want it to last for the rest of our lives.

Jan: Wow! Where are you going to pop the **question?**

Joe: I'm taking her to a **luxurious Indonesian** restaurant up in the hills so that we can see the city lights **shining** below. I asked the **chef** to put the ring in **Sasha's** wine glass, and the **musicians** will play our favorite song. I hope she won't get too **emotional.**

Joe: **She'll** be **emotional** for **sure**! **Sasha's** been waiting **patiently** for you to propose. **She's** put up with your **evasion** of the marriage **question** for a long time. Be **sure** to order **champagne** because she has to **fish** the ring out of the glass. And please, don't **stash** the ring in your **shoe**!

E. Activity: Fortune Cookies: Prediction or Superstition?

Roll the dice to find out what your fortune is. Unscramble the fortune so that you can read it.

1. uoy lliw dnif taerg noitcafsitas ni yna noitapucco uoy esoohc.

2. noitacude dna noitanimreted era eht syek ot rouy sseccus.

3. uoy lliw noos ekam a noisiced taht lliw deal uoy ni eht thgir niotcerid.

4. ruoy snoitaler evah sa hcum noitceffa rof uoy sa uoy evah rof meht.

5. uoy lliw teg a esirprus noitativni ot a noitarbelec.

6. uoy lliw dnif a neddih erusaert ni na lausunu ecalp.

7. ouy lliw tisiv ynam yawaraf snoitan dna ekam ynam snoitcennoc ereht.

8. uoy lliw niw eht noitarimda fo srehto hguorht ruoy ytsenoh dna noitacided.

9. uoy lliw edart niosnet rof niotaxaler dna noisufnoc rof gnidnatsrednu.

10. uoy lliw dnif noitelpmoc nehw uoy eusrup rouy tsetaerg noissap.

11. ruoy noitoved dna noissapmoc rof ruoy sdneirf lliw eb dedrawer.

12. ruoy efil lliw eb dellif htiw erusaelp dna erusiel.

F. Talk It Over

1. A New Year's **resolution** is a promise to make an improvement in your life during the coming year. **Usually** people make **resolutions** to lose weight, continue their **education**, find **closure** in a bad **relationship**, etc. What New Year's **resolution** did you make this year? What was the result?

2. Reality **television shows** are very popular because they give their stars **national exposure,** and viewers are given an **introduction** to these stars' personal lives and talents. The stars of these **shows** often become overnight **sensations** and sometimes even world-famous. Would you like to become a reality **television** star? Why or why not?

3. There is a famous **quotation** that says, "One man's **trash** is another man's **treasure.**" It means that a **possession** may not be worth a lot of money, but it has personal, sentimental value. Describe a **treasured possession** that has value only to you. Why is it so valuable to you?

4. Due to the economic **situation,** many people these days are taking "**staycations**" because going on **vacation** out of town is not an **option.** During their **staycations,** some people spend their **leisure** time at home or take **short excursions** to local sports **competitions,** art **exhibitions,** or **international** festivals. Other people's greatest **pleasure** is spending time on a hobby they enjoy. Some people will spend a day at a **luxurious** spa or relaxing by the **ocean.** What would you do on a **staycation?**

G. Speak Your Mind

1. Some experts have made the **observation** that strong **emotional** intelligence skills are as important as strong academic skills when it comes to being successful in life. **Emotional** intelligence includes our ability to understand and control our **emotions** and to understand the **emotions** of other people so that we can communicate with them effectively. Our level of **emotional** intelligence affects how well we work with others. Do you think that having strong **emotional** intelligence skills is as important as having strong academic skills to succeed at school or at work? Do you think that **emotional** intelligence skills should be taught in schools along with **traditional** subjects like reading and math?

2. People use the Internet for **communication** and **relaxation.** However, some people end up being online all day and don't pay **attention** to anything else. In fact, their **devotion** to the online world is so strong that psychologists say that these people are suffering from an **addiction** to the Internet. Do you think that Internet **addiction** is real?

H. The Pressure's On!

In this puzzle, find the 18 words from the lists in Part B. The words can be spelled horizontally (→), vertically (↓), or diagonally (↗↘). They can also be spelled forward or backward. When you have found all of the words, write them on the Word List. Check your answers with a partner.

```
M L U N A I C I T P O N
D E C I S I O N R H O V
O I E N S U R E C I C T
A S S U R E S N T E C E
D U M C P S L C I R A C
M R V R U E E P A U S H
I E E R U S A E M S I N
S R E H N S S D O O I
S M S N O I S I V L N C
I N O I T O M R O C T I
O A T T E N T I O N O A
N A I C I S U M L U C N
```

Word List

-CIAN (/ʃən/)	-TION (/ʃən/)	-SION (/ʃən/)	-SION (/ʒən/)	-SURE (/ʃɚ/)	-SURE (/ʒɚ/)
1.	4.	7.	10.	13.	16.
2.	5.	8.	11.	14.	17.
3.	6.	9.	12.	15.	18.

CHAPTER 36
Together, Baby (Review of Chapters 30–35)

A. ID Please

Match the sound in **bold** print with its IPA symbol. Write the letter in the blank.

A. ʃ   B. ʒ   C. tʃ   D. ð   E. θ

1. **th**is ____
2. **sh**ark ____
3. **ch**ew ____
4. **th**in ____
5. **g**enre ____

6. wat**ch**er ____
7. wa**sh**er ____
8. wi**th**out ____
9. lei**s**ure ____
10. lea**th**er ____

11. ma**th** ____
12. ma**tch** ____
13. ma**sh** ____
14. ba**th**e ____
15. bei**g**e ____

Write the correct IPA symbol for the sound in **bold** print.

θ   ð   tʃ   ʒ   ʃ   k

Easier:

1. **th**e ____
2. **ch**eer ____
3. fa**sh**ion ____
4. **th**ank ____
5. **Ch**ristmas ____

6. **sh**ow ____
7. trea**s**ure ____
8. **ch**ic ____
9. crea**t**ion ____
10. u**s**ual ____

Harder:

1. an**ch**or ____
2. na**t**ure ____
3. lu**x**ury ____
4. posse**ss**ion ____
5. occa**s**ion ____

6. physi**c**ian ____
7. mo**th**er ____
8. a**z**ure ____
9. bro**ch**ure ____
10. pa**th**way ____

B. Circle the Correct Answers

Be careful—there can be more than one correct answer for each question.

1. CH can sound like _____
   tʃ   k   ʃ   s   z   ʒ

2. -TURE can sound like _____
   sɚ   ʃɚ   zɚ   ʒɚ   tʃɚ   kɚ

3. -SURE can sound like _____
   sɚ   ʃɚ   zɚ   ʒɚ   tʃɚ   kɚ

4. -TION can sound like _____
   sən   ʃən   zən   ʒən   tʃən

5. -SION can sound like _____
   sən   ʃən   zən   ʒən   tʃən

6. TH can sound like _____
   t   d   θ   ð   s   z

C. Review the Rules

/s/, /z/, or /ɪz/?

a. In words that end in a voiced consonant or a vowel, -S sounds like
   s   z   ɪz

b. In words that end in an unvoiced consonant, -S sounds like
   s   z   ɪz

c. In words that end in /s/, /z/, /tʃ/, /dʒ/, /ʒ/, or /ʃ/, -S sounds like
   s   z   ɪz

Match the word group with the rule. Write the letter from above in the space.

1. dishes, sizes, edges   _____
2. shoes, runs, fills   _____
3. sits, taps, coughs   _____

/t/, /d/, or /ɪd/?

   a. In words that end in a voiced consonant or a vowel, -ED sounds like
       t   d   ɪd

   b. In words that end in an unvoiced consonant, -ED sounds like
       t   d   ɪd

   c. In words that end in /t/ or /d/, -ED sounds like
       t   d   ɪd

Match the word group with the rule. Write the letter from above in the space.

   4. kissed, wrapped, looked   _____

   5. lighted, weeded, rated   _____

   6. followed, tied, seemed   _____

D. Mix It Up: -S, -ES, and -ED

Work with a partner to fill in the chart below. Think about spelling also.

	Present Tense Verbs or Plural Nouns			**Past Tense Verbs**		
	/s/	/z/	/ɪz/	/t/	/d/	/ɪd/
1. cook	cooks			cooked		
2. change						
3. wish						
4. shock						
5. love						
6. walk						
7. shout						
8. show						
9. please						
10. fold						
11. laugh						
12. bat						
13. fade						
14. try						
15. load						
16. toss						
17. shine						
18. raise						
19. glow						

	Present Tense Verbs or Plural Nouns			Past Tense Verbs		
	/s/	/z/	/iz/	/t/	/d/	/id/
20. help						
21. save						
22. paste						
23. tip						
24. reach						
25. ask						

Use the Words

Work with a partner, and use the words from the chart to write 5 sentences together. Use as many words as you can. Share your sentences with your classmates.

1.

2.

3.

4.

5.

E. Sound Contrasts /ʃ/ and /tʃ/

Listen as your instructor reads the following sentences. Circle the word you hear. Check your answers with your partner's answers.

1. He and Cheryl are (watching washing) the TV.
2. We didn't eat (mush much) in Michigan.
3. That story about the (witch wish) was magical.
4. The fisherman stored his (catch cash) on his ship.
5. She put the peaches in the (dish ditch).
6. Shelly wants to (match mash) the potatoes.
7. The chimpanzee jumped into the (hash hatch).
8. Trisha got tired of (shopping chopping) all day.
9. After lunch, Richard showed us our (shores chores).

10. This (sherry cherry) is so sweet.

11. They should (shuck chuck) the corn.

12. Watch out for the (chards shards) under the table!

F. CH-CH Choo Choo Word Sorter

Work with a partner. Read the sentence aloud, and put the words with CH in them into the correct box. (HINT: There are 10 words for each sound).

1. Charles chaperoned the school chorus in Chicago.
2. Michael's mustache twitched as he chewed the crunchy Chinese chicken with chives.
3. The brochure says that the chrome coffee machine can churn out mocha lattes as light as chiffon.
4. Charlene scheduled her chemistry class before choosing a psychology class.
5. The echoes of the chef's chronic cough ricocheted throughout the chilly chalet.

CH sounds like /tʃ/	CH sounds like /ʃ/	CH sounds like /k/
1.	11.	21.
2.	12.	22.
3.	13.	23.
4.	14.	24.
5.	15.	25.
6.	16.	26.
7.	17.	27.
8.	18.	28.
9.	19.	29.
10.	20.	30.

G. I Am Shunned! /ʃ/ and /ʒ/

Match the first part of the word with the last part of the word. The first word is done for you. (Only one answer is correct in each row.)

	-TION /ʃən/	-CIAN /ʃən/	-SION /ʃən/	-SION /ʒən/
1. ac-	action			
2. vi-				vision
3. mis-			mission	
4. physi-		physician		
5. conclu-				conclusion
6. explo-				explosion
7. deci-				decision
8. posi-	position			
9. pas-			passion	
10. musi-		musician		
11. ten-			tension	
12. inva-				invasion
13. politi-		politician		
14. creat-	creation			
15. na-	nation			
16. techni-		technician		

Practice saying these sentences with a partner.

1. The musician's creations are a reflection of his passion for his art.
2. The lab technician left her position to become a physician.
3. The tension in the crowd became an explosion of anger when their landlord made the decision to sell their building.
4. The politician spoke about her vision for the nation's future.
5. Because Sheila took action quickly, the ants' invasion came to a conclusion.

H. Match Up

Match the first part of the word with the last part of the word. The first word is done for you.

	-TURE /tʃɚ/	-SURE /ʃɚ/	-SURE /ʒɚ/
1. cul-	culture		
2. pres-			
3. trea-			
4. na-			
5. plea-			
6. pic-			
7. mea-			
8. in-			
9. furni-			
10. lei-			
11. as-			
12. expo-			
13. tex-			
14. clo-			
15. cap-			
16. fea-			

Practice saying these sentences with a partner.

1. She enjoys capturing scenes from nature in her pictures.
2. The furniture is such a treasure that it's insured for $1 million.
3. The politician assured the anxious people that he would pressure the governor to stop the closure of the park.
4. In their leisure time, Jacques and Marie find pleasure in sharing their culture with their grandchildren.
5. To make a great cake, measure the ingredients carefully and limit the cake's exposure to cold air.

Chapter 36   Together, Baby *(Review of Chapters 30–35)*   **209**

I. Listen Up!

Listen as your instructor reads the following sentences. Circle the word you hear. Check your answers with your partner's answers.

1. Hurry! We're late for (math mass)!
2. Are (Dee's these) books for sale?
3. They didn't know it could (think sink).
4. Snakes can't (breed breathe) underwater.
5. Babies hate (teething teasing).
6. It's not a hit; it's a (miss myth).
7. John (Keats' Keith's) poems are romantic.
8. The (bath bass) made him sick.
9. You shouldn't read that (sick thick) book.
10. We bought this (though dough).
11. He studied (then Zen) in Japan.
12. This speech is (worthy wordy) enough for the event.

J. Think It Through

Practice saying these sentences with a partner.

1. Both of Arthur's brothers bother him with their pet python.
2. Soothe a toothache with a thimbleful of whisky.
3. The 30th is the last Thursday of the month.
4. Those athletes' math scores were rather pathetic, but their anthropology scores were better.
5. Mother and Father look healthy and youthful thanks to three weeks without the kids.
6. The thunderstorm threatened to thwart the birthday party, but they threw it anyway.
7. The weather's warmth gave Theo second thoughts about wearing his thick sweater.
8. Bertha loves the thrill of the hunt in thrift stores and vintage clothing shops.
9. Thomas turns thread, feathers, and leather into tasteful tablecloths.
10. Ruth thought that the author's talk was at another theater.

K. On a Roll /l/ and /r/

Practice saying these hard-to-pronounce /l/ and /r/ words:

roll	railroad	ruler	loyal	lyrics
liar	rely	rural	curl	real
rival	rattle	learn	rarely	roar
local	rear	world	lower	lawyer

L. Can You Guess It?

HINT: You can find all of the answers in the list above.

1. Lions and tigers make this sound
2. A king or a queen is a _____
3. The opposite of *higher*
4. Another word for *seldom*
5. Rock and _____ music
6. A car has front and _____ wheels
7. The opposite of *urban*
8. The opposite of *teach*
9. A person who doesn't tell the truth
10. A song's words
11. Another word for *opponent*
12. The opposite of *fake*

M. Do You Hear What I Hear? /l/ vs. /r/

Listen as your instructor reads the following sentences. Circle the word you hear. Check your answers with your partner's answers.

1. Flora is a fearless French (flyer fryer).
2. Those three birds will (clash crash).
3. People want their (lights rights).
4. Did the (mirror miller) arrive yesterday?
5. The (coal core) is almost black.
6. The (beer bill) was a surprise.
7. Burt's (limes rhymes) are often bad.
8. How did their (battle batter) turn out?
9. Larry isn't that (loyal lawyer).
10. They might (fill fear) the hall closet.

N. Rolling Along

Practice saying these sentences with a partner.

1. Rodney rolled the stroller around the corner.
2. Leonard hurled rude curses at Earl.
3. Don't overlook the little red letters.
4. Laura laughs loudly at Rick's ridiculous remarks.
5. Run to the store before Rollo realizes there's no beer!
6. Lemuel Gulliver loomed over the land of Lilliput.
7. Rhoda rocked forward and wrecked Rita's rubber tree.
8. The presents were wrapped in red paper and curly ribbons.
9. Lila's looking for love, so where's Mr. Right?
10. Caring for really long hair is a lot of trouble.

CHAPTER 37
You'll Jump for Joy (/dʒ/ and /y/)

A. Sound It Out

To make the /dʒ/ sound, start in the /d/ position with the tip of your tongue touching your tooth ridge. Then release the air and push your tongue forward to the /ʒ/ position.

To make the /y/ sound, your tongue is up and in the center of your mouth.

Note: The official IPA symbol for this sound is /j/ and you will find that symbol in some texts and dictionaries. We are using the symbol /y/ to avoid confusion.

B. Spell It Out

The /y/ sound is usually written with the letter Y.

    yellow   yarn   yard   yawn   yolk   year   yesterday

As noted in Chapter 19, the sound /y/ sometimes occurs before the sound /uw/ and a few other vowels:

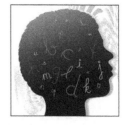

useful	monument
unity	volume
uniform	ambulance
university	communion
unique	communicate
utilities	review
Europe	refuse
Eugene	music
United States	cubicle
euthanasia	humorous
	beauty
	museum
	senior
	million

The /dʒ/ sound is usually written with the letters J or G.

Jeep   joy   jam   jet   jeopardy

giant   giraffe   agenda   agile   digestion

Some other spellings are:

-GE	-DGE	-DJ	-DU
wages	pledge	adjust	educate
oranges	edge	adjective	graduate
language	judge	adjourn	schedule

C. Listen Up!

Listen as your instructor reads one word from each row and circle the word you hear.

	/y/	/dʒ/
1.	yellow	jello
2.	yes	Jess
3.	yet	jet
4.	Yale	jail
5.	year	jeer
6.	yoke	joke
7.	yam	jam
8.	use	juice
9.	you'll	jewel
10.	years	jeers

D. Can You Guess It?

/y/

1. The opposite of *old*
2. A thread used for knitting
3. To shout loudly
4. The yellow part of an egg
5. A sweet potato
6. The day before today

7. The color of butter and lemons
8. A large boat used for pleasure
9. A period of twelve months
10. The contraction of *you will*
11. Delicious or appetizing

/dʒ/

1. The month after June
2. Another word for *prison*
3. A glass container used for storing food
4. A group of people in court who decide whether a person is guilty or innocent
5. Casual pants made out of denim
6. Rings, bracelets, or necklaces
7. A person in court who decides how the law should be applied
8. Another word for *diary*
9. Another word for *coat*
10. The lower part of your face
11. Someone of great size
12. A tall African animal with a long neck

E. Expressions

Work with a partner to explain the meaning of each expression. How would you use it in a sentence?

1. To keep up with the Joneses
2. In a jiffy
3. Jack-of-all trades
4. A tearjerker
5. Junk food
6. That's a joke
7. Jet lag
8. John or Jane Doe
9. A yummy food
10. A yucky food

11. A yuppie
12. Yin and yang
13. Yadda, yadda, yadda
14. Year in and year out
15. Yikes!

F. Silly Sentences

Practice saying these several times quickly.

1. Jess said, "Yes," when invited to go on Eugene's jet.
2. The mayor went to Yale, but his brother went to jail.
3. Orange-pineapple energy juice is my favorite juice.
4. Yogi Bear lives in Jellystone Park with his bear friends Juggles and Jack.
5. Young Jackson likes to drink yummy Yoohoo™.
6. Jade Young wore her yellow jacket to her job yesterday.
7. Juliette likes to yell, yodel, and jump when she sees the Yankees jog.

G. Sentence Practice

Mark all the /y/ and /dʒ/ sounds in these sentences. Then practice saying them.

1. John always yawns when he's bored.
2. George grew up in Yugoslavia.
3. Madge and Marge had high averages in school.
4. Gina is on a budget because they cut her wages at work.
5. Gene and Julia are going to host a party on the Fourth of July.
6. The door that leads to the yard is jammed.
7. Young Mr. Jung went to Yellowstone Park yesterday.
8. The jumbo jet has not arrived yet.
9. You'll like the jewels that Jane bought at the jewelry mart.
10. Last year we went to Jamaica with our friends Jen and Jim.

H. Food For Thought

Choose ten of these sayings and explain what you think they mean.

1. Don't judge a book by its cover.
2. Youth is wasted on the young.
3. Joyful is he who can age and still remain youthful.
4. When there is justice, truth prevails.
5. Generosity is giving from the heart joyfully.
6. I can lose my youth, but I will not lose my joy.
7. Life is often a joke, so let's laugh.

8. No man is an island, so join the crowd.
9. Love helps you stay young at any age.
10. A short man with a big heart is a giant.
11. One good gesture deserves another.
12. Yesterday is gone but there will be many tomorrows.
13. One person's generosity can save another man's life.
14. Judge others, and you will be judged.
15. Life is too short to hold grudges.
16. Don't be a yes–man.
17. Life should never be boring, so stop yawning.
18. Go to the gym, and you'll be fit and slim.
19. Your gender does not determine your success in life.
20. A gentle and genuine person will be loved by many.

I. A Shopping Spree

Let's go shopping. You have two shopping bags. Put all the products that have the /y/ sound in the first bag and those with the /dʒ/ sound in the second bag. Add additional food products that have either of these sounds.

/y/	/dʒ/

Yoohoo™ (chocolate drink)   onions   papayas

beef jerky   egg yolks   vegetable soup

yams   jelly beans   orange juice

jello   ginger   energy drinks

yuca   gin   jam

gelato   yogurt   vegetables

J. And the Verdict Is . . .

Mark all the words with the sound /y/ or /dʒ/. Then read the dialogue with a partner.

Yari:	Hi, Gian. Do you want to come to yoga class with me tomorrow morning? Visitors are welcome.
Gian:	I'd love to, Yari, but I have jury duty. I'm one of the jurors, and tomorrow we will decide whether the accused is innocent or guilty.
Yari:	How were the jurors selected?
Gian:	The lawyers asked the potential jurors questions to see who would be able to be impartial. Then the two lawyers decided which jurors would be on the final panel.
Yari:	Being an impartial juror is essential to make sure that the accused has a fair trial, right?
Gian:	Yes, jurors have a great responsibility in court cases.
Yari:	Do you enjoy being a juror?
Gian:	Yes, I had already been a juror in New York, and I found it to be very interesting. This time I have learned many things about the California judicial system. Sending a person to jail unjustly is not something you want on your conscience.
Yari:	I agree. A juror cannot be too judgmental. They must seek justice regardless of the accused person's background.
Gian:	That's right. Also, jurors can make their decisions only after all the evidence has been presented and examined carefully.
Yari:	Who makes the final decision about how a criminal should be punished?
Gian:	The judge is the person who determines what the punishment will be.
Yari:	I heard that you would like to be a lawyer or a judge someday.
Gian:	Yes, I would like to go to Yale University to study law.
Yari:	I would like to be on a jury someday. Thanks for sharing your experience. Call me when it's over, and we'll go to yoga class.

K. An Unusual Journey

Mark all the words with the sound /y/ or /dʒ/. Then read the story with a partner.

Jacqueline and Yolanda Jackson are identical twins. They have an unusual plan that started during their junior year in Yonkers College. Their youthful yearning will take them on a very joyous journey. They intend to visit different places whose names start with the same sounds as their names. Jacqueline plans to visit Japan, Jerusalem, Jamaica, and Jordan. Yolanda plans to visit Yugoslavia, the Yucatan Peninsula, Yokohama, and Yaoundé, the capital of Cameroon. Their journey will begin in New York City. Their travel agent, Junko Yamamoto, owner of Yokoso Travel Agency, will make sure that their tour is organized and exciting. Their trip will be during the months of June and July. Their journey will involve many forms of transportation, such as jets and yachts. Since this will be their dream luxury trip, they plan to rent a Jaguar to drive for part of their trip. Many joyous moments await them on this journey. Yonkers will never be the same after the Jackson twins return from their adventure.

If you were planning a journey based on the first letter of your name, what are some places you could visit? For example, if your name is Emiko, you could visit England, Estonia, and Ethiopia.

L. Talk It Over

1. Explain the meaning of the idiom "**You** can't **judge** a book by its cover." How do you feel about dating a person who has tattoos, body piercings, **strange** clothes, or other unusual adornments?

2. Some people are said to be "**Jack**-of-all trades and master of none." Explain what this idiom means. Do you know anyone who fits this description?

M. Speak Your Mind

A **jury** is a group of people who decide whether a person who is **charged** with a crime is innocent or guilty. Have you ever been on a **jury?** If you were chosen as a **juror,** could you be impartial in making your **judgment?** Would you be willing to serve as a **juror** in a criminal case related to a murder, rape, or other serious felony? How would you feel if the death penalty were involved?

CHAPTER 38
Ban the Van and Face the Pace (/b/, /v/, /f/, and /p/)

A. Sound It Out /b/ and /v/

The letters **B** and **V** can help you remember how to pronounce these two sounds. Look at the letter **B**. Can you see two lips there? You press your lips together to stop the air and then release them to make the sound /b/.

Now look at the letter **V**. Imagine a sharp tooth, like a shark's tooth. That will remind you that when you pronounce /v/ your teeth must lightly rest on your lower lip.

Both /b/ and /v/ are voiced. Can you tell which one is a stop and which one is a continuant? A stop sound can only be made once, while a continuant can be continued as long as you want. If you continue the /v/ sound for a minute, you should feel a lot of vibration on your lip.

Listen while your instructor reads the following words. Notice the position of your instructor's teeth and lips. If possible, practice saying these pairs of words while looking in a mirror.

1. best — vest
2. ban — van
3. base — vase
4. bat — vat
5. berry — very
6. bail — veil
7. boat — vote

B. Spell It Out

The sound /b/ is always spelled B and the sound /v/ is always spelled V. (See the chapter "Silence is Golden" for a few words that have a silent B.)

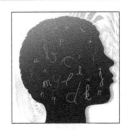

C. V is for Victory

Work with a partner and list as many words as you can think of in 3 minutes that begin with the sound /v/. Can you come up with some words that no one else in the class thought of?

1.
2.
3.
4.
5.
6.
7.
8.
9.
10.
11.
12.
13.
14.
15.
16.
17.
18.
19.
20.
21.
22.
23.
24.
25.

D. Silly Sentences

1. Van's vegetables were victorious in the voting.
2. Barry's berries are the very best berries.
3. The base of that vase is very big.
4. Vanessa likes the violet velvet vest best.
5. They banned vans on the Brooklyn Bridge.

E. Tongue Twister

Bobby Victor bought a bat.
Bobby bought a rubber ball.
With his bat he banged the ball
Banged it up against the wall.
But so boldly Bobby banged it
That he broke his rubber ball.
Now to beat his many troubles
Bobby Victor's blowing bubbles.
Bubble blowing brings him pleasure
More than playing bat and ball.
Bobby Victor's done with baseball
Batting balls against the wall.
He blows bubbles with no troubles
Leaning back against the wall.

F. Sound It Out /p/ and /f/

The sound /p/ is made in the same way as /b/, but /p/ is unvoiced. You press your lips together to stop the air and then release it to make the sound /p/. Because /p/ is a very soft sound, we add a lot of air (called aspiration) when the sound /p/ is at the beginning of a word. If you hold your hand or a sheet of paper in front of your mouth, you should feel or see a big puff of air when you pronounce words that begin with /p/.

Listen and repeat the following words. Notice the puff of air when you pronounce /p/.

1. bat   pat
2. bail   pail
3. big   pig
4. bad   pad
5. Ben   pen
6. buy   pie

The sound /f/ is made in the same way as /v/, but /f/ is unvoiced. Your teeth lightly touch your lower lip when you pronounce /f/. Air flows continuously. Listen to your instructor and notice the difference in lip and teeth in these words. If possible, look in a mirror as you pronounce words that begin with /f/.

1. pat   fat
2. pail   fail
3. pill   fill
4. put   foot
5. pull   full
6. Pete   feet
7. pan   fan
8. picks fix

G. Spell It Out

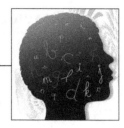

The sound /p/ is always spelled P. The sound /f/ is usually spelled F, but see section O below for /f/ spelled PH.

H. Silly Sentences

1. Pamela put pickles on her pizza.
2. Pedro put both feet flat on the floor.
3. Five fuzzy flies flew over the food.
4. Felicia found fancy flip-flops at the flip-flop factory.
5. Felix felt feverish following the party.
6. Four flags flapped in the breeze.

I. Tongue Twister

Peter Piper picked a pile of pickled peppers.
A pile of pickled peppers, Peter Piper picked.
If Peter Piper picked a pile of pickled peppers,
How many pickled peppers did Peter Piper pick?

J. Put It Together

Listen as your instructor reads the following words. Pay attention to the position of the instructor's lips and teeth.

/b/	/v/	/p/	/f/
bat	vat	pat	fat
big		pig	fig
buy	vie	pie	
ban	van	pan	fan
best	vest	pest	
	vine	pine	fine
bent	vent	pent	
base	vase	pace	face
beat		Pete	feet
backed		packed	fact
	view	pew	few
bull		pull	full

K. Can You Guess It?

The answers will be found in the chart on the previous page.

1. The opposite of *push*
2. A bench in a church
3. Something that is known for sure
4. A sweater without sleeves
5. The opposite of *empty*
6. A male cow
7. A place to keep flowers
8. Apple or cherry, for example
9. Another word for *crooked*
10. The opposite of *sell*
11. An animal that likes mud
12. A sweet fruit
13. You use it to play baseball
14. To hit, to win, or the rhythm of a song
15. At the bottom of your legs
16. The opposite of *worst*
17. You use it to stay cool
18. Something that annoys you
19. Softly touching a dog's head
20. Bigger than a car but smaller than a truck

L. Dizzy Dialogue

Circle all the words that contain the sound /p/, /b/, /f/, or /v/. Then practice the dialogue with a partner.

Vanessa: My family is coming over for dinner Friday.

Victor: That's fine. Who is coming?

Vanessa: Well, my cousins Peter and Paula, Felicia and Frank, Betty and Bill, and Valerie and Vance. And Frank's friend Fred. And of course, my favorite nephew Fergus.

Victor:	Hmmm, that's quite a few people! What kind of feast do you have in mind?
Vanessa:	Well, Valerie and Vance are vegetarians. And Frank is allergic to fish. Peter and Paula are vegans. And Bill offered to bring his favorite food: pickled beets.
Victor:	Maybe we can have a buffet out on the patio. I bought some fresh figs and fiddlehead ferns at the farmer's market this morning.
Vanessa:	That sounds good. And I will make some French fries from the potatoes I found on sale.
Victor:	I'll see if Paula would like to make a fresh fruit salad with bananas and berries.
Vanessa:	And we can serve peanuts and popcorn for a snack.
Victor:	What a fine feast this will be!

M. Talk It Over

1. What's your **favorite food?** Do you have a **favorite fruit?** A **favorite vegetable?**

2. What's your **family's favorite place for** a **vacation?** Describe your idea of a **perfect vacation.**

3. Who is the most **famous person** you have ever met? Is there a **famous person** you'd like to meet? Where's a good place to **find famous people?**

4. What kind of **films** (**movies**) are **popular** these days? What is your **favorite** type of **film?**

N. Speak Your Mind

Vegetarianism has **become** more **popular** recently in the United States. **People** choose to be **vegetarians** for a **variety** of reasons. Discuss the reasons **people** choose to **avoid** meat. What are some of the **benefits** of a **vegetarian** diet? Are there any **problems** with eating only **vegetarian foods?** How does a **vegan** diet **differ from** a **vegetarian** diet?

O. Not to Be Confused With. . . .

In English words borrowed from Greek, the sound /f/ is spelled PH. All of the following words come from Greek. Fill in the missing letters PH. Be sure to pronounce these words with the sound /f/.

1. You use a camera to take __otographs.
2. You buy medicine at the __armacy
3. You talk to your friends on the __one.
4. Your sister's son is your ne__ew.
5. A child with no parents is an or__an
6. An extreme fear is a __obia.
7. The shape of a ball or the earth is a s__ere.
8. A person who foretells the future is a pro__et.
9. The study of sounds is __onics.
10. The small line in a word like *X-ray* is called a hy__en.
11. A storm similar to a hurricane is called a ty__oon.
12. PE stands for __ysical education.

CHAPTER 39
We Will Win the Victory (/w/ and /v/)

A. Sound It Out

As explained in the previous chapter, when you pronounce the /v/ sound, your top teeth lightly touch your lower lip. When you pronounce the /w/ sound, your lips are rounded tightly and then unrounded.

B. Spell It Out

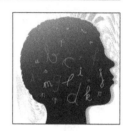

The sound /v/ is always spelled with the letter V. The only exception is the word *of*, pronounced /əv/. The letter V is always pronounced /v/.

The most common spellings for the sound /w/ is W.
    warm   wagon   wave   walk   weak

Other spellings are:
    WH: where   when   what
    O: one   someone   once
    U after Q: quick   question   queen   squirrel   square

At the end of words, the letter W is part of the vowel sound:
    grow   snow   thaw   saw

In words that begin with WR, the W is silent.
    wrist   wrinkle

C. Listen Up

Circle the word that you hear.

1. worse   verse
2. worry   very
3. wet   vet
4. whale   veil

5. wince   Vince
6. went   vent
7. west   vest
8. wane   vane
9. wine   vine
10. wow   vow

D. Can You Guess It?

/v/

1. Bright and colorful
2. A person's sight
3. To select a person for a political position
4. To spend time at someone's house
5. From the Colorado mountains, you see a spectacular _____
6. An animal doctor
7. A bride wears this on her head
8. Many people travel during their summer _____
9. When there is no room at a hotel the sign says "No _____"
10. The magician made the rabbit _____
11. A person who wanders without a place to live
12. When you leave for a trip, your friends say "bon _____"
13. The athletes celebrated their _____ as world champions
14. A movie or television program on tape
15. A string instrument used in classical concerts

/w/

1. Where you keep your cash and credit cards
2. When you have a birthday, you make a _____ and then blow out the candles
3. The opposite of *east*
4. When you are thirsty you drink _____
5. You _____ a hat on your head
6. Another word for *cry*
7. A ceremony to celebrate marriage

8. Air that moves quickly

9. A drink made from grapes

10. Husband and _____

11. The opposite of *lose*

12. The biggest ocean animal

13. People who give good advice are _____

14. Another word for *lady*

15. Lions and tigers are _____ animals

16. Another word for *labor*

17. Intense exercise at the gym

E. Tongue Twisters

1. Wayne went to Wales to watch walruses.

2. I wish to wish, you wish to wish,

   but if you wish the wish the witch wishes,

   I won't wish the wish you wish to wish.

3. When you write, you have the right to copyright the words you write.

4. Why do you cry, Willy?

   Why do you cry?

   Why, Willy?

   Why, Willy?

   Why, Willy? Why?

5. Wet weather is better than windy weather.

6. Wally Winkle wiggles his wrinkled white wig.

7. Wise women don't walk in the woods while wolves wander.

8. Vern Verve is well-versed in very vivid wordy verse.

9. Vinnie likes to view videos in his minivan.

10. Victor and Vince played varsity volleyball at Vernon Park.

11. Vinnie Vail voted for the vile villain of Victory Village.

12. Will Van wear wool or will Van wear velvet?

F. Silly Sentences

Circle all the /v/ and /w/ sounds in the following sentences. Then practice saying them with a partner.

1. Vultures devoured the vegetables with a visible vengeance.
2. Victoria wore her violet veil when she played her valuable violin in the vacant lot.
3. The volatile veteran had a verbal match with various ventriloquists.
4. The vain vagabond went on an adventurous voyage for his vacation.
5. The voracious vampire vigorously munches on vibrant vegetables.
6. The viper played the viola at Vagabond Inn.

G. Talk It Over

1. The following adjectives can be used to describe a person:

   - vivacious
   - volatile
   - versatile
   - vibrant
   - victorious
   - vigorous
   - vulnerable
   - witty
   - warm
   - wimpy
   - weak
   - weird
   - whimsical
   - wonderful

   Explain what each word means and give examples of people you know that have these character traits. Which words describe positive traits and which are negative? Would any of these words describe you?

2. In English, we use the expression "wow" to express amazement. Think of situations when you would use this to express your feelings about someone or something.

H. Speak Your Mind

Many **visitors** to the United States often notice that Americans seem **very wasteful.** Mention some examples of **ways** in which people in the United States **waste** resources such as **water** or food.

I. Story Time

Circle all the /v/ and /w/ sounds in the following stories. Then work with a partner and take turns reading them.

A Vacation in Venice

Last summer Walter and Vivian Wilson went on a vacation to Venice, Italy. Every morning they enjoyed their trip on the Venetian gondolas, taxis that travel on the waterways. Walter enjoyed visiting the museums, and Vivian spent some time watching the Venetian glass blowers. Later in the day, they went on the gondolas to see the sunset and listen to the gondoliers sing as they paddled down the  canal. Walter and Vivian took many morning walks around Piazza San Marcos and enjoyed meeting some of the local people. They also enjoyed feeding the voracious pigeons around the plaza. They had a wonderful vacation in beautiful Venice, the city of love and romance.

The Vicious Wolverine

Wolverines are interesting animals that live in northern forests in the United States, Canada, and other parts of the world. They are related to minks and otters. Wolverines are carnivorous, which means that they eat meat. The most surprising thing about wolverines is how strong they are.  Although only about the size of a medium-sized dog, they have been known to kill animals as large as moose. Are wolverines really vicious? Well, you don't want to get into a fight with one! They have powerful jaws, sharp claws, and thick fur and skin. There is a story that a 27-pound wolverine attempted to steal food from a 500-pound bear. Another story tells of a wolverine outsmarting a polar bear. The state of Michigan is known as the Wolverine State, and the University of Michigan football team is known as the Wolverines. Maybe they want their opponents to think they will be as victorious as real wolverines.

CHAPTER 40
Kin to the Golden King (/k/, /g/, /m/, /n/, and /ŋ/)

A. How Does It Sound?

When you pronounce the sound /k/, the center of your tongue comes up, touches the roof of your mouth, stops the air, and then releases it. The sound /k/ is unvoiced and there is a puff of air when /k/ is at the beginning of a word. The sound /g/ is made in the same way as /k/, but /g/ is voiced and /k/ is unvoiced.

Listen to the following pairs of contrasts:

	/k/	/g/
1.	came	game
2.	could	good
3.	kill	gill
4.	cap	gap
5.	cane	gain
6.	crowned	ground
7.	crow	grow
8.	curl	girl
9.	luck	lug
10.	lack	lag
11.	peck	peg

B. How Is It Spelled?

As you can see, at the beginning of words, the sound /k/ is often spelled with the letter C. As a rule, the letter C sounds like /k/ before the vowels A, O, and U and in consonant blends. The letter C sounds like /s/ before the vowels E, I, and Y. American students know these two sounds as soft *C* (/s/) and hard *C* /k/. (As you learned in Chapter 34, the letters CH are also pronounced /k/ in a few words such as *Christmas*.)

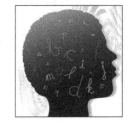

Read the following words that begin with the letter C and write /s/ or /k/ to indicate the sound you hear:

1. city   ___
2. country   ___
3. capital   ___

231

4. confused ___
5. century ___
6. citizen ___
7. cable ___
8. center ___
9. crown ___
10. could ___
11. certain ___
12. cave ___
13. circle ___
14. cent ___
15. cycle ___
16. climb ___
17. chorus ___
18. club ___
19. civilized ___
20. circus ___

The letter G also has two pronunciations. The sound /g/ is called *hard G*, and the sound /dʒ/ is known as *soft G* when it is spelled with the letter G. This sound is most often spelled with the letter J. (Notice that *jump* and *giant*, for example, start with the same sound.) Like C, the letter G usually sounds hard (/g/) before the vowels A, O, and U and in consonant blends. The letter G is often soft (/dʒ/) before the vowels E, I, and Y, but there are exceptions.

Read the following words that begin with the letter G and write /g/ or /dʒ/ to indicate the sound you hear:

1. gate ___
2. gum ___
3. gem ___
4. gentle ___
5. galaxy ___
6. goat ___
7. giant ___
8. gym ___
9. gender ___

10. giraffe ___
11. give ___
12. germ ___
13. ginger ___
14. get ___
15. gain ___
16. gallery ___
17. goose ___
18. geometry ___
19. general ___
20. Germany ___

C. Silly Sentences

1. There was a little girl
   Who had a little curl
   Right in the middle of her forehead;
   And when she was good, she was very very good
   And when she was bad, she was horrid.
2. The city girl could ride her cycle in circles, but the country girl was too confused by the sights of the city to get on a cycle.
3. Ginny likes gym class better than geometry or geography class.
4. George was a citizen of Germany, but he left his country and became a citizen of Ghana.
5. Columbus is the capital of Ohio, but Cleveland and Cincinnati are also large cities.

D. How Does It Sound?

The sounds /m/, /n/, and /ŋ/ are called nasal sounds because when we say them, the air comes out our nose instead of our mouth. Try this: make the sound /mmmm/ and then pinch your nose. See? You can't make the sound if your nose is closed. That's why you sound funny when you have a bad cold!

You make the sound /m/ by pressing your lips together and letting the air out through your nose. You make the sound /n/ by placing your tongue behind your teeth and letting the air out your nose. And you make the sound /ŋ/ by pressing the back of your tongue up and letting the air out your nose. Many languages have words that begin with the sound /ŋ/, but in English the sound /ŋ/ only occurs in the middle or end of words.

Listen to the contrast between /m/ and /n/ at the beginning of words. (Note: K is silent before N)

map	nap
mail	nail
met	net
mob	knob
mitt	knit

Now compare these words that end in /m/, /n/, or /ŋ/.

1.	ram	ran	rang
2.	Pam	pan	pang
3.	rum	run	rung
4.	sum	sun	sung
5.	dim	din	ding
6.	dumb	done	dung
7.	comb	cone	—
8.	—	thin	thing
9.	—	fan	fang
10.	brim	—	bring
11.	Kim	kin	king

E. How Is It Spelled?

The spelling of /m/, /n/, and /ŋ/ is almost completely regular. However, notice the difference in pronunciation of NG in the middle of words:

singer /sɪŋ ɚ/

bringer /brɪŋ ɚ/

stinger /stɪŋ ɚ/

longer /lɔŋ gɚ/

finger /fɪŋ gɚ/

danger /deyn dʒɚ/

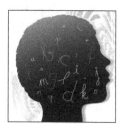

F. Droppin' Gs

The –ING ending is usually pronounced /ɪŋ/. But in very casual conversation, –ING is often reduced to /ɪn/. This is known as "dropping the G," although in reality, we are substituting /n/ for /ŋ/. Notice that this only happens to words that have an –ING ending added to a verb, not to words that always end with ING. So the word *playing* might be pronounced /pleyɪn/ but the word *bring* is never pronounced /brɪn/.

Read the following dialogue and circle the words that might "drop the G" in very casual conversation. Then try reading it that way.

Kim:	What are you planning to bring to the party?
Vin:	I'm thinking of bringing king crab and sparkling wine.
Kim:	Wow, that sounds amazing!
Vin:	Well, since winning the lottery, I've been trying to share some of my good luck with my friends!
Kim:	I heard that there's going to be some singing at the party, too. Do you like to sing?
Vin:	I'm not a good singer, but I'm inviting my new friend Beyoncé to come with me, so there will be some good singing.
Kim:	Beyoncé? You're kidding!
Vin:	Nope, I'm not pulling your leg. She's coming to the party with me.
Kim:	I hope there will be some dancing, too. I'd sure like a chance to dance with Beyoncé!
Vin:	Not a problem, Kim. There will be singing and dancing and eating and drinking all night long.
Kim:	It will certainly be an interesting party!

G. Can You Guess It?

Each answer will begin with /k/ or /g/:

1. An animal that meows
2. It shoots bullets
3. A baby cat
4. Another word for a birthday present
5. Mexico, Japan, and Italy are examples of _____
6. The child of your aunt and uncle is your _____
7. The force that makes apples fall from trees
8. The spirit of a dead person that haunts the earth
9. Like a mitten, but with 5 fingers
10. A baby bear or lion
11. This fruit is used to make wine
12. For good luck, some people carry a four-leaf _____

Each answer will begin with /m/ or /n/:

1. You earn it, save it, and spend it
2. A bird builds one for its eggs
3. The subject that studies numbers
4. The opposite of *something*
5. Pecans and cashews are types of _____
6. The part of your body between your head and your shoulders
7. How you feel before giving a speech
8. A person who assists doctors
9. You go to a concert to listen to _____
10. Sherlock Holmes tries to solve _____
11. The opposite of *father*
12. You use this body part to smell with
13. It shows the location of streets, cities, and countries

H. Talk It Over

1. Do you like to **sing**? Where are some places that you enjoy **singing**? Can everyone learn to **sing**? Should **singing** be taught in **elementary** school?

2. "What's **good** for the **goose** is **good** for the **gander**." Can you explain the meaning of this idiom? (A **gander** is a male **goose**.)

3. Have you ever been a **member** of a **club**? What **kinds** of **clubs** did your high school have? Is there a **club** at this school that you would like to **join**? What are some of the benefits of **joining** a **club**?

4. Sometimes we receive **gifts** that we don't really have any use for, and we may wonder what to do with these **gifts**. If you pass your **gift** on to someone else, it's called "**re-gifting**." Have you ever **re-gifted** a **gift** that you didn't like or didn't need?

5. In July 1969, the first **human** beings stepped on the **moon**. The last **human** visit to the **moon** was in **December** 1972. Do you think **humans** should return to the **moon**? Why or why not?

I. Speak Your Mind

One of the **most controversial** topics in the **United** States is **gun control**.

The **Second Amendment** says:

"A well regulated **militia** being **necessary** to the security of a free State, the right of the People to keep and bear **arms** shall not be **infringed**."

Some people believe that the **Second Amendment** gives every **American** the right to **own** a **gun**. Other people **maintain** that the **Second Amendment** only applies to those who are **members** of a **militia**.

How do you feel about the rights of an **individual** to own a **gun**? Would people in the United States be safer if **more** people owned **guns**, as some **claim**, or if **no** one were allowed to own a **gun** for personal use?

CHAPTER 41
Silence is Golden

We have learned the pronunciation and spelling patterns of many sounds in English, but our study would not be complete without noting that many English words have silent letters that are never pronounced, and other words tend to lose certain sounds in ordinary speech.

You have already noticed that the –E at the end of words is almost always silent:

    tape   these   like   home   cube

and that in 2-letter vowel combinations, the second vowel is usually silent:

    rain   each   pie   boat   true

In this chapter, we will focus on consonants that are always or often silent.

A. Silent Consonants

Silent B

The letter B is silent after M at the end of words and before T.

Listen as your instructor pronounces each word and draw a line through the letter B:

bomb	doubt	subtle
climb	dumb	thumb
comb	lamb	tomb
crumb	numb	
debt	plumber	

Remember, B is not *always* silent at the end of words! Pronounce each word, and cross out the B if it is silent:

1. rob
2. scrub
3. tomb
4. limb
5. curb
6. verb
7. thumb
8. bulb
9. job
10. crumb
11. subtle
12. subtitle

Silly Sentences

1. The dumb plumber climbed down into the tomb.
2. I doubt the bomb will be subtle.
3. Can you comb a lamb?
4. I am numb from all the debt I am in.

Silent C

A few words have a silent letter C:

science   scissors   scene   indict   muscle   czar   yacht (CH is silent), Connecticut (the second C is silent).

Silent D

The D is usually not pronounced in the words:

Wednesday   grandmother   grandfather   handsome   handkerchief

As noted in Chapter 37, when D is before U, the sound changes to /dʒ/:

educate   graduate   individual   schedule   gradual

Also D is pronounced /dʒ/ in:

soldier /sowl dʒɚ/ cordial /kɔr dʒəl/.

Silly Sentences

1. The handsome scientist showed us his muscles.
2. His grandfather and grandmother live in Connecticut.
3. The czar only went out in his yacht on Wednesdays.
4. The educated soldier cut up the handkerchief with scissors.
5. There was quite a scene when her grandmother was indicted.

Silent G and GH

The letter G is silent before the letter N:

> gnaw   gnat   gnarled   reign   foreign   sign   design   assignment
> sovereign   campaign   champagne

The letter combination GH is silent in most words. But in a few cases, it is pronounced /f/. The letters GH used to be pronounced in Middle English, with a sound like the ending of *Bach,* but English gradually lost this sound, so all that's left is either /f/ or nothing at all. So we can call these GHost letters to help us remember the correct spelling.

Listen to your instructor read the following words. If the GH is silent, draw a line through it. If it is pronounced /f/, write the letter F.

1. thought
2. tough
3. caught
4. taught
5. bright
6. cough
7. might
8. light
9. enough
10. rough
11. fought
12. weigh
13. through
14. sigh
15. laughter
16. eight
17. frighten
18. night
19. ought
20. neighbor
21. daughter
22. dough

(Note: When GH is at the beginning of a word, it is pronounced /g/):

ghost   ghastly   ghetto

GH is also pronounced /g/ in:

aghast   afghan   Afghanistan

By the way, someone once joked that the word *fish* could be spelled GHOTI based on English spelling rules. How?

- GH pronounced /f/ as in *tough*
- O pronounced /ɪ/ as in *women*
- TI pronounced /ʃ/ as in *nation*

Okay, English spelling and pronunciation rules are bad, but not quite that bad!

Silly Sentences

1. Star light, star bright, first star I see tonight

   Wish I may, wish I might

   Have the wish I wish tonight.

2. You might be caught if you laugh at your neighbor.

3. Her daughter taught her to weigh the dough.

Silent H

In a few words, the letter H is silent at the beginning of the word.

Listen to your instructor read the following words. If the H is silent, draw a line through it. If the H is pronounced, underline it.

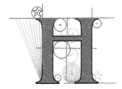

1. hour	6. handsome	11. horror
2. heavy	7. herb	12. honor
3. heir	8. Herbert	13. history
4. hair	9. honest	14. happy
5. hat	10. home	

Also, see Reductions, section E.

Silent K

The letter K is silent before N:

know/knew/known	kneel/knelt	knell
knowledge	knock	knoll
knight	knuckle	knob
knot	knead	doorknob
knife/knives	knit	unknown

Silly Sentences

1. The knight knelt down on the grassy knoll.
2. His knobby knees knocked together.
3. She knocked on the door and then turned the doorknob.
4. He cut his knuckle on the sharp knife when he was kneading bread dough.
5. This new knowledge will solve that knotty problem.
6. She knows how to knit, but not with yarn full of knots!

Silent L

The letter L is usually silent before K and M and in a few other words as well. Draw a line through the silent L as your instructor reads each word:

chalk	calm	half/halves
talk	palm	calf/calves
walk	psalm	could
stalk	balm	should
folks	salmon	would
polka dot	yolk	

Note: Some native speakers of American English may pronounce the L in a few of these words.

Silly Sentences

1. That calm calf is covered with polka dots!
2. She made a sauce for the salmon out of egg yolks.
3. Some folks can't walk and talk at the same time.
4. She held half a piece of chalk in the palm of her hand.
5. This balm should help calm the itch.
6. I knew I should, I knew I could, but I doubted if I would.

Silent N

In words that end in MN, the N is silent.

autumn	hymn	solemn
damn	column	

Note that in some cases, the N is pronounced in longer forms of the word:

    damnation   autumnal   hymnal   solemnity

Silent P

There is a small group of words borrowed from Greek that begin with a silent P.

psalm	psychiatrist	pseudonym
psychic	psychology	pneumonia

Silly Sentences (Silent N and P)

1. The psychic predicted I'd have pneumonia next autumn.
2. The solemn psychologist sang a psalm from the hymnal.
3. The newspaper column was published under a pseudonym.

Silent S

The letter S is silent in:

isle   island   aisle

It is also silent at the end of a few words borrowed from French:

corps (both the P and the S are silent)

debris

rendezvous (the Z is also silent: /rɔn dei vuw/)

Names of some places in the United States are based on French names and have a silent S:

Illinois

Arkansas

Des Moines

Louisville

Silly Sentences

1. A young man from Des Moines couldn't decide whether to join the Peace Corps or the Marine Corps!
2. The tornado left debris across the state of Arkansas.
3. Should we rendezvous in Louisville or somewhere in Illinois?
4. We walked up and down the aisles in the supermarket until we found some coffee called Island Gold.

Silent T

Listen as your instructor reads the following words and cross out the silent T in each word.

often	moisten	ballet
Christmas	glisten	buffet
listen	wrestle	beret
whistle	mortgage	depot
fasten	apostle	bouquet
hasten	epistle	debut
hustle	christen	gourmet
bustle	castle	ricochet
soften	chestnut	crochet

(Note: TH is silent in *clothes* and *asthma*. Some people pronounce the T in *often*.)

Silly Sentences

1. The hustle and bustle of Christmas shopping often causes us to forget the real meaning of this holiday.
2. The gourmet hastened to the buffet.
3. This cream will soften and moisten your skin so that it glistens.
4. She wrestled with learning to crochet so that she could learn how to make a beret.
5. The bullets ricocheted off the castle.
6. This is her debut performance in the ballet.
7. The train whistle was heard in the depot.

Silent W

The letter W is silent before the letter R and in a few other words.

wrist	wreath	wreck
wrap	write/wrote/written	answer
wrong	wrestle	sword
wrench	wrinkle	

Silly Sentences

1. Do you need a wrench to make a wreath?
2. The wrestler was so old he was wrinkled.
3. The cheater wrote the answer on his wrist, but the answer he wrote was wrong!
4. He wrecked his sword by hitting it against a stone.

B. Can You Guess It?

The answer to each clue will be a word with a silent letter.

1. If you owe a lot of money, you are in _____
2. I'm not sure; I still have some _____
3. The opposite of *question*
4. A French hat
5. A king might live in a _____
6. A chess piece that looks like a horse
7. A person who fixes leaky pipes
8. The day after Tuesday

9. Chicago is in the state of _____

10. Parsley, basil, and cilantro are all _____

11. The yellow part of an egg

12. A country other than our own is called a _____ country

13. A young sheep

14. A song that you sing in church

15. 50%

16. December 25th

17. Land that is surrounded by water on all sides

18. Sparkling wine that people drink at weddings and other celebrations

19. A person who can predict the future or read your mind

20. You use it to untangle your hair

21. A young cow

22. Another name for the fall season

23. The past tense of *bring*

24. The past tense of *teach*

25. The past tense of *think*

C. Disappearing Sounds

When T is close to /n/, most Americans do not pronounce the /t/ sound in normal speech, though they might pronounce it if they are speaking slowly and carefully. Your instructor will read each word twice, once with slow and careful pronunciation and then more quickly in a sentence. Notice the disappearing T. Draw a line through the missing T sound.

mountain…We flew over the Rocky Mountains.

fountain….No one can find the Fountain of Youth!

twenty…He owes me twenty dollars.

plenty….You have plenty of time for this test.

mitten….The weather is cold in Chicago, so don't forget your mittens!

kitten….I wish I could get a puppy or a kitten.

bitten….Have you ever been bitten by a spider?

romantic….They went away for a romantic weekend.

frantic…I was frantic when I couldn't find my son at Disneyland!

enlighten….The full name of the Statue of Liberty is Liberty Enlightening the World.

frighten....That movie really frightened me.

Atlanta...The Atlanta airport is one of the busiest airports in the world.

Atlantic...Columbus crossed the Atlantic Ocean searching for India.

Toronto...Toronto is the largest city in Canada.

Santa Barbara...She attends the University of California in Santa Barbara.

Santa Claus....Do your children believe in Santa Claus?

D. Disappearing Syllables

Not only do sounds disappear from words in relaxed American speech, but whole syllables also disappear as well. Listen to your instructor say each of the following words and tap out the syllables you hear:

favorite	interesting	camera
vegetable	different	laboratory
chocolate	every	business
family	beverage	comfortable

Listen again and draw a line through the vowel/syllable that disappears.

Silly Sentences

1. Every member of the family writes a letter to Santa Claus at Christmas.
2. Two little kittens have lost their mittens.
3. His favorite vegetable is broccoli.
4. We took a romantic vacation in the mountains of Santa Fe.
5. Twenty dollars is plenty of money to buy chocolate.
6. I need a new camera for my business.
7. The new laboratory is different from the old one.
8. I know Santa Barbara is on the Pacific coast, but is Atlanta on the Atlantic coast?

E. Price Reductions? No, Sound Reductions!

The /h/ in *he, his, him,* and *her* is often silent in normal relaxed speech:

Did he do it?	→ Did /iy/ do it?
I think he likes her.	→ I think /iy/ likes /ɚ/
I asked him his name.	→ I asked /ɪm/ /ɪz/ name
I don't think he can do it.	→ I don't think /iy/ can do it.

(Note: The /t/ at the end of *don't* may also disappear because it is close to the θ in *think*.)

The TH in *them* is sometimes silent in relaxed speech. As a result, it may be impossible to tell the difference between *him* and *them*.

| I asked him for help | → I asked /əm/ for help. |
| I asked them for help | → I asked /əm/ for help. |

The word *and* is often reduced to just /n/, especially in pairs of words that are often together. Some familiar phrases are sometimes spelled 'n' to show this.

salt and pepper	→ salt 'n' pepper
husband and wife	→ husband 'n' wife
rock and roll	→ rock 'n' roll
fish and chips	→ fish 'n' chips
meat and potatoes	→ meat 'n' potatoes
me and him	→ me 'n' him
you and me	→ you 'n' me

Notice the reductions that happen to the word *to*:

to	→ tə
got to	→ gotta
want to	→ wanna
have to	→ hafta
has to	→ hasta
going to	→ goin' tə → gonna

Note: These spellings are sometimes used in humorous or very informal writing, but they are not standard English, so you should not use them in school assignments or other formal writing.

The /v/ sound at the end of the word *of* often disappears: *of* → /ə/

a piece of cake	→ a piece /ə/ cake
a lot of work	→ a lot /ə/ work
some of my friends	→ some /ə/ my friends

Practice saying the following sentences in relaxed English.

1. Some of my friends think algebra is a piece of cake, but I think it's a lot of work.
2. If you want to be successful in business, you're going to have to work hard.
3. Before he can learn to surf, he has to learn to swim!
4. She thought they were brother and sister, but actually they were husband and wife.
5. Listening to rock and roll made me and him very excited.
6. He's taller than you and me, but he isn't as strong.

7. This soup tastes terrible. You've got to add some salt and pepper.
8. I don't like fancy meals. Just give me plain old meat and potatoes.
9. You can't fool all of the people all of the time.
10. When the police stopped him for speeding, he ended up in a lot of trouble because he didn't even have a license!

CHAPTER 42
Together at Last (Review of All Consonants)

A. Match Up

Write the symbols that match each description of how you pronounce it: /dʒ/, /y/, /w/, /v/, /b/, /f/, and /p/

(Note: Most have more than one answer. The number of spaces indicates the number of answers.)

1. Round lips   __
2. Teeth on bottom lip __ __
3. Two lips together   __ __
4. Unvoiced   __ __
5. Voiced   __ __ __ __ __

B. Silly Sentences

1. Yellow jello is better than other jello.
2. That vent where the mouse went is bent.
3. I want a big bowl of Very Berry ice cream.
4. Five fine pigs found five big figs.
5. The base of that famous vase is wide.
6. The finest wines come from the finest vines.
7. We wove the vines into a basket.
8. This verse is worse than that verse.
9. She bought the best vest in the west.
10. It's just the job for you.
11. They banned vans in the park.
12. Julie is younger than John.
13. Jane made juicy jam out of yellow yams.
14. Jasmine's yarn is red and white.

C. Rhyme Time

Using the sounds /dʒ/, /y/, /w/, /v/, /b/, /f/, or /p/, how many rhyming words can you think of?

Example: wig: big   pig   fig   jig

1. van:
2. white:
3. purse:
4. fat:
5. jet:
6. jay:
7. won:
8. jest:
9. gin:
10. wool:

D. Listen Up!

Circle the word your instructor says in each sentence:

1. Her brother went to **Yale**/**jail**.
2. They were **wed**/**red**.
3. She touched the **base**/**vase**.
4. Your **vote**/**boat** is very valuable.
5. There's something wrong with his **vowels**/**bowels**.
6. We took a **bow**/**vow**.
7. Did she say *yet/jet*?
8. That machine is for **bending**/**vending**.
9. He measured the **bolts**/**volts**.
10. That one is **verse**/**worse**.
11. She thinks her little brother is the **best**/**pest**.
12. What does *jewel/you'll* mean?
13. I need a better **fan**/**pan**.
14. She looked at the **pig**/**fig**.
15. She asked him to spell *pail/fail*.

16. We paid for the **fine**/**vine**/**wine**.

17. I thought she said *wheel*/*veal*/*feel*.

18. I looked at the **bill**/**pill**.

19. He wrote the word *went*/*vent*/*bent*.

20. Can you spell *while*/*vial*/*bile*?

E. Can You Guess It?

Answers will begin with /dʒ/, /y/, /w/, /v/, /b/, /f/, or /p/.

1. Pickles come in a _____
2. You knit or crochet it
3. The opposite of *tame*
4. People who help or work without pay
5. A popular sport in which you throw the ball through a hoop
6. A popular sport played on the beach
7. Chairs, tables, beds, etc.
8. Taking a lunch to eat in the park
9. You have five on each hand
10. The people in court who decide who is innocent or guilty
11. Another name for your work
12. The largest animal in the ocean
13. Brides traditionally wear this on their heads
14. The opposite of *succeed*
15. The opposite of *old*
16. Useless stuff ("My garage is full of _____")
17. You use it to write
18. You sit on it in a park
19. It keeps dogs out of your yard
20. Another word for *prison*
21. A machine to clean the carpet
22. A sweater without sleeves
23. Humans have hair, but animals have _____
24. A wild animal like a dog that howls at the moon
25. Fish use these to swim

F. Match Up

Match the symbols to the description: /s/, /z/, /θ/, /ð/, /t/, /d/

(Note: The number of spaces indicates the number of answers.)

1. Unvoiced   ___ ___ ___
2. Voiced   ___ ___ ___
3. Tongue behind your teeth   ___ ___ ___ ___
4. Tongue shows between your teeth   ___ ___
5. Continuant (you can continue making the sound)   ___ ___ ___ ___
6. Stop (you can only make the sound once)   ___ ___

G. Think or Swim

Circle the word that your instructor says:

1. He didn't **think** / **sink**.
2. I want the **thin** / **tin** one.
3. There are a lot of **trees** / **threes**.
4. Be sure you have enough **thread** / **tread**.
5. I got the **letter** / **leather**.
6. I thought she said *Zen* / *then*.
7. Do you know what **load** / **loathe** means?
8. I admire her **face** / **faith**.
9. She forgot how to spell *those* / *doze*.
10. They expected more **tanks** / **thanks**.

H. Silly Sentences /s/, /z/, /θ/, /ð/, /t/, /d/

1. Those three thirsty sisters thoughtfully sipped their tea.
2. She bought six thin sweaters and three thicker sweaters.
3. Thirteen seamstresses used three thimbles and thirty spools of thread.
4. Thumbelina was a tiny thing, no bigger than a thumb.
5. Bang the drum but don't bang your thumb!
6. They teased the three-year-old and called him a thumb-sucker.
7. This thread is too thick and that thread is too thin.
8. Thanks! I'll see you at three-thirty on Thursday.
9. Two tall trees are surrounded by three thick thistles and six sharp thornbushes.
10. This soup is so thin I think it's simply broth.

I. Family Tree

Work with a partner to figure out the name for each family member. (Many but not all of the answers contain the sound /ð/.)

1. Your male sibling is your _____.
2. Your female parent is your _____.
3. Your husband or wife's mother is your _____.
4. If your mother re-marries, her husband is your _____.
5. Your sister's husband is your _____.
6. Your female child is your _____.
7. Your father's father is your _____.
8. Your husband or wife's sister is your _____.
9. If your father has a son who has a different mother than you, this son is your _____.
10. Your grandmother's mother is your _____.
11. Your mother's brother is your _____.
12. Your uncle's children are your _____.
13. Your grandmother's brother is your _____.
14. If your father marries a woman who has a son, that boy is your _____.

J. Right or Wrong? /l/ or /r/

Circle the word that makes sense.

1. If you're not on time, you are **late / rate**.
2. The amount of interest you pay for a loan is called the interest **late / rate**.
3. She made a refreshing drink out of **limes / rhymes**.
4. The word *cat* **limes / rhymes** with *mat*.
5. You can skate at a skating **link / rink**.
6. On the Internet, you can click on a **link / rink** and go to another website.
7. My favorite color is **led / red**.
8. My pencil is out of **lead / read**.
9. A baby sheep is called a **lamb / ram**.
10. A male sheep is called a **lamb / ram**, which is also the name of a sturdy truck and a football team.
11. She turned on the **lamp / ramp** when it got dark.

12. They pushed the cart up the **lamp / ramp** and into the building.

13. I know my answer on the test was **light / right**.

14. Don't turn left, turn **light / right**.

K. Sheep, Jeep, or Cheap?

Write the symbol /ʃ/, /tʃ/, or /dʒ/ for each word:

1. sheep____
2. cheap ____
3. jeep____
4. chin____
5. shin____
6. gin____
7. Jack____
8. shack____

9. share____
10. chair____
11. chef____
12. champion____
13. ginger____
14. sugar____
15. genius____
16. passion____

17. champagne ____
18. geometry____
19. sure____
20. shoot____
21. chute____

L. Silly Sentences: /ʃ/, /tʃ/, and /dʒ/

1. You can put **sheep** on a **ship,** but you can't put a **ship** on a **sheep.**
2. **Sheila should choose** a **Chevrolet** instead of a **Jeep.**
3. **Shinya** won the Top **Chef championship** when he created a dessert that combined **ginger** and **champagne.**
4. **Jack** is a **genuine genius** at **geometry.**
5. Can you **touch** your **chin** to your **shin?**
6. That school is so overcrowded that two students have to **share** one **chair.**

M. What's the Difference? /s/ or /z/

Write the symbol for the pronunciation of the letter S in each word:

1. rose   ____
2. his   ____
3. miss   ____
4. misery ____
5. mystery ____
6. less   ____

7. Lee's   ____
8. zeroes ____
9. post   ____
10. suppose ____
11. house   ____
12. cousin ____

13. reason ____
14. lease ____
15. please ____

N. What's the Difference? /t/, /d/, or /id/

Write the symbol for the pronunciation of the –ED ending in each word:

1. voted _____
2. looked _____
3. played _____
4. tipped _____
5. created _____
6. snowed _____
7. pushed _____
8. lived _____
9. coughed _____
10. loaned _____
11. wanted _____
12. pretended _____
13. ended _____
14. amazed _____
15. obeyed _____

O. Categories

Work with a partner to fill in a word in each category that starts with the sound on the left. When everyone is finished, read your answers to the class. You get 1 point for each word, 2 points for a word that no one else had, and 5 points if you have an answer and no one else had an answer at all in that box.

	Foods	Countries	Musical Instruments	Girls' Names	Animals
/l/					
/r/					
/dʒ/					
/tʃ/					
/p/					
/v/					
/f/					

P. Put It All Together

Work with a partner to write 5 words that begin or end with each consonant sound:

1. /b/

2. /d/

3. /f/

4. /g/

5. /h/

6. /dʒ/

7. /k/

8. /l/

9. /m/

10. /n/

11. /ŋ/ (ending sound)

12. /p/

13. /r/

14. /s/

15. /t/

16. /v/

17. /w/

18. /y/

19. /z/

20. /tʃ/

21. /ʃ/

22. /ð/

23. /θ/

24. /ʒ/ (ending sound)

Q. Ultimate Challenge

Match each word with the correct symbol for the first sound in the word. You will use each sound at least once.

1. pneumonia ____	• /aw/
2. wrap ____	• /ɔ/ or /a/
3. chemistry ____	• /f/
4. knife ____	• /g/
5. history ____	• /h/
6. United States ____	• /k/
7. ghost ____	• /n/
8. phobia ____	• /p/
9. chauffeur ____	• /r/
10. honest ____	• /s/
11. knitting ____	• /ʃ/
12. psychic ____	• /tʃ/
13. photo ____	• /w/
14. Europe ____	• /y/
15. knowledge ____	• /dʒ/
16. hour ____	• /ʒ/
17. chef ____	
18. want ____	
19. patriotic ____	
20. giant ____	
21. uniform ____	
22. knuckle ____	
23. psychology ____	
24. wrinkle ____	
25. church ____	
26. genre ____	

PART 4

Projects for Practice and Improvement

CHAPTER 43
Listening Logs

Going to see a movie, following the latest news, understanding lectures in history or science classes, feeling comfortable in daily conversations—you need good listening comprehension skills to accomplish any of these goals. Even students who have studied English for many years are sometimes dismayed and discouraged by how much difficulty they have in understanding what is being said. Like any other skill, listening requires practice. Listening Logs provide this practice.

What is a Listening Log?

A log is like a diary or journal in which you record what you did. A Listening Log is a record of what you listened to and what you learned from it. You should take notes as you listen, and then complete your Listening Log form afterward.

For best results, you need to practice listening to something that is not too hard and not too easy, but like Goldilocks' porridge, just right. Think about physical exercise—if I decided that I wanted to run a marathon, I would need to practice (a lot!) If I started out by walking for 10 minutes a day, I wouldn't get any closer to my goal, because I can *already* walk for 10 minutes without any effort. It's too easy, so it's not going to make me any stronger than I am now. On the other hand, if I started out by trying to run 10 miles, I would most likely injure myself, or at the very least, give up. It's too far above my current abilities. I need to do *a little more than what I can do now*. And I need to increase the challenge gradually.

The same thing applies to listening. You need to push yourself to do *a little more than what you can do now*. You need to go beyond your comfort zone, but not too far beyond. Luckily, you won't injure yourself if you try something that's too hard for you, but you might discourage yourself.

The Benefits of Listening Logs

One benefit of Listening Logs is that you can choose material that is just right *for you*. And you can choose material that fits your own interests. When you listen to topics that interest you and about which you have some background knowledge, you will be able understand more and improve your skills.

We are fortunate today to have access to a wide variety of materials online as well as in other formats, making it possible to personalize your listening practice.

Suggestions for Listening Logs

- Voice of America
  http://www.voanews.com/specialenglish/index.cfm
  The Voice of America is sponsored by the United States government. Originally it was only a radio broadcast, but it is now also available on the Internet. VOA produces many programs in what they call Special English. Special English uses a basic vocabulary of 1500 words. It uses simple grammar and avoids idioms. The announcers also speak at a slower rate, about two-thirds the speed of standard English. In addition, VOA provides a written transcript of each program, so that you can preview the topic, follow along, or check your comprehension. Current news, science, daily life, literature, and idiom study are all available. If you need to start with something simple, this is the place to begin.

  Some specific pages that you might like:
  Words and Their Stories
  http://www1.voanews.com/learningenglish/home/words-stories/)

  Information about Studying in the U.S.
  http://www1.voanews.com/learningenglish/home/foreign-students/

  Stories about American Literature
  http://www1.voanews.com/learningenglish/home/american-life/literature/

- California Distance Learning Project
  http://www.cdlponline.org
  This resource was created to help both ESL and other adult students improve their reading skills as well as listening skills. Some of the stories include a video, and some have the same story in two versions, the original story and a simplified version called Basic. Each story also has vocabulary and comprehension activities to help you practice what you have learned. CDLP includes stories on law, education, nature, family life, and work, among others.

- ESL Podcasts
  http://www.eslpod.com
  ESL Podcasts are created by a private company, and not everything on the site is free. You can listen to a wide variety of podcasts (stories) for free, using either your computer or an iPod™, but if you want the transcripts and other learning activities, you have to pay to subscribe. You can also buy "packs" of podcasts and learning guides about American history and government and daily life.

- National Public Radio
  http://www.npr.org
  NPR is a radio network that receives funding from listeners as well as some government funding. Their website provides pictures and further information about stories that are broadcast on the radio. Many of the stories also have an icon that indicates you can *Listen to the Story*. The written story is not exactly the same as the story you hear. But it

can help you preview or review what you hear, and you can read names and other difficult vocabulary. NPR is not specifically for ESL students, so it is more challenging, but the speaking style is clear and distinct.

- Public Radio International
  http://www.pri.org/
  Similar to NPR, but PRI also includes many programs from the BBC (British Broadcasting Company), if you want to listen to a wider range of accents.

- From the White House
  http://www.whitehouse.gov/briefing-room/speeches-and-remarks
  You can watch videos of many of the president's speeches and remarks and read transcripts of what he said.

- This American Life
  http://www.thisamericanlife.org

- The Story
  http://www.thestory.org

- Story Corps
  http://www.storycorps.org
  The three sites listed above all contain stories about the daily life and experiences of American people of all backgrounds and ethnicity. They use ordinary spoken American English and they do not include transcripts.

- The Discovery Channel
  http://dsc.discovery.com/

- Animal Planet
  http://animal.discovery.com/
  These two science-based sites have short video clips from their television shows that you can watch online.

- The Splendid Table
  http://splendidtable.publicradio.org/
  This is an hour-long show about food and wine, places to eat, and questions and answers about cooking.

This is just a starting point, and you can find many other resources online as well. In addition to talking dogs and funny babies, there are many worthwhile videos on Youtube.com, for example.

Do not limit yourself only to online resources, either! If you are in an English-speaking environment, you are surrounded by radio, television, movies, and people speaking English. The world is your classroom!

Here are some other suggestions for Listening Log topics:

- Do you have a library card from your local public library? If not, visit your nearest library and ask for information about how to get a card and what materials are available.
- Do you attend religious services? Perhaps you could attend a service in English rather than your native language.
- Do you like watching movies on television, DVD, or through your cable or satellite company? If you usually use captions in your native language, try English captions. If you use English captions, try watching without captions. Or choose a short scene and watch it several times, with and then without captions.
- Have you been to a movie at a movie theatre? This is more challenging than other listening experiences, and you won't be able to take notes or listen several times, but it's a great experience.
- Is there a lecture, drama, debate, or information session being offered on campus or in your community? Give it a try!
- Do you have an opportunity to chat with a neighbor or friend in English for 20 or 30 minutes?

Some Comments from Other Students

Our students have told us that doing 12 or more Listening Logs during a semester increased their enjoyment of living in the United States. They used this assignment to push themselves to meet people, try new things, and gain confidence in their listening ability.

One important thing we learned from our students is that if you are trying to listen to something with a lot of new vocabulary, the material will be too hard for you. Everyone knows that unfamiliar names are very difficult to "hear." In the same way, if you are trying to "hear" unfamiliar scientific terms or technical vocabulary, it will be very difficult.

To avoid this frustration, you can read a transcript first and look up unfamiliar words before (or after) you listen, or you can choose topics that you know very well. For example, a student who listened to a story in English about news from her home country found it very easy to understand—because she had enough background to understand the content. But a story about American politics would be much more difficult.

It can help to listen 3 or 4 times to a short piece, but it is also good to listen to longer pieces sometimes and to focus on just getting the main idea. In real life, no one remembers everything they hear. You don't have to have perfect listening comprehension. Be realistic!

It is very difficult even for native speakers to catch the words in some movies, so don't be discouraged. Many students find that comedy is more difficult to understand than other topics. Also, students often want to try to catch all the words in a song, but this is also very difficult. Perhaps find a copy of the lyrics (words) first, and then listen and see if you can hear the words being said.

Listening Log Guidelines

Your instructor will decide how to assign and grade your Listening Logs. The following are some suggestions:

- One Listening Log is due at the beginning of each week. You must listen for a minimum of 30 minutes for each Listening Log. However, if you choose a movie or other presentation that lasts longer than 30 minutes, it still counts as only one Listening Log.
- The presentation must be in English! (Yes, a couple of students over the years told us that English was too hard for them, so they were listening to programs in their native language. Understandable maybe, but not very helpful!)
- Definitions of vocabulary and idioms may be in English or in your native language.
- Try to include as much variety in your Listening Log as possible. Listening to at least 4 different types of listening experiences during the semester is reasonable.
- Listening done in other classes cannot be used as a Listening Log. The goal is to do *more* than what you are already doing.

To be beneficial, Listening Logs must be done week by week. Handing in 5 or 6 Listening Logs at once at the end of the semester is not going to be beneficial. Your instructor might choose to accept no more than 2 Listening Logs in any one week, so that students who may have missed 1 assignment can still get credit, but students who get behind cannot try to hand in a month's work in 1 day!

Name: _____
Listening Log # _____ Date: _____
Title: _____
Format: TV _____ DVD _____ Movie in theatre _____ Radio _____
Speech, sermon, drama, or other live performance _____ Personal Conversation _____
Internet http://www._____

Brief Summary: What was the story about or what topics were discussed?

Personal Reaction: What did you learn? How did you like it? How do you feel about the topics discussed or issues raised?

New Vocabulary or Idioms:

Self-Evaluation: How well did you understand this material? How do you feel about your ability as a listener? What did you do to try to understand better?

© N. Llado, D. Mochidome and E. Uyemura. Permission is granted to make up to 20 copies of this page for personal use by the owner of this textbook only.

Possible Grading Rubric

25 points:

Listening Log is complete, neat, and easy to read.
Student paid attention and took careful notes.
Several new words or idioms are included.
Self-evaluation is thoughtful.
Student is making a great deal of effort to understand more.

22 points:

Some details are omitted or unclear.
Student paid attention and took careful notes.
Only one or two new words are included.
Student is making an average amount of effort.

20 points:

Listening Log is carelessly completed.
Student does not appear to have taken notes but is relying on memory.
or No new words or idioms noted.
or Listening Log was handed in late.

15 points:

Listening Log is messy, hard to read, unclear.
Careless work, but it appears that the student did listen as required.
Student is not able to explain any details of the story or topic.
No new words or idioms (or faked ones).

10 points:

Student listened but is copying description from the DVD packaging, Internet, or TV Guide.

5 points:

Not enough detail to indicate that the listening assignment was completed.

0 points:

Copying from another student.

Other Suggestions for the Instructor

When you collect the Listening Logs, ask students to share informally what they chose and how they liked it. If *you* have seen a movie or interesting show, share your thoughts with the class as a model of how they might also share what they have seen.

You might choose to require more formal reports in which students share what they chose for their Listening Log, how to locate it, and what they learned.

You could choose a specific story from one of the ESL sites and assign the entire class to listen to it independently and then discuss it in class.

If you have computer access in your classroom, you can choose a story with a transcript and use it to create a cloze exercise. One missing word per three lines of text is a suggested pace.

At the end of the course, ask students to evaluate how Listening Logs have helped them.

CHAPTER 44
Two Thumbs Up

Going to the movies or watching a film at home can be fun, especially if you share your movie experience with friends. You don't have to be a movie critic to evaluate a movie or to write a movie review. All you have to do is decide what genre of movie you want to see, think about the plot and the actors' performances, and finally, give your opinion about the movie. This chapter includes several kinds of movie reviews, and your instructor may ask you to try one or more of these ways of responding to a movie you watched.

What is a Movie Review?

A movie review is an analysis of several aspects of a movie. You include the title and list the main characters and the actors who play them, briefly summarize the plot, discuss the theme (the ideas that the writer and director want to get across), comment on the visual and musical effects that highlight the theme, and make any other comments regarding the film. A movie review should be more than just a plot summary (telling what happened in the movie). Good movie critics are always careful to tell us just enough to capture our interest without including any "spoilers" that give away the ending.

Why Write a Movie Review?

Watching and discussing films in and out of class can help you learn to analyze elements such as plot, setting, character, tone, and theme, which you will also do in your reading, literature, and art classes. You can share your ideas and opinions with your classmates, and you will gain a deeper understanding of the movie by writing a review.

What are the Language and Cultural Benefits of Movie Reviews?

When you watch a movie, you have to listen carefully to understand the dialogue, which may contain new vocabulary words and idiomatic expressions. Movies give a vivid picture of a culture, but as you know, it might not always be accurate. If you only learned about American culture from movies, you might think everyone is glamorous and wealthy and that car chases happen every day of the week! But if you choose good movies, you can learn a lot about the thoughts and beliefs of American people.

A. Movie Match-up

Movies are often classified by genres, and some people know exactly what kind of movie they like best. Can you match these film genres with the content of each?

_____ 1. action   a. deals with themes of love
_____ 2. adventure   b. should make you laugh
_____ 3. fantasy   c. involves danger and risk, such as car crashes
_____ 4. comedy   d. involves tension or excitement between people
_____ 5. romance   e. depicts real-life situations
_____ 6. drama   f. occurs in a fictional time and place
_____ 7. horror   g. combines song and dance to support the plot
_____ 8. mystery   h. creates terror in the audience
_____ 9. documentary   i. involves discovering clues to solve a problem
_____ 10. musical   j. creates interaction between "good" and "bad" characters, often in an exotic location

B. Film Feelings

Let's talk about our movie preferences. Answer the questions and then discuss your answers in a small group.

1. What genres do you like? Circle all that apply. Can you give an example of some of your favorite types of movies?

Action	Mystery
Adventure	Romance
Animation	Romantic Comedy
Comedy	Sci-Fi (Science Fiction)
Documentary	Sports
Drama	Thriller
Fantasy	War
Horror	Western
Musical	

2. Do you have any favorite actors? Who are they? What do you like about them?

3. Have you seen any movies lately or in the past that you really liked?

4. Do you prefer to watch movies at the theater or at home? Why?

5. How often do you watch movies?
   _____ several times a week
   _____ once a week
   _____ once a month
   _____ occasionally
   _____ never or almost never

6. What movies do you prefer to see?
   _____ American films
   _____ Films from your own country
   _____ other

7. How are movies rated in your country? Does your country use a system like the American movie rating system? (G, PG, PG-13, R, NC-17)

8. What are some benefits of watching movies? Can you think of any drawbacks?

C. And the Oscar Winners Are . . .

The following is a list of the Academy Award winners for Best Picture (2000–2011). Look up these Oscar-winning movies on the Web and write the year and the genre of each of these films.

Movie	Year	Genre
Chicago	_____	_____
The Departed	_____	_____
The Hurt Locker	_____	_____
A Beautiful Mind	_____	_____
No Country for Old Men	_____	_____
Million Dollar Baby	_____	_____
Slumdog Millionaire	_____	_____
The Lord of the Rings	_____	_____
Black Swan	_____	_____

Crash _____ _____

Gladiator _____ _____

Avitar _____ _____

Which of these movies have you seen? You may want to select one of these films for your movie review.

D. Movie Memories

Working with a partner, interview each other about the best movie you have ever seen. You can ask questions such as:

- What is the title of the movie? Who were the stars?
- How long ago did you see it?
- What was it about?
- Why did you like it so much?
- How did this movie make you feel? Did it make you laugh? Did it make you cry? Why?
- Was there something about this movie that was important to you on a personal level? What was it about this movie that made such a strong impression on you?

Your instructor may ask pairs of students to share their answers with the class.

E. Some Suggestions for Movies to Review

Action
The Hurt Locker
Inglourious Basterds
Invictus
Sugar
Whip It
Universal Soldier 3
Clash of the Titans
Robin Hood
Prince of Persia
The Sounds of Time
Karate Kid
Salt
From Paris with Love
The Expendables

Comedy
The Hangover
World's Greatest Dad
The Informant
It's Complicated
When in Rome
Our Family Wedding
Bounty Hunter
Date Night
Ramona and Beezus
The Winning Season
Lottery Ticket
Youth in Revolt
Spy Next Door
City Island
Solitary Man
Death at a Funeral

Romance

Nine

Crazy Heart

Valentine's Day

The Yellow Handkerchief

Remember Me

Charlie St. Cloud

Dear John

Leap Year

The Back-Up Plan

Going the Distance

The Switch

Drama

Up in the Air

The Cove

A Serious Man

The Messenger

The Blind Side

Julie & Julia

Sherlock Holmes

Michael Jackson's This Is It

Green Zone

Eat, Pray, Love

The American

Conviction

You Will Meet A Tall, Dark Stranger

Creation

Brooklyn's Finest

The Social Network

Letters to God

The Ghost Writer

Animation/Adventure

Coraline

Up

The Princess and the Frog

Harry Potter and the Half-Blood Prince

Cloudy With a Chance of Meatballs

Toy Story

Legend of the Guardians

Alice in Wonderland

Furry Vengeance

Despicable Me

Centurion

Clash of the Titans

Science Fiction

Star Trek

District 9

The Road

Moon

Repo Man

Iron Man 2

Inception

Avatar

The Book of Eli

Quantum Quest: A Cassini Space Odyssey

Legend of the Guardians: The Owls of Ga'Hoole

F. How to Write a Movie Review

1. Choose a movie that you would like to see. It could be a classic, such as *It's a Wonderful Life,* a comedy such as *Wedding Crashers,* a romantic film such as *Under the Tuscan Sun,* an action movie such as *The American,* or any other film of your choice.
2. Watch the movie for its overall content. Write down what you liked or disliked about the film.
3. Watch the movie a second time and write down as much as you can about the movie.
4. Use the Internet to find some basic information about the film, such as the year, the rating, and the names of the actors and director.
5. Start with a basic summary of the movie, but don't give away the ending. Make sure you don't copy the plot summary from the DVD cover or the Internet!
6. Present your movie review to the class for discussion.

Name:_____

G. Movie Review

1. Name and year of the film _____

2. Characters and actors _____

3. Setting (time and place) _____

4. Type of film (comedy, adventure, etc.) _____

5. Rating of the film G _____ PG _____ PG-13 _____ R _____ NC-17 _____

6. Plot summary (limit the events to five and don't reveal the ending)

   _____
   _____
   _____
   _____
   _____
   _____
   _____
   _____

7. Your response to the film

   _____
   _____
   _____
   _____
   _____
   _____
   _____

© E. Uyemura, N. Llado, D. Mochidome. Permission is granted for the owner of this book to make a copy of this page.

H. Sample Movie Review

1. Name of the film *August Rush* (2007)

2. Characters and Actors

Evan/August	(Freddie Highmore)
The Wizard	(Robin Williams)
Lyla	(Kerri Russell)
Louis	(Jonathan Rhys Meyers)
Lyla's father	(William Sadler)

3. Setting New York

4. Type of film Drama and romance

5. Rating of the film PG

6. Plot summary:

    Evan's parents are musicians, and they meet when they are playing at different music arenas nearby. Lyla is a cellist and Louis is an Irish rock singer. They spend the night together and promise to meet, but her father forces her to leave town to pursue her career. They have no way to contact each other. She is pregnant, but her father tells her the baby boy has died and sends him to an orphanage. The father does not let anything interfere with Lyla's career. The boy, Evan, manages to run away from the orphanage and go to New York. He meets some street musicians in Washington Square, picks up a guitar, and it turns out that he is gifted. Will he ever be reunited with his parents?

7. Response to the film:

    This movie is a great romantic story. It is a story of love, music, and much more. It made me cry at times and laugh at others. There was also drama in the film with Lyla trying to find her son, Louis trying to find Lyla, and Evan trying to find both parents. I really enjoyed this movie.

I. Just One More Question

Choose a famous person from the list below or a person of your choice and create an imaginary interview. First, you will research the person, and then write your questions and the answers you think this person would give based on what you have learned. After you have written your interview questions and answers, you will take turns role-playing interviewer and interviewee with a classmate. Your final activity will be to present your interviews to the class.

Here are some suggestions for your research:

Composers	Directors	Actors	Actresses
John Williams	Steven Spielberg	Tom Hanks	Angelina Jolie
Quincy Jones	Francis Ford Coppola	Harrison Ford	Drew Barrymore
Burt Bacharach	Frank Capra	Tom Cruise	Jennifer López
Jerry Goldsmith	Spike Lee	Matt Damon	Gwyneth Paltrow
Henry Mancini	Quentin Tarantino	Brad Pitt	Kate Hudson
John Barry		Will Smith	Sandra Bullock
Tim Rice		Robin Williams	Hilary Swank
		Edward Norton	Diane Lane
		Morgan Freeman	Julia Roberts
		Denzel Washington	Jennifer Aniston
		John Travolta	Meg Ryan
		Jim Carrey	Diane Lane
		Leonardo DiCaprio	Kate Winslet
		Richard Gere	Susan Sarandon
		Russell Crowe	Renée Zellweger

J. An Imaginary Interview with a Film Giant

Steven Spielberg is one of the most influential personalities in the history of film. Let's get to know him better by reading the responses given to the interviewer's questions.

Interviewer: Mr. Spielberg, it is an honor to be interviewing one of the best-known directors in Hollywood.

Mr. Spielberg: Thank you. I really enjoy reading your reviews.

Interviewer: Besides being a director, what other credits do you have to your name?

Mr. Spielberg: I am a producer and a writer.

Interviewer: Where were you born?

Mr. Spielberg: I was born in Cincinnati, Ohio.

Interviewer: What are some of the movies that you have directed?

Mr. Spielberg: I directed *The Sugarland Express, Jaws, Close Encounters of the Third Kind, Raiders of the Lost Ark, Poltergeist,* and *E.T.: The Extra-Terrestrial.*

Interviewer:	I know that you were also one of the pioneers in special effects movies, like *E.T.* and *Close Encounters.*
Mr. Spielberg:	Yes, special effects really did make a difference in films.
Interviewer:	What other projects did you do that used these special effects?
Mr. Spielberg:	Well, there was *Indiana Jones and the Temple of Doom,* which was a big success, and *Back to the Future,* which made Michael J. Fox an instant superstar, among others. I also directed *The Color Purple,* based on the novel. Whoopi Goldberg and Oprah Winfrey made this movie a success. Now it is considered a classic.
Interviewer:	In the late 1980s, you took on some other projects.
Mr. Spielberg:	Yes, I started directing animated and action films like *Who Framed Roger Rabbit?*, *Indiana Jones and the Last Crusade,* and *Back to the Future Part II.*
Interviewer:	What was the highest paying movie in the 90s?
Mr. Spielberg:	It was *Jurassic Park,* which I directed.
Interviewer:	What was the most important film you ever directed?
Mr. Spielberg:	That was *Schindler's List,* based on the true story of a man who risked his life to save 1,100 Jews from the Holocaust.
Interviewer:	As a producer, you also had many accomplishments.
Mr. Spielberg:	Yes, I produced films like *Men in Black, Saving Private Ryan, Shrek,* and *Artificial Intelligence.*
Interviewer:	Mr. Spielberg, you are indeed an amazing man. You have made movies, TV series, documentaries, and much more. You have certainly made amazing contributions to the film and television industry.
Mr. Spielberg:	Thank you for your kind words. Entertainment is a great part of my life, and I enjoy every one of my endeavors.
Interviewer:	It has been an honor to interview one of the greatest figures in entertainment. Thank you for your time.
Mr. Spielberg:	My pleasure.

K. Group Movie Review

1. Your instructor will give the class a suggested list of movies.
2. You will work with a group of three or four and choose a movie that everyone would like to watch.
3. Each member of your group will watch that movie at home or at a movie theater and complete the movie review sheet.
4. After watching the movie, members of the group will discuss the movie and work together to prepare a group report. Each person will focus on one aspect of the movie (plot, character, visual effects, music, etc). As a group, you will evaluate the movie for its overall content, acting, music, special effects, or any other element.

CHAPTER 45
Getting to Know You

Interview Project

Have you ever wished that you could sit down with someone who is a native speaker and ask him or her all the questions you want? Well, that's just what this project will give you the opportunity to do! We've all seen interviews of politicians on television or read interviews of famous stars in magazines, but most of us have probably never interviewed anyone. For this project, you will plan and conduct your own interview. This is a great opportunity to practice speaking and listening in English, and it can also help you in other ways as well. Read on!

What is Your Purpose?

In order to plan a meaningful interview, you need to have a goal or purpose in mind. Are you planning to be a nurse, an accountant, a graphic designer, or some other career? Many students choose to interview someone who is working in a career that they are interested in.

Other students don't have career plans just yet but are planning to transfer to a university and could learn about that through an interview. If you are a parent, you may be interested in talking to another parent to learn more about their parenting style. If you participate in a sport or other activity, you might want to get insight from your coach or instructor.

Maybe you have a friend or relative who shares your culture but who was born and grew up here. Elderly people often like to talk about their lives, and they may have more free time than working people. You could ask about how life has changed over the past 50 years or more.

Who Can You Interview?

One of the goals of this project is to speak English with someone who is very fluent in English. The person can be a native speaker or someone who has lived in an English-speaking country for a long time and whose English skills are very strong. You could interview one of your teachers, but you should not interview an ESL teacher. ESL teachers are used to communicating with ESL students, and you want more of a challenge!

Spend some time brainstorming and think about who you know that you would like to talk to and learn from. It is possible to approach a stranger, but in most cases, it works better if you interview an acquaintance.

Your boss, a co-worker, or an employee would probably be happy to spend some time being interviewed. How about your child's teacher or coach, your spouse's friend, a neighbor, an acquaintance from another class (not an ESL class), your yoga or karate teacher, or someone you know from church or other organization?

You should contact the person ahead of time and make sure that they can spend about 30 minutes talking to you. Be sure to tell them that this is an assignment for a class you are taking—many people are happy to help if they know why you want to ask them questions. You might make a plan to meet at a coffee shop—maybe offer to buy them a cup of coffee or tea in exchange for their time and patience.

How Will You Do the Interview?

If at all possible, try to conduct the interview face-to-face. Talking by telephone is much more difficult and stressful. The purpose of this project is to practice listening and speaking, so e-mail, text messaging, or instant messaging is not acceptable. If you can arrange a video chat, that will work.

You will prepare questions ahead of time and use them to guide the conversation. But your goal is to have a conversation, not just to get answers to your questions. Start informally and try to make the other person comfortable. This isn't a police interrogation!

You can take a few notes during the interview if you want to, but do *not* try to write down everything they say. If you do that, the person will speak more and more slowly and might even end up grabbing your list of questions and just writing down the answers. Don't let that happen! It's important to look at the person and pay attention to what she or he is saying. After the interview is over, you can add to your notes to help you remember what you learned.

During the interview, you may find that your interviewee has already answered one of your questions. For example, if you ask, "How long have you worked here?" she might say, "I started here in 2004. I love this job so much that I could do this for the rest of my life!" If your next question is, "Do you like your job?" skip that question and move on to the next one! Or better yet, ask a follow-up question: "Why do you say that?"

What Questions Should I Ask?

Planning your questions is the most important part of doing an interview. At home, you should brainstorm as many questions as possible—12 to 20 questions. It is much easier to skip a few questions than it is to think up new ones if you run out of things to ask.

You will probably want to start the interview with a few basic factual questions: How long have you lived here? How many children do you have?

But most of the questions should be open-ended rather than yes/no or information questions. What do you like most about . . .? What is the most difficult part of . . .? Why did you choose . . .? What advice would you give . . .? Can you tell me about a time when you felt . . .? What would you do differently . . .? What is your philosophy of . . .? Would you want your children to work as a . . .?

Many Americans will be uncomfortable if you ask their age and especially if you ask questions about money. Rather than asking, "How much money do you make?" ask more indirectly: "What kind of salary could I expect to make if I became a nurse?"

What is the Schedule for this Project?

Your instructor will probably allow 1½ to 2 weeks for you to plan and complete your interview and write up your report. Here's a suggested schedule:

Class meeting 1: Discuss Interview Project, brainstorm ideas, ask and answer any questions about the procedure. (20–30 minutes)

Class meeting 2: Your choice of the person you plan to interview is due. (5 minutes)

Class meeting 3: A list of at least 10 questions is due. Students can share their questions and plans for the interview in small groups while the instructor goes around and checks questions for clarity and grammar. Students can help each other plan more and better questions. (30–45 minutes)

Class meeting 3 or 4: Students can role-play doing an interview, or the instructor could have the class interview him or her for practice. (20 minutes or more)

If possible, your instructor will schedule the due date for the interview report so that you have a weekend to conduct the interview.

Class meeting 5: Interview reports due.

Some Suggestions

After your instructor has checked your interview questions, type them up or write them neatly, leaving an inch or two (several centimeters) between each question. As you ask your questions, you can write a few notes in the space. Remember: the goal is not to write everything down; it is to have a conversation! If taking notes is slowing down the interview, stop writing and just listen. You can write your notes later.

Your instructor might choose to collect your questions but not the answers you wrote down. Again, the most important part of the interview is not the answers, but your experience asking them and listening to the answers.

A Final Thought

A book called *What Color is Your Parachute?* has been offering advice for finding your perfect career for over 30 years. One of the techniques this book suggests is to find someone who is doing the job you are interested in and interview that person. One of the authors of this textbook took that advice back in 1983 and called a local community college to learn more about teaching English as a Second Language. During the conversation, she asked if she could volunteer in a class, and the program director offered her a paid job as a teacher's aide. After working as a teacher's aide for a year, she started taking classes to qualify as a teacher herself, and she has been teaching ever since.

Maybe the interview you conduct can be the beginning of something new for you, too! This project will be as useful to you as you make it.

Interview Report

Your name: _____

Who did you interview?

Why did you choose to interview this person?

What did you learn from the person you interviewed?

How did you feel about the interview? What was successful? What could you improve?

© E. Uyemura, N. Lladó, D. Mochidome. Permission is granted for the owner of this book to make a copy of this page.

CHAPTER 46
On the Hot Seat

One of the most important skills you need is being prepared for a job interview. The job interview helps employers form their first impression of you, and this impression will last for a long time. So it's important to put your best foot forward. You may even be the one interviewing a prospective employee.

It's All About You

It may be difficult for you to "sell" your talents and accomplishments to an employer, but in American culture, you must do it. During the interview, it's important for you to let the interviewer know as much as possible about your talents and strengths. Your answers to each interview question should be about 3 to 5 sentences long.

Don't worry; no one will think that you're being boastful. In fact, an interviewer will be impressed with the range of abilities you have and the benefits that you will bring to the company. For example, as an ESL student, you already have the ability to speak two or more languages and the experience of living in two or more countries. In this competitive global economy, companies want employees who are multilingual and multicultural, so don't hesitate to tell an interviewer that these two words describe you.

At the same time, you must be careful to tell the truth. You may be tempted to make your skills and accomplishments sound better than they really are. However, you need to remember that prospective employers will check your background information and your references, and if they find out that you aren't telling the truth, you will not get the job.

The Little Things Count—Body Language and Dressing for Success

Even though we're taught not to "judge a book by its cover," an interviewer will notice how you dress and carry yourself. Therefore, you should come to the interview "dressed for success."

For non-office jobs, dress neatly and avoid jeans. Wear a shirt with a collar.

For an office job, women and men should wear

- Conservative business attire
- A watch
- No strong perfume or cologne
- No visible tattoos
- No large or jangly jewelry

Men should wear

- A suit (or a sports coat and slacks) and a shirt and a tie
- Dark socks and leather shoes

Women should wear

- A suit, a dress or skirt and blouse with a jacket, or a pantsuit—nothing too revealing
- Closed-toe shoes

In the United States, a firm handshake is very important when you meet someone new. If you grasp a person's hand like a "dead fish," that person will think you're weak or you don't want to shake hands. If you grasp a person's hand too tightly, you may hurt someone! The amount of pressure that you need to hold a tennis racket is the same amount as for shaking hands.

As you shake hands, you should look into the other person's eyes. If you don't do this, the other person will think you are not trustworthy or that you aren't self-confident. If you feel uncomfortable looking into someone's eyes, try looking at her eyebrows instead. Also, while you are speaking with an interviewer, maintain eye contact with her. That way, she will know that you are listening carefully, and you can see how she is reacting to what you are saying.

While you are speaking with the interviewer

- Sit up straight
- Don't cross your arms
- Don't fidget, play with your hair, tap your foot, or make any other nervous gestures

Don't forget to shake hands with the interviewer after the interview, too.

Let's Get Personal

When you apply for a job, the employer may ask you to submit a cover letter and a résumé. In a cover letter, you introduce yourself to a prospective employer, and you describe the type of job you're interested in. A résumé lists your work experience, education, special skills, etc. See the samples at the end of this chapter.

The first question in a job interview is often

- Tell me about yourself.

The best way to respond to, "Tell me about yourself," is not to repeat information that you talked about in the cover letter and the résumé but to talk about your additional job-related talents and abilities instead. If you repeat the same information over and over, the interviewer will think that you don't have much to offer the company. So be prepared to give more information about your talents and strengths in the interview.

If you are applying for a job that requires specific skills, you will probably be asked questions about your experience and training. However, many interviews also include behavioral questions. These are questions about how you have behaved or would behave in a variety of job-related situations. For example:

- Describe a time when you were faced with a stressful situation and how you handled it.
- Tell us about a time when you set a goal and achieved it.

- Tell about a situation in which you had to go beyond the call of duty to get a job done.
- Give an example of a time when you took the initiative to make improvements.

Although some of these questions may seem personal, it is best to keep your answers in the area of work and business. For example, if the interviewer asks you about a time when you had to make a tough decision, this is not the time to talk about choosing between two people who wanted to marry you!

It is helpful to have a plan for how to answer such questions. One such plan is called SOAR. The letters stand for:

- **S**ituation
- **O**bstacle
- **A**ction
- **R**esult

If you are asked about how you handled stress, start by explaining briefly what the Situation was. What was your job and what were your responsibilities? Then explain what the Obstacle was. Obstacle means problem or roadblock. In a sentence or two, explain the problem that came up. Next explain the Action you took. It is important that you focus on your actions, not what other people did. If it took help from others to resolve the problem, keep the focus on your part in making that happen. Finally, end your response by explaining the Result you got.

So let's consider an example:

Ms. Natale: Tell me about a time when you faced a stressful situation and how you handled it.

Tuan: Well, one stressful situation that I had to deal with was the time when I first came to this country, and I got a job delivering pizzas. The pizza company guaranteed that the pizza would be at the customer's door in 30 minutes, which meant that I only had about 15 minutes to drive from the store to the customer's house. If I got lost or confused, the customer would get the pizza free, the company would lose money, and I would lose my job! But I also couldn't speed because a traffic ticket would make me late for sure. So whenever I had free time at work, I would study maps of the area so that I became very familiar with all the streets. And if I was given a delivery to a location that I was unsure of, I would take the time before I went out the door to double-check the map and make sure of one or two possible routes to get there. As a result, I never had to give away a single free pizza, and I saved the company a lot of money. My boss said I was the best driver they had.

Notice how Tuan starts by describing the overall situation (the job) and the obstacle he faced (pressure to make the delivery in a very short amount of time). Then he explains the specific actions he took to deal with that problem, and the outcome or result, emphasizing how his efforts helped the company he worked for. Notice also that he could use this same story to answer a number of different questions that might be asked (a time you took initiative, a time you went beyond the call of duty). So think ahead of time of all the ways that you have used your skills to get a good result.

If you are asked about a situation that you have not actually faced at work, you can use examples from volunteer work or situations that came up in club or other activities, or you can talk about what you would do. But using real-life examples is always best.

And remember that the point of the question, and your answer to it, is to show your good qualities as a worker. So even if the question seems to ask about a failure or a negative situation, look for ways to show your positive qualities and strengths.

Some personal questions that you may be asked include:

- What do you hope a former boss would say about you?
- What motivates you?
- What do you see yourself doing 5 years from now?
- What is an important decision you've made in your professional life? Why was it important?

You should also know that there are some subjects that are illegal for an interviewer to ask you about. These subjects include

- Your age
- What country you are from
- Your religion
- Your marital status, sexuality, or children

If an interviewer asks you a question about one of these subjects, you can ask

- How is this question related to the job?

Don't worry about making the interviewer uncomfortable; it is your right to ask this question.

Accentuate the Positive

The interviewer may ask some questions that make you feel like you will have to give a negative answer. Examples of these types of questions are:

- Why did you leave your last job?
- Do you have any limitations that may prevent you from fulfilling the duties of the position?
- What is a major disappointment in your professional life?
- What do you consider your weaknesses?

Be prepared to answer these questions with a positive spin. Compare these responses to the same question:

Mr. Ochoa: Can you tell me why you left your last job?

Mira: Well, I left Superbox because I felt I wasn't paid enough. I was also stuck in a dead-end job, and there weren't any opportunities for advancement, so I quit.

Mira is telling Mr. Ochoa the truth, but her answer sounds very negative. She should tell the truth but put a more positive spin on it:

Mr. Ochoa: Can you tell me why you left your last job?

Mira: Well, that's a good question. I liked my job at Superbox, but I always want to try new things and learn new skills, so at that point in my life, I was ready for a change. I feel that Astromall will provide me with the opportunities that I've been seeking. For instance, your management training program sounds great . . .

In this response, Mira begins by giving herself a few seconds to think when she says, "Well, that's a good question." Some other sentences of this type include

- Hmmm . . . let me think for a moment.
- Just so I understand, you want to know [*repeat the question*].
- So, what you're asking me is [*repeat the question*].

Then, Mira focuses on the advantages of working for Astromall rather than on her problems at Superbox. She also adds some information that she found while researching the company.

Everybody has weaknesses, but if you are asked about a weakness, try your best to turn even that question in a positive direction. For example, you might be tempted to say that your English skills are your biggest weakness. But that will just give the interviewer a reason not to hire you. So turn your weakness into a strength:

Shin: Some people might say that my language skills are my biggest weakness, but I feel that since coming to this country, it is a challenge that I have worked hard to overcome. In the process, I have had to learn patience, with myself and other people, and I have found that I can master anything if I work hard enough. Becoming bilingual has really made me grow as a person.

In this response, Shin is honest, but he uses the question to talk about his hard work and determination and also manages to remind the interviewer that he is bilingual, which is a strength, not a weakness.

Do Your Homework—Research the Company

Before your interview, you should check the company's website to learn about the company and its most recent projects. An interviewer will almost always make a few comments about the company during the interview, and these comments are your cues to let the interviewer know that you have some knowledge of the company. Some of these questions can include

- What do you know about our company?
- Why do you want to work for our company?
- What can you do to contribute to our company?
- Are you willing to go anywhere the company sends you?
- How do you evaluate a company when you're looking for a job?

The last question in any job interview is almost always

- Do you have any questions?

You should always have one or two questions to ask the interviewer. But there are some questions you should NOT ask. For example

- How much money will I make?
- What kind of health insurance will I get?
- Can you schedule me while my children are in school?
- I planned a vacation in August, so is it okay if I take time off then?

In other words, don't ask about your pay, hours, etc., and don't ask for any special favors.

Instead, you should ask thoughtful questions about the company that will allow the interviewer to talk about the company in detail. For example, if you have some experience volunteering with a youth group, you can ask a question like

- I noticed that your company has started a community outreach program to mentor inner-city youth. Can you give me some details about this program and what the company's long-term goals are regarding this program?

This type of question shows that you are interested in more than just getting a job; you're also interested in the good deeds that the company does for the community. It also gives you the opportunity to tell the interviewer about your experience and commitment to working with young people. You want to end your interview on a strong positive note, and asking carefully-researched, thoughtful questions is a great way to do this.

Follow up

After a job interview, you should always write a thank-you note to the interviewer. Make sure you find out the interviewer's full name, title, and e-mail address. Within 24 hours, send an e-mail thanking the interviewer for her time. If you have thought of an answer that slipped your mind at the interview, you can also mention that in the e-mail. Don't apologize, though! A short, positive note is all that is required. See the sample at the end of the chapter.

It's natural to want to know immediately if you got the job. But you should be patient and wait about a week after the interview for the employer or a company representative to contact you. Usually, an employer needs a week to make a decision as to who gets the job. If a week goes by, and you don't hear anything, you can call the company to see if they've made their decision.

Finally, if you did not get the job, you can ask what you can do to improve your interview skills. That way, you can find out about any mistakes you may have made and how to correct them. Thank the interviewer again, and remind him to keep you in mind if there is another job opening in the future.

Use What You've Learned—The Job Interview

1. Form a group of 3–5 people.

2. As a group, decide if all of you are applying for the same job or if you want each group member to apply for the job of his or her choice.

3. Do some research online to find job listings.

4. Make copies for your interview panel of these job listings and, if you have them, your cover letter and résumé. (See samples at the end of the chapter.)

5. Before the interview, familiarize yourselves with the job you'll be applying for.

6. During the interview period, the panel will take turns interviewing one applicant at a time until everyone in the group has been both an applicant and an interviewer.

7. As an applicant, you must be ready to answer a total of 5–7 questions:
   - Tell me about yourself.
   - 3–5 questions of the interviewers' choice. In other words, the applicant won't know which questions will be asked, just like in a real job interview. Interviewers can choose questions from the list of interview questions at the end of this chapter.
   - Do you have any questions for us?

8. During an interview, each interviewer will fill out an Interviewer's Notes sheet to rate the applicant's interview skills and to make comments.

9. The rest of the class will quietly observe the interviews. They can fill out Interviewer's Notes sheets as well (optional).

10. After the panel has interviewed all of its members, the panel and the rest of the class can discuss the interviews together.

11. Your grade will be based on:
    - Your panel's (and your classmates') totals for the items on the Interviewer's Notes sheet
    - Your answers to interviewers' questions (when you are the applicant)
    - Your responses to applicants' answers as they are speaking (when you are the interviewer)
    - Your Interviewer's Notes for the applicants you interviewed.

12. Be ready, be confident, and above all, good luck!

Interviewer's Notes

Applicant's Name:_____ Date: _____

Interviewer's Name:_____

Rating Scale: 5 = Excellent   4 = Good   3 = Average
                2 = Needs Improvement   1 = Unacceptable

Criteria	Rating	Comments
Greeted the interviewer and shook his/her hand firmly		
Spoke with confidence and enthusiasm		
Maintained good eye contact with the interviewer throughout the interview		
Answered questions directly and completely with answers of an appropriate length		
Turned negative statements and situations into positive ones		
Asked the interviewer appropriate and relevant questions		
Ended the interview in a friendly manner and thanked the interviewer		

Additional Comments

Interview Questions

1. What do you hope a former boss would say about you?
2. What motivates you to do your best?
3. What qualities do you have that make you suitable for this job?
4. What do you see yourself doing 5 years from now?
5. What is an important decision you've made in your professional life?
6. Why did you choose this field?
7. Tell about a mistake you made and how you resolved it.
8. Are you a team player?
9. What is a skill you'd like to improve?
10. What is more important to you, the type of work you do or the hours you work?
11. What do you know about our company?
12. Why do you want to work for our company?
13. What can you do to contribute to our company?
14. Are you willing to go anywhere the company sends you?
15. In your opinion, how is our company different from our competitors?
16. How has your education prepared you for this job?
17. Do you think your grades accurately reflect your academic achievement?
18. What changes would you make in your education, if any?
19. Which academic courses did you like the most?
20. Do you think that on-the-job experience is more important than academic knowledge?
21. What skills have you developed over the last year?
22. Explain any gaps in your résumé.
23. What was the most rewarding part of your previous job?
24. What do you think it takes to be successful in this job?
25. Describe your favorite boss.
26. How do you persuade someone to do something?
27. How do you handle criticism?
28. What do you do if you are unsure about an assignment at work?
29. What do you do if a co-worker doesn't do his or her work?
30. Describe a time when you had to use creativity to solve a problem.
31. Describe a time when you were faced with a stressful situation and how you handled it.
32. Tell us about a time when you set a goal and achieved it.
33. Tell about a situation in which you had to go beyond the call of duty to get a job done.
34. Give an example of a time when you took the initiative to make improvements.
35. Tell me about a difficult decision you've had to make.

Sample Résumé

First Name Last Name
333 W. 300th Street
Somewhere, CA 90001
(333) 555-1111
my-email@gmail.com

Objective: A full-time position with opportunity for advancement.

Education
El Camino College
Torrance CA 90506
Cumulative GPA: 3.2/4.0
Associate's Degree expected June, 2012
Courses in graphic design, Computer Information Systems, and accounting

FarAway High School
Beijing, China
Overall average 91%
Diploma, June, 2006

Work Experience
Math Tutor
Mathematics Department, El Camino College
August, 2009–present
Starting pay: $7.50 an hour. Current pay: $9.00 an hour.

Tutor
Torrance Public Library
September, 2008–June, 2009
Volunteer position, approximately 10 hours per week

Skills
- Read, write, and speak Chinese and English
- Word, Excel, Photoshop, Powerpoint
- Adobe Creative Suite (Illustrator, Photoshop, InDesign, Flash, Acrobat Pro)
- Authorized to work in the United States

Sample Cover Letter

First Name Last Name
333 W. 300th Street
Somewhere, CA 90001
(333) 555-1111
my-email@gmail.com

Mr. Jun Kawasaki
ABC Corporation
2222 W. Main Street
Torrance, CA 90504

Dear Mr. Kawasaki,

I am responding to your job listing for an office assistant. I believe that my background and experience match your needs.

I am skilled at word processing and Excel. My typing speed is 80 words per minute, and I am familiar with both PC and Mac applications.

In addition, my language skills will be an asset to your company since you deal with many customers throughout Asia.

I look forward to meeting with you soon to learn more about the opportunities your company offers and to discuss with you how my skills can meet your needs.

Sincerely,

Sample Thank You Letter

To: JKawasaki
Fr: PJChang
Re: Yesterday's Interview

Dear Mr. Kawasaki,

I would like to thank you for the time you spent with me discussing the office assistant position at ABC Corporation. I am very excited about this position and I am confident that my skills will be perfect for this job.

I meant to mention during the interview that I have taken classes in Windows 7 and Microsoft Office Word 2007. I received a grade of A in both classes, and I am very efficient in all word processing applications.

Please contact me if you have any questions about my ability with Windows 7 or about any of my other qualifications.

I look forward to hearing from you soon about the position, and I want to thank you again for meeting with me.

Sincerely,

Polly Chang

CHAPTER 47
May I Ask You a Few Questions?

Have you ever been stopped at the mall and asked to give your opinion on a new product? Has anyone ever called you to ask who you planned to vote for? Have you ever shared your opinion by answering questions online? If so, you have participated in a survey. For this project, you will work with a small group of classmates to plan, conduct, analyze, and report on a survey about a topic of your choice. It's a great opportunity to talk to people in your community in a structured way. So let's get started.

Class 1: (60 minutes)

Step 1: The first thing you need to decide is what topic you would like to focus on. Here are some suggestions:

- sports
- health
- food
- television
- the Internet
- political issues
- the economy
- jobs
- fashion
- marriage
- parents and children
- another topic of your choice, with the approval of your instructor. (Topics such as religious or sexual issues, while interesting, can be too controversial in some situations, so check with your instructor for approval.)

Since this is a group project, your instructor may want to put several choices on the board and have the class form groups to work on the topic they prefer. Each group should have 5 to 8 members.

Step 2: Get together with your group and start thinking about what questions you want to ask. Think about your purpose. What are you trying to learn about Americans' opinions? As you think about questions, also think about what choices you will give for answers. For this survey, you need to have multiple–choice answers. Let's look at an example. Suppose you choose the topic Marriage. One question you are interested in is what age people believe is the best age to get married. So you create a question:

1. In your opinion, what is the best age for a person to get married?

Now you need some answers. Let's say you try these possible responses:

    a. 18   b. 21   c. 25   d. 30

Not bad, but maybe some people would want to answer 23 or 35 or older. You haven't given them that option. It works best if you provide a range rather than a single number in your answers. So let's try again.

    a. 18–20   b. 21–25   c. 26–30   d. 31–35   e. 36 or older

Now you have covered all the reasonable choices, and you will get useful information as to what age people really think is the ideal age to get married. Notice that we did not put 21–25 and 25–30, because that would put age 25 in two different responses.

As you can see, creating the responses is perhaps more challenging than creating the questions.

Here's another example. Suppose the topic you have chosen is Sports, and you want to ask about people's favorite sport to watch. But there are a lot of sports in the world, and you can't include them all. So let's try this:

1. What sport do you enjoy watching the most?
    a. American football   b. baseball   c. basketball   d. soccer   e. some other sport

By including the answer "some other sport" we provide an answer for hockey and golf fans.

So on Day 1, your group should brainstorm ideas about what you want to ask and think about the responses to include.

At Home: Your homework is to work on your own and write at least 5 possible survey questions, each with 4 or 5 possible responses.

Class 2: (60–90 minutes)

Step 1: Get together with your group and share the ideas you came up with for homework. The goal today is to agree on 5 to 8 questions with responses that the whole group will use for their survey. (It works well if there are the same number of questions as there are members in the group, but this is not essential.) If several people have similar questions, decide exactly how to ask that question and what responses you will include. If you are having a hard time agreeing, your instructor can help you out. The whole group must use the exact same survey questions and the exact same responses in the same order.

Step 2: When you have your final list of questions and responses, your instructor will check it for grammar, spelling, and clarity. After your questions and responses are approved, every member of the group will copy the questions and responses exactly.

Step 3: Make predictions about what answers you think your respondents will give. After conducting the survey, you will compare your predictions with the actual results.

At Home: Neatly type or write the questions and the responses into the Survey Sheet. Every member of the group must have the same numbering, the responses in the same order, the same wording, etc. Do not conduct the survey yet!

Class 3: (45 minutes)

Get together with your group and double check to make sure that everyone has their questions and responses and that they are all the same. Discuss how you will conduct the survey—who will you ask, will you look for people of a certain age range or gender? Will you ask only native-speakers of English or will you include non-native speakers?

The instructor will ask for volunteers to role-play conducting a survey. At first, the instructor may answer one student's questions, and then students from two different groups will role-play asking and answering the questions. Discuss with your instructor guidelines for etiquette and safety in conducting the survey.

Here are some suggestions:

- You may *not* include the students or instructor from this class in your survey.
- You may *not* include students or instructors from your other ESL classes in your survey.
- You *may* include students or instructors from non-ESL classes that you are taking.
- You *may* include students who are studying in the library or hanging out in the cafeteria or student lounge.
- You *may* include people you know, such as neighbors or co-workers.
- Malls and coffee shops are good places to approach people and ask questions.
- Be sure to explain that this is a school assignment, and that it will only take 5 minutes of their time.
- Make sure that you read the questions and possible responses to the person you are surveying. Don't just hand them the paper and ask them to fill it out!
- You might need to ask a preliminary question to see if the person will be able to answer your survey. For example, if you are doing a survey on sports, you might want to ask, "Are you interested in sports?" And if the answer is "No," just say "Thank you" and move on to another person.

At Home: Now you are ready to conduct the survey. Your assignment is to ask **10 people** your survey questions. Record the answers people give you under the questions. Your instructor will probably give you **one week** to complete the survey. If you have questions or concerns, ask your instructor for help.

Class 4: (60 minutes)

Your survey results are due today! It is very important that every member of the group complete the survey on time. Don't let your group down. Today you are going to combine the information from all the members of the group. Using one Analysis Sheet for each question, add up the responses from all the members of the group.

Once you have the results, discuss them. Did people's answers turn out the way you predicted? Are there any surprises?

Each member of the group will prepare an oral report based on one of the questions you asked. If necessary, some students can analyze two questions, or one student can introduce the group and explain the overall topic.

At Home: Prepare a clear visual to explain the question you asked and the results you got. Plan a 1- to 3-minute presentation that will help the class understand your results. Some students may know how to use *Excel* to create a pie chart or bar graph. Be sure to explain what the results mean, as well as the actual numbers, and how your results compared to your predictions.

Class 5: (60–90 minutes) Group presentations

Each group will come up to the front of the class and present their results. Each member of the group will have 1 to 3 minutes to explain one question that their group asked, the possible responses, and what the results were.

Afterward: Each student should complete a Survey Reflection Sheet and hand it in along with the Analysis Sheet.

Survey Sheet

Student's Name:_____

Question 1:				
a.	b.	c.	d.	e.

Responses:

Question 2:				
a.	b.	c.	d.	e.

Responses:

Question 3:				
a.	b.	c.	d.	e.

Responses:

© E. Uyemura, N. Llado, D. Mochidome. Permission is granted for the owner of this book to copy this worksheet as needed for this assignment.

Question 4:				
a.	b.	c.	d.	e.

Responses:

Question 5:				
a.	b.	c.	d.	e.

Responses:

Question 6:				
a.	b.	c.	d.	e.

Responses:

© E. Uyemura, N. Llado, D. Mochidome. Permission is granted for the owner of this book to copy this worksheet as needed for this assignment.

Question 7:				
a.	b.	c.	d.	e.

Responses:

Question 8:				
a.	b.	c.	d.	e.

Responses:

© E. Uyemura, N. Lladó, D. Mochidome. Permission is granted for the owner of this book to copy this worksheet as needed for this assignment.

Analysis Sheet

Student's Name: _____

Question I am Analyzing:

Our Prediction:

Classmates' Names ↓	Response a.	Response b.	Response c.	Response d.	Response e.
Totals →					

© E. Uyemura, N. Llado, D. Mochidome. Permission is granted for the owner of this book to copy this page as needed for this assignment.

Survey Reflection Sheet

Student's Name:_____

1. How did you feel about the way your group worked together to create the survey? Were you satisfied with the topic and the questions you created?

2. How did you feel about conducting the survey? Is there anything that you would do differently the next time?

3. How did you feel about your group's presentation? Were you able to explain your question and responses clearly to the class?

4. What did you learn from doing this survey?

CHAPTER 48
Room for Debate

What is a Debate?

A debate is a contest to see which person or team has the most convincing arguments. You may engage in debates about the economy, presidential elections, stem-cell research, human cloning, immigration laws, the legalization of marijuana, and many other controversial topics. You might debate at home, at work, at school, and even online. It doesn't matter whether you win or lose, but what you learn through the process. When debating, you are not necessarily expressing your own personal opinion about an issue. Good debaters learn to argue both sides of an issue depending on the position that they have been assigned. Debating is very popular in American universities and high schools as it is in many countries around the world. Therefore, learning the art of persuasion will help you succeed in a variety of academic and professional circles.

What are the Benefits of Debating?

Debating requires that you learn how to work as part of a team, develop critical thinking skills, organize ideas based on your research, prepare notes and outlines for your presentation, select the most persuasive arguments, and present them in the most convincing way possible. Class participation is important in the United States, so having the ability to express and support your opinion is beneficial for all students who want to do well in content classes such as history or psychology. High school and college students often participate in regional, national, and even international debate tournaments.

How to Prepare for a Debate

The most important part of a debate is the preparation. First, you must choose which topic you will work on and the position you will defend. Then you will begin to search through books, periodicals, journals, websites, and other sources to find the information needed to support your arguments. You will look not only for the arguments that support your position, but also for arguments that your opponents may present, so that you can respond to them. You should write your notes on index cards to present your position in a well-organized manner.

You may find it helpful to divide up the research. The following are some "fields of inquiry" that you may find useful:

- scientific reasons
- health reasons

- financial reasons
- moral or religious reasons
- psychological reasons
- social reasons
- political reasons
- emotional reasons
- philosophical reasons
- cultural reasons

For example, if you were arguing that cigarette smoking should be banned, you might divide up your research into health reasons, social reasons, and financial reasons. Those arguing against banning cigarette smoking might present philosophical, political, and social reasons.

After you gather your information, you will get together with your team members to make sure you are not duplicating ideas and to check that the information you present is reliable. Choose the most convincing arguments to present to the audience. You should also think about the possible arguments that the opposing team might present and prepare to respond to them.

What are the Do's and Don'ts of Debating?

Do's

- Choose issues that people have different opinions about. For example, crime is a serious problem, but we all agree that crime is bad, so there's not much to debate.
- Research and study your facts carefully before you present them. Cite statistics if available.
- Prepare notes in your own words.
- Anticipate what your opponent is going to say and be ready to respond.
- Be polite and treat your opponents with courtesy and respect.
- Speak with confidence.
- Manage your time carefully.
- Discuss with your instructor whether you can use charts or other visual aids.

Don'ts

- Don't read from your notes or worse yet, from something you printed from the Internet. You should prepare effectively so that you just need a quick glance at your notes to remind you of what you want to say.
- Don't attack your opponent personally.
- Don't raise your voice or get angry.
- Don't speak too fast.
- Don't repeat the same points over and over.

What is the Format of a Debate?

There are two teams of debaters for each topic. The affirmative team is the side that answers the question Yes, and the negative team is the side that answers No. There are two to four students on each team. Your instructor may serve as moderator and timekeeper, or she may assign a student to fill that role.

Both teams have an equal amount of time to speak. The affirmative side speaks first and last. If you are on the affirmative side, you must present convincing arguments to prove that your statement is true. These arguments should be based on facts from your research.

If you are on the negative side, you must present your counter arguments to try to prove that the affirmative team's position is weak, unclear, wrong, or unsubstantiated. Remember that there are no right or wrong answers, just stronger or less convincing arguments. When the debate is over, the class will decide which team was most convincing.

Time Frame for a Debate

The following is a suggested format for a debate that lasts approximately 30 minutes:

First affirmative speaker	5 minutes
First negative speaker	5 minutes
Second affirmative speaker	5 minutes
Second negative speaker	5 minutes
Final statement: negative	3 minutes
Final statement: positive	3 minutes
Questions from audience	4 minutes
Vote by closed ballot or show of hands	1 minute

If the groups have more than 3 members, you may decide to add more time to the debate or to shorten the time each speaker is allotted. In any case, both sides should have the same total amount of time.

After the vote, the instructor and the students may want to take a few minutes to comment on the strengths and weaknesses of the arguments and the presentation.

Sample Debate Outline

Question:

Our Position: Yes… or No…

Reason 1:

Reason 2:

Reason 3:

Reason 4:

Our opponents may argue:

1.

Our Response:

2.

Our Response:

Conclusion:

Sample Grading Rubric for a Debate

Question: _____   _____ Affirmative   _____ Negative

Members: _____
_____
_____
_____

a.	Content of the arguments (research, selection of most convincing arguments)	5 +	4	3	2	1 −
b.	Organization of ideas (well-organized notes)	5 +	4	3	2	1 −
c.	Debating skills (responding to arguments)	5 +	4	3	2	1 −
d.	Language use (clarity, conciseness, speed of delivery, tone of voice)	5 +	4	3	2	1 −
e.	Delivery (eye contact, not reading, time management)	5 +	4	3	2	1 −

Total: _____ (25 pts.)

Comments: _____

_____

_____

_____

25–23 A
22–20 B
19–17 C

Sample Debate Topics

- Should prayer be allowed in public schools?
- Should women be allowed to participate in combat?
- Should high school students be tested for drug use?
- Should same-sex marriage be legal?
- Should same-sex couples be allowed to adopt children?
- Should tattooing be allowed for middle school and high school students?
- Should animal organs be used in human transplant?
- Should marijuana be legalized?
- Should assisted suicide by people who are terminally ill be allowed?
- Should genetically engineered foods be allowed?
- Should children born in the United States to undocumented parents be citizens of the United States?
- Should texting while driving be legal?
- Does the use of computers contribute to anti-social behavior?
- Should the United States require carmakers to make more cars using alternative fuels?
- Should governments limit use of carbon-based fuels to fight global warming?
- Should parents be allowed to home-school their children?
- Should parents be allowed to use physical punishment to discipline their children?
- Should teenagers be allowed to get credit cards?
- Should drunk drivers receive a jail sentence?
- Should money be spent on Olympic Games, the World Cup, the Miss Universe contest and similar activities during a recession?
- Should the use of animal fur in clothing be banned?
- Should animals be used in medical research?
- Should the legal age for drinking alcohol be lowered from 21 to 18?
- Are airport security measures too intrusive on personal privacy?
- Should nuclear power be used in this country?

CHAPTER 49
Think on Your Feet

We never know when and where we may be called upon to speak in front of a group without having adequate time to prepare our remarks and to practice them beforehand. Therefore, being able to speak for several minutes without much preparation time is a real gift.

Probably the easiest way to get started is to think of a specific example from your own life that reflects the topic in some way. The most important—and difficult—part of impromptu speaking is sticking to the topic. When we feel a bit nervous, we may go away from the topic and start talking about unrelated topics. If we aren't careful, before we know it, we are talking about a completely different subject than the one we began with. As a result, we may end up with a speech that seems unfocused and disorganized. Therefore, it is important to have a plan before you start speaking so that you know which points you want to emphasize and how you want to end your speech.

A good basic format for an impromptu speech is

- Introduction to the topic
- First example OR story
- Second example OR story
- Third example OR story
- Conclusion that ties everything together

Here is an example of an outline for an impromptu speech on the next page:

Impromptu Speech Outline

Introduction

Copy the quotation and its author, if any, here:
"No pain, no gain"

What does this quotation mean to you?
You will get into shape if you work out until your body hurts = You must work hard and endure hardships to be successful

Your first example/story about this quotation:
My weight problem in college—was 25 pounds overweight—clothes didn't fit anymore, had trouble climbing stairs, knees hurt
Loved to eat but went on a strict vegetarian diet for 6 months—watched people eat pepperoni pizza, Thanksgiving dinner—I ate steamed vegetables and salads (which I don't like)
Worked out every day—took aerobics (hated it), ran around ECC track (boring), lifted weights (sore muscles)
Finally was in the best shape of my life and felt great!

Your second example/story about this quotation:
Greg—wanted to study art, but his parents wanted him to study business and kicked him out of the house without any money
Paid for school with 3 part-time jobs—deliveryman, store clerk, bartender—for 6 years
Lived in a crowded apartment in a dangerous neighborhood, ate instant noodles and peanut butter sandwiches
Finally, after graduating, got a well-paying job at a design company

Your third example/story about this quotation:
Grandma came to the U.S.—couldn't speak English, was very poor
Worked hard—took care of 6 kids, worked in the fields, supported the family financially when Grandpa was sick
Cried while the family was asleep—her back hurt, had mean co-workers—but never complained, got stronger, and was respected by all
Finally saved enough money to buy the farm her children have today

Conclusion

What is the lesson you want the audience to get from your speech?
As you can see, we can gain success after we experience pain in our lives. When we survive a period of stress and hard work, any accomplishments we achieve are much sweeter.

Now You Try It—Quotations

- You have 10 minutes to prepare for this speech
- Before you speak, make an outline so that you have a basic plan for your speech
- Your speech should be 1–3 minutes long
- Draw one quotation out of a box to see which quotation you will speak about:

1. "It is only with the heart that one can see clearly. The most important things are invisible to the eyes." (Antoine de Saint-Exupéry)

2. "Laughter is the best medicine."

3. "If you enjoy what you do, you'll never work another day in your life."

4. "The trouble with doing something right the first time is that nobody appreciates how difficult it was." (Walt West)

5. "I do not know the key to success, but the key to failure is trying to please everyone." (Bill Cosby)

6. "A loving person lives in a loving world. A hostile person lives in a hostile world. Everyone you meet is your mirror." (Ken Keyes)

7. "My best friend is the one who brings out the best in me." (Henry Ford)

8. "Being defeated is only a temporary condition. Giving up is what makes it permanent."

9. "It is important to remember that the entire population of the universe, with one minor exception, is composed of others." (Andrew J. Holmes)

10. "Wisdom is knowing what to do, skill is knowing how to do it, and virtue is doing it."

11. "We receive three educations: one from our parents, one from our teachers, and one from the world. The third one contradicts everything the first two teach us."

12. "Experience is the name we give our mistakes." (Oscar Wilde)

13. "The love of money is the root of all evil." (St. Paul in the Bible, I Tim. 6:10)

14. "A friend in need is a friend indeed."

15. "When there's a will, there's a way."

16. "Don't count your chickens before they're hatched."

17. "Haste makes waste."

18. "Two heads are better than one."

19. "You can't judge a book by its cover."

20. "It's better to be safe than sorry."

21. "Out of sight, out of mind."

22. "Absence makes the heart grow fonder."

23. "Money can't buy happiness."

24. "Too many cooks spoil the soup."

25. "Every cloud has a silver lining."
26. "Beauty is only skin deep."
27. "Penny wise but pound foolish."
28. "You get what you pay for."
29. "If you snooze, you lose."
30. "What goes around, comes around."
31. "If the world were perfect, it wouldn't be." (Yogi Berra, baseball star)
32. "I'm the straw that stirs the drink." (Reggie Jackson, baseball star)
33. "Fight fire with fire."
34. "Love is blind."
35. "When in Rome, do as the Romans do."
36. "Do as I say, not as I do."

Impromptu Speech Outline

Introduction:
(Copy the quotation and its author, if any, here):

What does this quotation mean to you?

Your first example/story about this quotation:

Your second example/story about this quotation:

Your third example/story about this quotation:

Conclusion:
What is the lesson you want the audience to get from your speech?

CHAPTER 50
Going Solo

Standing in front of the class to deliver a speech can be an intimidating experience. It's not easy to give a speech even in your native language, and doing it in your second language is a real challenge. You may worry that you will get nervous and forget what you are going to say. But with preparation and practice, you can overcome your fears and learn to communicate with confidence and clarity. You may be called upon to give a speech or presentation in other classes and in your career. In this class, you will have a friendly and sympathetic audience, so it's a great opportunity to get some experience.

Let's take it step by step. The first decision you have to make is what to talk about. Choose a topic that you know well and that you think your classmates would be interested in. You may not be an expert on global issues, but everyone is an expert on something. Sharing your expertise with your classmates is exciting.

Here are some general ideas for topics:

- Something related to your job or career
- Something related to your major
- A hobby or special interest
- Something you know how to make, fix, or do
- A specific place to visit in your country
- One holiday or one custom from your country or culture
- A place you have visited in the United States
- A plan for the perfect day in a vacation spot

As you think about your topic, you need to keep in mind that your speech should be approximately 5 minutes long. That means you need to choose a topic that you can cover in 5 minutes. Some topics are much too broad, and some might be too narrow.

Your first thought might be: My country or my culture. Don't do it! You cannot tell us about your entire country or culture in 5 minutes, and as a result, your speech will be vague and boring. Instead, choose one specific aspect of your culture, or one particular location in your country.

You may need to do a little bit of research as you prepare your speech, but your topic should be something that you are already familiar with. You will not have time to become an expert on an unfamiliar topic, and you may end up copying too much information from the Internet.

Some topics might be too narrow to talk about for 5 minutes or too hard to describe. Suppose you tried to explain how to tie your shoes or ride a bicycle. It's not easy to put into words, and it's too detailed.

Here are some topics that our students have chosen for successful speeches:

- How to make chocolate chip cookies
- A game to help you improve your English
- How to solve Rubik's Cube™
- Why you should adopt a dog
- Planning a visit to Yosemite National Park
- How to have a good time at Disneyland
- How to do CPR
- How to avoid getting the flu
- How to take a person's blood pressure
- Why we Muslim women wear hijab
- The real meaning of Easter
- A romantic weekend in San Francisco
- Obon festival in Japan
- New Year's in Vietnam
- Las Posadas in Mexico
- Teacher's Day in my country
- How to read food nutrition labels
- Why you should be a vegetarian
- How to make your own greeting cards
- Being an international nanny
- How to change a flat tire
- How to make flower sushi
- How to dance salsa
- My journey to the Himalayas
- Enjoy your visit to Hearst Castle
- How to visit New York City without spending a fortune
- A trip to Mount Rushmore
- Places to see in Washington DC for free
- The volcano in my hometown
- How to be a successful waitress
- How to cook rice without a rice cooker
- How to draw a person's face
- Spend a day in Tokyo
- How to keep your kids happy on a 14-hour plane trip
- An easy and delicious salad
- You can change your own oil in your car
- How to buy a car without getting ripped off
- Planning a great "staycation"
- How to wear hanbok
- Setting the table for Nowruz
- A special party for a one-year old baby in my culture

- What to do on your first trip to Las Vegas
- Different styles of Japanese kimono
- What to eat to live a longer life
- How to improve your golf game
- How to make an origami toy
- A traditional Indian wedding
- How to personalize your computer
- What a make-up artist can do
- Some easy ideas for your kids' Halloween costumes

After choosing your topic, start to think about your visual element. For this assignment, you are required to prepare some sort of visual aid to support your topic. You can make a Powerpoint™ or you can use an overhead projector. Consider including pictures, photos, charts, maps, or actual objects. The visual aid is important, but it is only an aid. The speech itself is more important than the visual aid, so don't spend all your time on the Powerpoint™ and then forget to practice your speech!

There should be very few words in your visual aid. If you are writing whole sentences in your Powerpoint,™ you are probably going to end up reading them, so don't let that happen.

Once you've chosen an interesting topic and prepared some visual aids, you need to plan your speech. You should make an outline or a few notes about key words to remind you of what you want to say. Don't write out the entire speech! You are not going to read your speech, and you are not going to memorize it. Reading makes a speech really boring. Your pronunciation is worse when you read, and your classmates will fall asleep if you are looking down at a piece of paper and reading to them.

Memorizing is even worse! When students try to memorize their speech, they usually get stuck at some point. Then they stand there, staring at the ceiling, unable to say a word, or they start over and speak faster and faster, trying to get the words out quickly before they forget them. Don't be the person standing in front of the class like a deer in the headlights!

So if you aren't supposed to read your speech or memorize it or even write it out, how are you going to know what to say? Well, there's an old joke that gives the answer:

A little boy carrying a violin case asks a man on the street: How do you get to Carnegie Hall (a famous concert hall in New York City)?

The wise old man answers him: Practice, practice, practice!

That's what you need to do to prepare for your speech as well. You have to practice it. That means not just imagining yourself saying it, but actually saying the words out loud. Successful speakers practice out loud at least 5 times. Lock your door, sit in your car, or hide in the bathroom if you must, but find a time and place to actually say your speech several times. Time yourself or have a friend listen and time you. If you can't finish the speech in 5 minutes, decide what you need to cut. If you finish up in 2 minutes flat, think about what you could add to make it more complete.

As you plan, prepare, and practice, think about the things that good speakers do (or the mistakes that bad speakers make). Here are some characteristics of a good speech:

- Loud, clear voice: If we can't hear you, nothing else will matter! Speaking in a soft voice only makes you look (and feel) more nervous.

- Eye contact: Look at your audience as you speak. And look at the whole audience, not just the instructor or a couple of your friends. Move your eyes around from one part of the audience to another as you give your speech. Don't turn your back on your audience to look at the board or screen!

- Body language: We've all seen speakers who rock back and forth, lean on the podium, look at their feet or the ceiling, or move around too much or too little. Practice standing up straight with your hands resting lightly on the podium or table. You can move if you have a reason to move, but don't pace back and forth like a lion in a cage! Don't tap a pencil or twist your hair.

- Fluency: Don't you, um, hate it uh, uh, uh, when someone is, like, um, you know, talking and they um, uh, fill their speech with empty sounds while they search for words (or worse yet, ask their classmates to translate the word for them!) How can you speak more smoothly? Practice, practice, practice!

- Vocabulary: As you prepare your speech, you need to make sure you know the vocabulary you need for your topic. Write down key words. If you are describing how to cook your favorite recipe, the middle of the speech is not the time to be learning the names of the ingredients or techniques!

- Pronunciation: No one's pronunciation is going to be perfect. But as with vocabulary, you can practice in advance the pronunciation of any difficult words.

- Visuals: Make sure ahead of time that your visual will work. Don't start your speech with 5 minutes of struggling with the computer. Do not use other people's videos (from youtube.com, for example) in your speech.

Rubric for Speech

Topic and Content 10 points	• Your topic is interesting and appropriate for the audience • Your speech is informative; information is clearly presented • Your topic is focused, not too broad or too narrow • You show good knowledge of the topic
Visual Aid 10 points	• Your visuals are neat, visually attractive, readable, easy to see • Your visuals are useful in helping your audience understand your topic • Your visual aid does not contain the text of your speech • You do not spend so much time getting your visual to work that it detracts from your speech
Preparation 10 points	• You are ready on time • It is obvious that you have practiced and prepared effectively
Presentation 30 points	• You speak with a loud, clear voice • You make good eye contact and look around at audience • Your body language is good—no distracting actions, not turning away from audience to look at screen • You are not reading; you did not memorize; you use notes effectively
Pronunciation 20 points	• Your overall pronunciation is understandable • You use stress and intonation to help audience understand • Your key words have been practiced so that they are understandable • Specific sounds are as correct as possible and don't interfere with understanding
Grammar and Vocabulary 10 points	• Your vocabulary is adequate for clear communication • Your grammar is adequate for clear communication
Length and Fluency 10 points	• Your speech is 4–6 minutes long (You will lose points for a speech that is too short OR too long) • You speak at a good rate, no long pauses or distracting sounds (ummm, ummm)

Grading Sheet for Speech

Topic and Content 10 points	
Visual Aid 10 points	
Preparation 10 points	
Presentation 30 points	
Pronunciation 20 points	
Grammar and Vocabulary 10 points	
Length and Fluency 10 points	

CHAPTER 51
A Panel of Experts

What is a Panel Discussion?

A panel discussion is a guided discussion by a group of four to six speakers who exchange their points of view on a topic. The subject should be of interest not only to the members of the panel but also to the audience. As students, you have many concerns about your academic and professional goals and contemporary social issues that may affect your lives. Panel discussions are an excellent opportunity for you to enhance your critical thinking and speaking skills.

How to Prepare for a Panel Discussion

A panel consists of a group of experts on a specific topic. Even though you may not feel like an expert, you can become knowledgeable about your topic through Internet research, newspaper and magazine articles, videos, or information gathered from experts.

After you and your team members have completed your research, you will work with the moderator to plan the discussion. You should not read from a prepared speech. Speaking naturally and using well-organized notes will make your presentation more interesting. You do not need visual aids or a Powerpoint™ presentation.

Think about the seating arrangement. A semi-circle of chairs will allow the panelists to see each other and the audience. The moderator should sit in the middle of the group.

Guidelines for a Panel Discussion

- Your panel will consist of four to six members.
- The panelists should represent a variety of opinions on the topic.
- You will each have a time limit, perhaps five minutes, to present your point of view.
- There should be 10 to 15 minutes for questions and answers after the panelists have led their discussion.
- The audience should be respectful and allow panelists to speak without interruption.
- The overall panel discussion should not last more than thirty minutes.

How to Conduct a Panel Discussion

1. The moderator introduces the topic or theme of the discussion to the audience and begins the discussion.

2. The panel members are called in a pre-determined order to explain their points.
3. After all panel members have presented their ideas, any panel member may react to or add to views presented by the other panelists.
4. At the end of the panel discussion, the moderator briefly summarizes the different points of view.
5. Finally, the audience can ask additional questions.

The Role of the Moderator

The moderator may be the instructor or a student who is well-informed about the issue being discussed. The main role of the moderator is to keep the panel discussion going, without taking sides.

After all the members of the panel have spoken, the moderator will ask for questions from the audience. She may need to re-word the questions to make them clearer. The moderator will try to keep the questions focused so that more questions can be answered in a short period of time. If there are no questions from the audience, the moderator should be prepared to ask a few questions herself.

It's important to make sure that the panel discussion stays within the allotted time. There should be time for the team to present their information, answer questions, and provide closing remarks. The moderator needs to check the time and remind the panel how much time is left.

Sample Panel Discussion Topics

- Television and movies can have positive or negative effects on children's behavior. What criteria should parents use when deciding what their children can or cannot watch? Should the same criteria apply to teenagers?
- What has been the impact of the large number of immigrants on the United States?
- Teenage suicide has increased in the last ten years. What are the reasons for this social problem and what can be done to prevent it?
- Anorexia and bulimia are very common eating disorders among teenagers and adults. What are the possible causes and solutions?
- What are the possible effects of same-sex marriages on children?
- What are the major problems related to global warming? What measures should be taken to control this problem?
- What are the dangers of cell phone use? What restrictions are needed?
- What are the privacy issues raised by social networking sites like Facebook™?
- What are the advantages and disadvantages of cell phones, mp3 players, iPods™, and other electronic devices for society in general?
- Should teachers be allowed to use physical punishment to discipline children? Should parents?
- What should be the consequences for students who copy research papers or plagiarize in other ways?
- What are the advantages and disadvantages of bilingual education?

- How can schools and parents help prevent bullying?
- What are the advantages and disadvantages of debt consolidation and/or declaring bankruptcy in today's economy?
- What factors should be considered when choosing a career? What careers will be the most popular and most lucrative in the years ahead?
- How can society balance security concerns and privacy rights?
- What are the effects of violent video games on young people? Should limits be placed on these games?
- Should the government fund space research? How can the costs and potential benefits be balanced?

Evaluation Form for a Panel Discussion

Topic _____

Presenter's Name _____

1. The points presented were well-researched	5 +	4	3	2	1 −
2. The points were presented in a well-organized and succinct manner	5 +	4	3	2	1 −
3. The presenter adhered to the assigned time frame	5 +	4	3	2	1 −
4. The points were presented clearly and audibly, not read	5 +	4	3	2	1 −
5. The speaker made appropriate eye contact with panel members and audience	5 +	4	3	2	1 −

Total: _____

25–23 A
22–20 B
19–17 C

Comments: _____

_____

_____

_____

_____

CHAPTER 52
Scenes from American History

Putting on a play (also called a drama) for your classmates is a great way to work on your pronunciation. Most of the time, you read a sentence only once and then move on to something else, but when preparing for a drama, you will practice saying your lines over and over. You can work carefully on individual sounds, the correct pronunciation of the words, and your overall intonation in the sentences.

You will also learn about American history and culture as you practice and present these plays. And you and your fellow cast members will have a lot of fun at the same time.

Preparing for Your Performance

You do **not** have to memorize your lines. This is called reader's theatre, meaning that the actors read from scripts. But you do need to practice so that you can read smoothly and make eye contact with each other and the audience. The more you practice, the better your performance will be!

Here's a suggested schedule for practice:

Day 1: Decide which dramas to do and who will be in each group. Sit in a circle with your group and read through your entire drama, taking turns around the circle to read each section, but do not assign roles yet. At home, read the whole script through again. Make sure you understand and can pronounce all the vocabulary. (approximately 30 minutes of class time)

Day 2: Decide who will take each role. Mark the lines of your role with a highlighter. Sit in a circle and read through the drama several times. Your instructor will work with each group to give corrections and suggestions on pronunciation and intonation. At home, practice saying your lines out loud. (approximately 45 minutes of class time)

Days 3 and 4: Discuss any props that you might want to use (a book, an article of clothing, etc.) Could you include any pictures or music to add to your drama? Today, stand up as you practice your drama several times. The instructor will move from group to group offering help and suggestions as needed. (30–45 minutes of class time.)

Day 5: Bring any props or other materials that you plan to use. Today you will "block" the drama, which means you will plan who will stand where, what actions you will use, make sure that you aren't turning your back to the audience, etc. Run through the entire drama at least twice. (45–60 minutes of class time.) Continue to practice your lines out loud at home several times.

Day 6: Showtime! You should be very familiar with your lines so that you can look up from your script and say the words smoothly and with feeling. Each drama presentation will take about 10 minutes, but allow at least 20 minutes to be sure everyone has enough time to get set up and to receive the applause of their classmates!

Some Suggestions for the Instructor

You can assign specific dramas and roles, but another suggestion is to allow students to choose which dramas they want to do. Put the titles on the board, explain each topic and the number of roles, and then invite students to put their name under the one they like the most. You will probably have to do a little re-organizing and re-negotiating to get the right number of students in each play.

There is some flexibility in the number of players in each drama. You can have 3 or more narrators if you need more roles, or you can have one player take several of the smaller roles if you have fewer students. If your class is small, you can do 2 dramas, with half the class watching while the other half performs. If you have a large group, you will be able to do 3 or 4 of the dramas.

Once students have been divided into groups, they can work together to decide who will take each role, or you can help with this. Some groups prefer to draw names, while others want to give the lead roles to the strongest members. If there are students whose attendance is irregular, you might give them a smaller role, which could be filled by another student if they are absent. You could assign one student in the group as the director, or a leader might arise spontaneously. Female students are sometimes more willing to play male roles than vice versa. You might want to explain the practice of color-blind and gender-blind casting to your class if that is a concern.

With a little encouragement, students can be quite creative in adding personal touches to their dramas—they might want to do some background research and prepare a Powerpoint™ with illustrations, or use lights and music to add a theatrical touch. Some students may even choose to memorize their lines. Costumes are not necessary, but simple props such as a hat or shawl can add interest. Also, consider video-recording or taking and sharing photographs.

If practical, it's helpful to let students practice in empty classrooms or outside or in the hallway for the last few run-throughs, to keep the element of surprise.

If your class meets 5 days a week, you could complete the entire activity in just over a week, but in most situations, it will help to spread the practice over 2 or even 3 weeks. In classes that last 2 or 3 hours, you will probably want to schedule the drama practice for the last 45 minutes or so of each class, and students can run through the drama at least twice each time. If your class time is 50 or 60 minutes, schedule several 20 minute practices, which will only allow a single read-through in most cases.

This is a great culminating activity for the semester, integrating everything students have worked on and leaving them with a warm glow. You might schedule it for the last day of class and serve simple refreshments at the end.

Permission is granted for each student to make one photocopy of one play to use as a script. If the pages are stapled twice on the left side like a booklet, the script is easier to handle. These plays may be performed in classroom settings only. For any other use, contact the publisher for permission.

Drama #1: Benjamin Franklin: Inventor and Patriot

Drama #2: The Wright Brothers: First to Fly

Drama #3: Rosa Parks and the Montgomery Bus Boycott

Drama #4: John F. Kennedy: A Life Cut Short

DRAMA 1
Benjamin Franklin: Inventor and Patriot

Characters: 9 players (6 major roles, 3 small roles)

Narrator 1
Narrator 2
Josiah Franklin, Ben's father
Young Ben
Friend 1 (small role)
Friend 2 (small role)
James Franklin, Ben's older brother
Older Ben
John Hancock (small role)

Narrator 1: Benjamin Franklin is one of the most amazing men in American history. During his long life, he made many scientific discoveries and inventions. His writings influenced the American people's ideas not only during his lifetime, but ever since. And he helped create the American government. As a result, he is sometimes called The First American.

Narrator 2: Ben Franklin was born in Boston, in the Massachusetts colony, in 1706. His father, Josiah Franklin, had been born in England, but Josiah immigrated to Boston in 1683. Josiah had 17 children. Benjamin was number 15. To support his large family, Mr. Franklin ran a small business making soap and candles from animal fat. When Ben was 10 years old, his father began to think about a career for the boy.

Father: Ben, you have been in school now for two whole years. It is time for you to learn a trade. Do you want to work with me making soap and candles?

Young Ben: Sir, there's so much I want to learn. Can't I stay in school?

Father: Perhaps you would like to become a minister? I could try to find the money for you to study to become a pastor.

Young Ben: I appreciate that, sir, but I don't want to be a minister. I just want to learn as much as I can.

Father: I'm sorry Ben, but in that case, you will begin working with me to learn my trade.

Young Ben: The smell of animal bones and fat being melted to make soap and candles makes me feel ill!

Father: As long as you live under my roof, you will help me with my work and learn a useful trade.

Narrator 1:	So Benjamin left school after only two years of formal education. But for the rest of his life, he read everything he could get his hands on.
Narrator 2:	For the next two years, young Ben worked in his father's hot, smelly workplace. In his free time, Ben learned to swim and had fun with his friends.
Young Ben:	Feel how strongly the wind pulls on this kite. I wonder what would happen if....
Friend 1:	(looking into the distance) What in the world?
Friend 2:	Isn't that Ben Franklin out there in the pond?
Friend 1:	But how is he moving so fast?
Friend 2:	I know he's a good swimmer, but no one can swim that fast! Look, he's just lying on his back and holding onto a string!
Young Ben:	I had an idea that if I used a kite, I could hold onto it and let it pull me across the water. And it worked! I loved inventing new ideas. But I did not love working for my father.
Narrator 1:	Finally, when he was 12, Ben spoke to his father again about his future. His half-brother James, who was 9 years older than Ben, had a new printing business.
Young Ben:	Father, I have worked hard for you and tried my best. But this is not the work I want to do. My brother James is looking for an apprentice in his printing shop. I want to work with books and ink. Will you apprentice me to him?
Father:	You will be required to work for him until you are 21 in exchange for your room and board. You must respect and obey him. In return, he will teach you a trade that will allow you to make your living for the rest of your life.
Young Ben:	I promise I will work hard! I'll do whatever he tells me.
Narrator 2:	So Ben went to work for his brother James. He loved the work of a printer. James started a newspaper, expressing his opinions to the world. Ben also wanted to write for the paper. But James wasn't interested in the ideas of his little brother.
James:	*The New England Courant* is a new kind of newspaper. It is independent and I can publish whatever I want.
Young Ben:	Sir, please look at the letter I have written. Would you include this in this week's paper?
James:	You are only 15 years old! No one wants to read the opinions of an apprentice. Pay attention to your work and let me do the thinking and the writing.
Young Ben:	Yes, sir.
Narrator 1:	But Ben didn't give up so easily.

James:	A letter arrived today from Mrs. Silence Dogood. She is a middle-aged widow and her letter is so amusing that I'm sure our readers will enjoy it. I will include it in this week's paper.
Young Ben:	(an aside to the audience) At last! My very own words in print! Even if I did have to pretend to be a woman named Mrs. Dogood to fool my brother!
James:	Everyone is asking about Widow Dogood. Several men have approached me to ask about marrying her! But I had to tell them that her identity is a mystery to me. All I know is that every other week, a new letter is slipped under my door.
Narrator 2:	James was not a man with a good sense of humor. When he discovered that his little brother Ben was the one writing the Mrs. Dogood letters, he was furious.
James:	Benjamin! You have made me the laughingstock of all of Boston! You lied and you disobeyed me! You will be punished for this.
Narrator 1:	Benjamin didn't stay around to receive his punishment. He ran away from his brother and moved to Philadelphia, over 300 miles away.
Narrator 2:	A few years later, Benjamin Franklin had his own printing business. He began publishing an annual book that he called *Poor Richard's Almanack*. In addition to predictions about the weather and other useful information, he included the proverbs for which he became well-known.
Older Ben:	A penny saved is a penny earned . . . Early to bed and early to rise makes a man healthy, wealthy, and wise . . . Well done is better than well said . . . Nothing is certain except death and taxes . . . Fish and visitors smell after three days . . . Beware of little expenses. A small leak will sink a great ship.
Narrator 1:	In the 1750s, when Franklin was in his 40s, he wrote a letter about an experiment with a kite and a key proving that lightning was electricity.
Older Ben:	(writing) When rain has wet the kite twine so that it can conduct the electric fire freely, you will find it streams out plentifully from the key, at the approach of your knuckle, . . . and therefore the sameness of the electrical matter with that of lightening is completely demonstrated.
Narrator 2:	Most likely, Ben did not actually stand in the rain and pull electricity out of a thunderstorm, because other men who tried the experiment were killed! But the image of Ben Franklin flying a kite will always remain in our imagination. Some of his other inventions are not as well known, but they were just as important.
Older Ben:	(holding a pair of glasses) I call these bifocals, because they allow me to see both near and far. If you want to keep your home from being struck by lightning, you should try my lightning rod. It pulls the lightning safely into the ground. And do you want to keep your home warm? My Franklin stove is much more efficient than any fireplace.

Narrator 1: Franklin spent many years of his life in Europe, but his heart was always in America, and when he learned that the American patriots were rebelling against Britain in 1775, he knew he had to return to America. He was chosen to help write the Declaration of Independence, along with Thomas Jefferson, John Adams, and two other men. But an illness called gout left him in pain.

Older Ben: Owww, my foot is too painful to touch! Let me see what Tom and John have written here: "We hold these truths to be self-evident, that all men are created equal, that they are endowed by their Creator with certain unalienable Rights, that among these are Life, Liberty and the pursuit of Happiness." Hmm, I couldn't have said it better myself!

Narrator 2: A few days later, the most prominent men in America signed their name to this document, declaring that the 13 American colonies were an independent country. It was a serious moment, because Britain would surely not let its colonies go without a fight, but Ben kept his sense of humor, making a clever joke.

John Hancock: (writing) John Hancock. There, my signature is big enough that King George won't need his glasses to read it. Now we all must hang together.

Older Ben: Yes, we must, indeed, all hang together, or most assuredly we shall all hang separately.

Narrator 1: Ben Franklin was not hanged by the British king. Throughout the American War of Independence, he served as Ambassador to France, representing his young country. He returned to America in 1785 to assist with writing the United States Constitution.

Narrator 2: When Benjamin Franklin died in 1790 at the age of 84, over 20,000 people attended his funeral. George Washington is known as the father of his country, but Benjamin Franklin might also deserve that title. He was never president, but his ideas influenced America and the world. Not bad for the youngest son of a candle-maker, who only attended school for 2 years!

DRAMA 2
Wilbur and Orville Wright: The First to Fly

Characters: 8 players (6 major roles, 2 small roles)

Narrator 1
Narrator 2
Young Wilbur Wright
Young Orville Wright
Father Wright (small role)
Friend (small role)
Adult Wilbur Wright
Adult Orville Wright

Narrator 1: For thousands of years, humans looked at birds and dreamed of flying. An ancient story told about a young man named Icarus, who attached feathers to his arms with wax and flew. But Icarus flew too close to the sun, which melted the wax. The feathers fell off, and Icarus fell into the sea and drowned.

Narrator 2: Two young men in Dayton, Ohio, also dreamed of flying. Wilbur Wright was born in 1867 and his younger brother Orville in 1871. Their dream of flying started when they were eleven and seven years old. Their father brought home a gift for his two youngest sons.

Father: Look what I've brought you!

Young Wilbur: A stick with a rubber band and a propeller?

Young Orville: What is it? How does it work?

Father: You twist it like this and then let it go and . . .

Young Wilbur: It flies!

Young Orville: What is it called?

Father: It's a helicopter.

Young Wilbur: Come on, Orville, let's take this outside and play!

Narrator 1: The two boys played with their wonderful new toy for days, until the little machine fell apart. Then they had another idea.

Young Wilbur: Let's make an even bigger one! Maybe it can lift a stone into the air.

Young Orville: We can make it twice as big and it should be twice as strong.

339

Narrator 2: But it didn't work. When they made a bigger version of the toy helicopter, it wouldn't fly. The boys didn't know it, but a helicopter twice as large needed 8 times as much energy to fly. They continued to work on toys that could fly, however.

Young Orville: I need a little money, but Father says I have to earn it myself.

Young Wilbur: What about those kites you are always making? Maybe some of our friends would like to buy a kite.

Young Orville: It costs too much to buy the wood for the frame. But maybe if I cut each piece in half and made it thinner…

Narrator 1: The wood in Orville's kites was so light that the wood bent when he flew it.

Young Orville: Look at it go! This is the best kite ever!

Young Wilbur: The thin wood curves and the curved kite flies better than other kites. Hmm, I wonder why?

Friend: How much do you want for a kite like that?

Narrator 2: Wilbur and Orville had learned two important lessons: new methods might work better than the usual methods, and new ideas could make an inventor some money!

Narrator 1: Wilbur and Orville both attended high school, but neither one graduated or went to college. Instead, they started a business.

Adult Orville: Look, I made my own printing press. I went to the junkyard and found some parts, and it really works.

Friend: What can you do with it?

Adult Wilbur: We can help Father by printing the church newspaper on it. But suppose we took some wood and the top of an old folding wagon top . . . we could print more pages per hour and fold them automatically too.

Narrator 2: Amazingly, the hand-made printing press the two brothers made really did work, and they were in business for themselves. They started a newspaper when Orville was just 18 years old and his brother Wilbur was 22. They hired their friend Ed to help out.

Narrator 1: But a new hobby suddenly caught their interest—bicycles! Bicycles were just becoming popular, and naturally, two young men who loved mechanical things were excited. They left their friend Ed in charge of the printing business and opened a new shop.

Adult Wilbur: There how does that look? "Wright Cycle Company."

Adult Orville: It's a great shop, Will. But instead of just selling and repairing bicycles, I think we can build them ourselves. Then we can offer our customers personalized bicycles to meet their needs.

Narrator 2: Their bicycle shop was a great success, but several years later, Orville became seriously ill with typhoid fever. Wilbur sat with his brother day and night, and

	to pass the time, he read to him about an inventor who was trying to create a flying machine.
Adult Wilbur:	Listen to this, Orv. A man in Germany named Otto Lilienthal has invented a glider. He has made thousands of flights, jumping off a hill and gliding safely to the ground.
Adult Orville:	I'd love to give that a try. But jumping off hills will never get you anywhere. A machine that can fly needs an engine.
Adult Wilbur:	It says here that Otto *did* add an engine to his glider, but that's when he crashed and died. I am going to write to the Smithsonian Institute in Washington to get all the information I can about what other inventors have tried.
Narrator 1:	After Orville got better, the two brothers started working on building kites, to learn more about flying. One day they stood outside watching a hawk fly.
Adult Orville:	Look, Will. The hawk lifts the tip of one wing and dips the other wing, and it can fly in a circle.
Adult Wilbur:	Hmmm, it reminds me of a long thin box, like the ones bicycle chains come in. If I twist one end, the other end twists the opposite way.
Adult Orville:	We could try this out on a kite.
Narrator 2:	Their kite, controlled by sticks from the ground worked great. They got to work building a kite large enough to hold a man. They wrote to the US Weather bureau, looking for the windiest place in America, to test their new invention.
Adult Wilbur:	A letter from the Weather Bureau arrived today.
Adult Orville:	What does it say?
Adult Wilbur:	There's a place called Kitty Hawk, North Carolina, a sandy beach on a hilly island, where the wind blows 10 to 20 miles per hour almost all the time.
Adult Orville:	It sounds perfect. Don't tell anyone what we're doing. We need to keep our research a secret or someone might steal our ideas.
Narrator 1:	In September, 1900, the two brothers began their experiments at Kitty Hawk. They lived in tents and cooked their own food. They played the harmonica and the mandolin for entertainment. They took photographs and careful notes of all their experiments.
Adult Wilbur:	There she is—our first glider. That cotton fabric on the top and bottom wings looks pretty nice. 17 feet wide. Total cost: $15.
Adult Orville:	Hop on, Will. I'll time you.
Narrator 2:	That first day, their glider with controls like a hawk's wings carried Wilbur on a dozen flights.
Adult Wilbur:	How far was that one, Orv?
Adult Orville:	400 feet in 20 seconds.

Narrator 1: It wasn't much, but the brothers were learning how to control their flight, rather than just being carried by the wind.

Narrator 2: The following two years, the brothers returned again and again to Kitty Hawk, testing out their ideas and conducting experiments. But something was wrong.

Adult Wilbur: According to the tables published by Otto Lilienthal, we ought to be getting more lift.

Adult Orville: Do you suppose there could be a mistake in his calculations?

Adult Wilbur: There's only one way to find out. We will have to run our own tests and create our own tables.

Narrator 1: So the brothers spent many hours back in Dayton, building a wind tunnel, testing and re-testing, keeping careful records. They discovered that an equation that had been used for over 100 years was incorrect: it said lift was .005, but they found that it was actually .003. That tiny number explained a lot!

Narrator 2: Finally, in December, 1903, after many tests, the brothers were ready. They had developed a light but powerful engine and a way to control the plane as it flew.

Adult Orville: Who will fly it first?

Adult Wilbur: Heads I go, tails you go.

Orville: (flipping a coin) Looks like it's you, Will.

Narrator 1: The two brothers gathered a small group of local men to assist and to serve as witnesses. Then Wilbur Wright climbed into the two-winged airplane and powered it up.

Friend: He's going . . . oh no!

Narrator 2: The first flight, if you can call it that, lasted just 3½ seconds and ended with a crash that damaged the plane. It took two days to repair the wings.

Narrator 1: On December 17, 1903, it was time to try again. Now it was Orville's turn.

Friend: There he goes! He's flying! I got the photograph.

Adult Wilbur: 12 seconds! 120 feet! And a safe landing!

Adult Orville: Your turn, Wilbur. . . . Amazing! 852 feet in 59 seconds! Almost a full minute in the air.

Narrator 2: That evening, the two brothers went to the telegraph office, and using a dollar that their father had given them for that purpose, they sent him a telegram.

Adult Orville: (writing) "Success. Four flights Thursday morning . . . average speed through air, thirty one miles per hour. Longest 59 seconds. Inform press. Home for Christmas."

Narrator 1: The age of flight had begun. The brothers spent several years making sure that they received patents that would allow them to profit from their discovery. Sadly, Wilbur fell ill with typhoid fever and he passed away in 1912 at the age of just 45.

Narrator 2: Orville lived long enough to see his great invention used in World War I and World War II, when airplanes were used to bomb cities throughout Europe and Asia, including the two atomic bombs dropped on Hiroshima and Nagasaki.

Adult Orville: I don't have any regrets about my part in the invention of the airplane, but no one deplores more than I do the destruction it has caused.

DRAMA #3
Rosa Parks and the Montgomery Bus Boycott

Characters: 11 players
(8 major roles, 3 small roles)

Narrator 1
Narrator 2
Claudette Colvin, age 15
E. D. Nixon
Bus Driver
Rosa Parks
Jo Ann Robinson
Dr. Martin Luther King, Jr.
Black Woman (small role)
White Woman (small role)
Pastor Adams (small role)

Narrator 1: In 1865, at the end of the American Civil War, all people who had been slaves became free. And for a few years, it looked as if African-Americans had achieved freedom. But little by little, states and cities began passing laws known as Jim Crow laws that required segregation, or separation between white and black people.

Narrator 2: In 1955, in the southern city of Montgomery, Alabama, all the buses were segregated. Both white and black people rode the same buses, but all the bus drivers were white. White people sat in the front of the bus, but black people had to sit in the back. Claudette Colvin, a 15-year-old African American girl, explains how the system worked:

Claudette Colvin: We all pay the same bus fares. After we pay, the white folks walk right on and sit in the front of the bus. But we colored folks, as we are called, have to step off the bus, walk to the back door, and sit as far back as possible. As the bus fills up, the white section and the black section meet in the middle. Then the bus driver walks back, moves the sign that says "Colored" further back, and makes the colored people stand up to allow white people to sit down.

E. D. Nixon: I am president of the local NAACP, the National Association for the Advancement of Colored People. We want to change the Jim Crow rules on the buses.

Narrator 1: One day Claudette was on the bus when the bus driver came to the back and told her to move.

Bus Driver:	Girl, get up and move to the back. Let the white man sit down.
Claudette:	No sir.
Bus Driver:	Are you defying me, girl? I'm gonna have your black butt arrested!
Claudette:	I'm not afraid of you. I paid my fare and I'm sitting in the colored section.
Bus Driver:	Not anymore you ain't. This is a white row now.
Narrator 2:	So Claudette was arrested. E. D. Nixon, the NAACP president, thought this might be his chance to try to get the law changed.
E. D. Nixon:	Claudette, is there anything in your background that will make us look bad?
Claudette:	Um, well, I just found out I'm going to have a baby.
E. D. Nixon:	And you're not married?
Claudette:	No, sir, I'm not.
E. D. Nixon:	(sighing) This won't work. The white people will laugh at us if we defend a 15-year-old unmarried mother. I need someone that everyone will respect.
Narrator 1:	On December 1, 1955, for the second time that year, the police were called to arrest a woman on a city bus for refusing to obey the Jim Crow law.
Bus Driver:	(moving sign) All you four coloreds, stand up and move to the back. There's white people who need these seats.
Narrator 2:	The other three African Americans quietly obeyed and moved. But when Rosa Parks saw the bus driver's face, she remembered him from an incident 12 years earlier. That day, after she had paid her fare and was walking to the back door, he had slammed the doors shut and driven away laughing.
Rosa Parks:	No, sir.
Bus Driver:	Come on now, I'll have you arrested if you don't move.
Rosa Parks:	You may do that.
Narrator 1:	So once again, the police were called and they took a woman to jail for refusing to give up her seat on the bus. Rosa Parks was fingerprinted, photographed, and found guilty. She was fined a total of $14. Maybe this was the case E. D. Nixon had been looking for.
E. D Nixon:	It looks like they picked the wrong one to arrest this time. Rosa, I know you, but I have to be sure—is there anything that would embarrass us if we appeal?
Rosa Parks:	I am 43 years old. I am a high school graduate and I work as a seamstress, doing alterations on clothing at the Montgomery Fair department store downtown. I am married to Raymond Parks, who works as a barber. We have no children. Neither of us has ever been in any sort of trouble. We work hard, live quietly, and attend church. As you know, we have both been active in the NAACP for many years.

E. D. Nixon:	This won't be easy on you, Rosa. Are you ready to face the trouble that will come?
Rosa:	Yes sir, I am, and my husband is 100% behind me.
E. D.:	All right then. Here's the plan. Jo Ann Robinson, head of the Women's Political Council, will help us organize a one-day boycott of all the city buses by the colored people. Maybe if we hit them in the pocketbook, they'll get the point.
Jo Ann Robinson:	I typed up a notice and made hundreds of copies. It said:
	Another woman has been arrested and thrown in jail because she refused to get up out of her seat on the bus for a white person to sit down. . . . This has to be stopped. Negroes have rights too, for if Negroes did not ride the buses, they could not operate. Three-fourths of the riders are Negro . . . If we do not do something to stop these arrests, they will continue. The next time it may be you, or your daughter, or mother.
	Rosa Parks' case will come up on Monday. We are asking every Negro to stay off the buses Monday in protest of the arrest and trial. Don't ride the buses to work, to town, to school, or anywhere on Monday. You can afford to stay out of school for one day . . . You can also afford to stay out of town for one day. If you work, take a cab, or walk. But please, children and grown-ups, don't ride the bus at all on Monday. Please stay off all buses Monday.
Narrator 1:	Jo Ann Robinson brought the notice to all the black churches in town. At the Dexter Street Baptist church, she met the new young minister in town, the Reverend Martin Luther King Jr. He was only 25 years old and had only been in town for less than a year. But he offered his church as headquarters for the boycott, and he was chosen as the leader.
MLK:	We only planned a one-day boycott, but after the first day, we held a meeting to decide what to do next.
Black Woman:	My feet are tired, but my soul is rested. We have suffered long enough. We can walk a few more miles for freedom!
MLK:	The one-day boycott was so successful that we decided to continue it. It was a miracle, really. Hundreds and thousands of Negro people who worked hard for a living walked miles to work. Or they car-pooled with a neighbor who had a car. The bus fare was 10 cents, so black taxi services lowered their fares to 10 cents so that poor people could afford them.
Jo Ann:	As the days turned into weeks, the white women who employed colored maids started secretly driving out to the colored neighborhoods to pick them up and bring them to work.

"Don't Ride the Bus" by Jo Ann Gibson Robinson, December 2, 1955. Copyright by University of Tennessee Press. Reprinted by permission.

White Woman: I believe in segregation as much as the next person. But what am I supposed to do? My Mary does all my washing and cleaning and watches the baby when I get together with my friends. I'm lost without her. So I pick her up. Of course she sits in the back seat. But I know she appreciates it. Just don't tell my husband!

MLK: We had church meetings almost every night. We sang and prayed and I preached. The police did everything to harass the boycotters. If a black driver went 1 mile above the speed limit, he'd be stopped and given a speeding ticket. They even claimed that it was illegal for taxis to charge less than 45 cents for a ride. But when some white men threw a firebomb into my house, I wondered how much longer my wife and children could hold up.

Narrator 2: After 381 days of walking and hoping and praying, the black people of Montgomery got their answer. The U.S. Supreme Court ruled that the segregation of buses was unconstitutional. Black people could sit anywhere they wanted on the bus. Rosa Parks was photographed sitting quietly on a bus in front of a white man, and the picture was published in newspapers across the country.

Rosa Parks: They asked me why I did what I did. I told them I was just tired of it. The reporter wrote that I stayed in my seat because I was too tired to get up. But what I was tired of was segregation. I was tired of injustice. I was tired of giving in. After the boycott, my husband and I moved north to Detroit. We had to work to make our living, and no one would hire us in Montgomery.

Narrator 1: Rosa Parks died in 2005. At her funeral, Charles Adams, pastor of Detroit's Hartford Memorial Baptist Church, spoke.

Pastor Adams: Custom said, 'Get up.' Society said, 'Get up.' Politics said, 'Get up.' The bus driver said, 'Get up.' But God gave her the power to stay seated. She heard His voice. Because she sat where she sat, we are now sitting in Congress. We are sitting in the Supreme Court. We are sitting as CEOs and heads of universities.

Narrator 2: But even Pastor Adams didn't know that because Rosa Parks stayed seated, a black man would also sit in the White House in 2009, only 4 years after her death.

DRAMA 4
John F. Kennedy: A Life Cut Short

Characters: 11 players (4 major roles, 7 small roles)

Narrator 1
Narrator 2
Joe Kennedy (small role)
Young John Kennedy
Father Joseph P. Kennedy (small role)
JFK (mature John F. Kennedy)
Jackie Kennedy (small role)
School Child (small role)
Teacher (small role)
Mrs. Connolly (small role)
TV Announcer (small role)

Narrator 1: John Fitzgerald Kennedy was born in 1917 to one of the wealthiest families in America. The family had nine children in all.

Narrator 2: Joseph Kennedy hoped that his oldest son, Joe Junior, might become president of the United States some day. But in 1941, the United States entered World War II. Both Joe and John enlisted in the military.

Joe: Listen John, I want to fly bombers. I'm joining up.

Young John: The Army turned me down. They said I have a bad back. But I'm not going to sit at home while a war is going on, Joe. Maybe the Navy will have me.

Narrator 1: The Navy did take John Kennedy. He was sent to the Pacific, where he piloted a patrol boat. But in August, 1943, he was severely injured. His back problems got much worse.

Narrator 2: However, his older brother Joe faced even worse dangers as a pilot, and he was killed in August, 1944. When the war ended, his father turned his hopes to John, as the oldest surviving son.

Joseph Kennedy: John, let me help you get started in politics. It won't be easy. Some people don't trust us because we are Irish Americans and Catholics, but I believe that you will make a great president some day.

Young John: President? One step at a time, Dad! I'm not even 30 years old yet. But I will run for Congress.

Narrator 1: Kennedy was elected to the House of Representatives in 1946, and 6 years later ran for the Senate and won.

Narrator 2: In 1960, when Kennedy was just 42 years old, he was ready to try to fulfill his father's dream. He announced his candidacy for President of the United States.

JFK: (*speaking to a crowd*) You ask why I am running for president. I am running because the problems are not all solved and the battles are not all won—and we stand today on the edge of a New Frontier . . . But the New Frontier of which I speak is not a set of promises—it is a set of challenges. It sums up not what I intend to offer the American people, but what I intend to ask of them.

Narrator 1: The 1960 election was very close, but in the end, Kennedy defeated Richard Nixon to become the youngest president ever elected and the first and only Catholic president. He was also the first president born in the 20th century. At his inauguration, he said:

JFK: Let the word go forth from this time and place, to friend and foe alike, that the torch has been passed to a new generation of Americans, born in this century, tempered by war, disciplined by a hard and bitter peace, proud of our ancient heritage, and unwilling to witness or permit the slow undoing of human rights.

Let every nation know, whether it wishes us well or ill, that we shall pay any price, bear any burden, meet any hardship, support any friend, oppose any foe, to assure the survival and the success of liberty.

Narrator 2: He ended his speech with these famous words:

JFK: And so, my fellow Americans: ask not what your country can do for you—ask what you can do for your country.

Narrator 1: When John Kennedy became president, his wife Jackie was only 31 years old. She was well-educated and wanted to emphasize art and literature. She began by redecorating the White House.

Jackie: Where are all the beautiful art works that should decorate the White House? Everything in the White House should be the best.

Narrator 2: Kennedy had many important challenges in mind. He created the Peace Corps, challenging young Americans to serve their country, not only in war but in peace, by volunteering two years of their life to help others.

JFK: Life in the Peace Corps will not be easy. But it will be satisfying. Every young American who participates in the Peace Corps will know that he or she is sharing in the great common task of bringing to man that decent way of life which is the foundation of freedom and a condition of peace.

Narrator 1: Kennedy also had another dream—to send a man to the moon! In May 1961, he said:

JFK: I believe that this nation should commit itself to achieving the goal, before this decade is out, of landing a man on the moon and returning him safely to the earth. It will not be one man going to the moon—it will be an entire nation. For all of us must work to put him there.

Narrator 2:	It was hard to imagine that NASA could acquire the skills and build the rockets to get safely to the moon in less than 10 years. But no one imagined that President Kennedy himself would not live to see the goal accomplished.
Narrator 1:	Kennedy faced many other challenges during his short time as president. A planned invasion of Cuba failed, and a few years later in October 1962, the Soviet Union began placing nuclear missiles in Cuba, only 90 miles from the coast of the United States. Fear filled the nation and the world held its breath.
School Child:	Are we all going to die? Are the Russians going to bomb us?
Teacher:	If we hear a siren, we must all duck our heads under our desks for protection.
School Child:	Will that keep us safe from the bomb?
Teacher:	Let's just hope we don't have to find out.
JFK:	I call upon Chairman Khrushchev to halt and eliminate this threat to world peace and to stable relations between our two nations. He has an opportunity now to move the world back from the abyss of destruction—by withdrawing these weapons from Cuba—by refraining from any action which will widen or deepen the present crisis—and then by participating in a search for peaceful and permanent solutions.
Narrator 2:	The world breathed a sigh of relief when Kennedy announced two weeks later on November 2, 1962:
JFK:	The Soviet missile bases in Cuba are being dismantled, their missiles and related equipment are being crated, and the fixed installations at these sites are being destroyed.
Narrator 1:	Kennedy made many difficult decisions during his 3 years as president. He sent American troops to South Vietnam, beginning the U.S. involvement in the Vietnam War. And he proposed the law that became the Civil Rights Act of 1964, promising equality to all citizens of the United States, regardless of their race or color. But he didn't live long enough to see that dream fulfilled either.
Narrator 2:	On November 22, 1963, Kennedy and his wife traveled to Dallas, Texas. He would be running for re-election within a year, and he needed more political support in the South. A motorcade was planned through the city.
Narrator 1:	An open car carried President John Kennedy, Mrs. Kennedy, John Connolly, the governor of Texas, and the governor's wife drove slowly through Dealey Plaza in downtown Dallas.
Jackie:	Look at all the crowds of people who have come out!
Mrs. Connolly:	Mr. President, you can't say Dallas doesn't love you.
John:	That's true!
Narrator 2:	Suddenly shots rang out.

TV Announcer: The President has been shot!

Narrator 1: The nation was stunned by the news that their vibrant young president had been shot. A short time later the news got worse.

TV Announcer: President John F. Kennedy died at approximately 1 p.m. Central Standard Time in Dallas. He died of a gunshot wound in the brain. I have no other details of the assassination.

Narrator 2: Over the next several days, the American people and people around the world sat in front of their televisions, watching in disbelief as vice president Lyndon Johnson was sworn in as president. They watched as the accused assassin, Lee Harvey Oswald, was himself shot and killed inside a Dallas police station. They watched as the widow and two young children of John F. Kennedy bravely attended his funeral.

Narrator 1: Those who were alive that day will always remember where they were when they heard that the president had been shot, just as those who witnessed 9/11 will never forget that awful morning. But they will also remember John Kennedy's most famous words:

JFK: Ask not what your country can do for you; ask what you can do for your country.

APPENDIX
Can You or Can't You?

Many people have a hard time hearing the difference between the important words *can* and *can't*. It seems very difficult to hear the /t/ sound at the end of *can't*, especially if the word that follows it begins with the sound /t/, as in *We can't talk*. In fact, instead of listening for the /t/ sound at the end of *can't*, you should focus on the vowel sound. The word *can't* is usually stressed, so the vowel sound is stretched. The word *can* is usually unstressed, and is pronounced very lightly, with a reduced vowel sound.

Listen as your instructor reads the following sentences:

    I /**kæ:nt**/ speak Italian.   I /kɪn/ **speak** Spanish.

    He /**kæ:nt**/ swim very well.   **He** /kɪn/ **swim** very well.

Notice the stress on **can't** in the first sentence, and the stress on the subject and main verb in the second sentence. The less you stress the word *can*, the easier it will be for people to understand what you mean.

A.

Listen to the instructor and write the correct word:

1. He _____ ski.
2. She _____ speak Spanish.
3. We _____ come tomorrow.
4. She _____ help you.
5. You _____ sit here.
6. They _____ hear you.
7. I _____ understand what you said.
8. He _____ swim.
9. Susan _____ change the oil in her car.

B. Now You Try It

Work in pairs. One student will choose answers for A and the other student will choose answers for B. (Don't let your partner see your answers.) Then take turns reading your sentences to your partner and see if he or she understands you correctly. Remember to reduce the vowel in **can** and to lengthen it in **can't**.

Student A

1. I _____ run very fast.
2. She _____ complete a marathon.
3. You _____ borrow $10 from me.
4. I _____ fix it.
5. We _____ go later.
6. They _____ speak French.
7. They _____ lend us $50.
8. I _____ change a tire on my car.

Student B

1. She _____ eat raw fish.
2. I _____ believe it!
3. He _____ go to the movies tonight.
4. Most people _____ swim one mile.
5. I _____ wait for you.
6. She _____ help us.
7. He _____ escape from jail.
8. They _____ speak three languages.

C. Can We Talk?

Work with a partner to discuss each topic. Remember to reduce the vowel in **can** and to lengthen the vowel in **can't**.

1. What can a citizen do that a non-citizen can't do?
2. What can a baby do that an adult can't do?
3. What can an adult do that a child can't do?
4. What can a cat do that a dog can't do?
5. What can a dog do that a human can't do?
6. What can you do with a smart phone that you can't do with a regular phone?
7. What can we do today that we couldn't do 100 years ago?
8. What will we be able to do in the future that we can't do now?
9. What can many men do that most women can't do?
10. What can many women do that most men can't do?

CPSIA information can be obtained
at www.ICGtesting.com
Printed in the USA
LVHW061310071120
670970LV00002B/2

9 780757 588907